Managing PeopleSoft on the Oracle Cloud

Best Practices with PeopleSoft Cloud Manager

Aaron Engelsrud

Apress®

Managing PeopleSoft on the Oracle Cloud: Best Practices with PeopleSoft Cloud Manager

Aaron Engelsrud
Saint Paul, MN, USA

ISBN-13 (pbk): 978-1-4842-4545-3
https://doi.org/10.1007/978-1-4842-4546-0

ISBN-13 (electronic): 978-1-4842-4546-0

Managing Director, Apress Media LLC: Welmoed Spahr
Acquisitions Editor: Jonathan Gennick
Development Editor: Laura Berendson
Coordinating Editor: Jill Balzano

Cover image designed by Freepik (www.freepik.com)

Distributed to the book trade worldwide by Springer Science+Business Media New York, 233 Spring Street, 6th Floor, New York, NY 10013. Phone 1-800-SPRINGER, fax (201) 348-4505, e-mail orders-ny@springer-sbm.com, or visit www.springeronline.com. Apress Media, LLC is a California LLC and the sole member (owner) is Springer Science + Business Media Finance Inc (SSBM Finance Inc). SSBM Finance Inc is a **Delaware** corporation.

For information on translations, please e-mail rights@apress.com, or visit http://www.apress.com/rights-permissions.

Apress titles may be purchased in bulk for academic, corporate, or promotional use. eBook versions and licenses are also available for most titles. For more information, reference our Print and eBook Bulk Sales web page at http://www.apress.com/bulk-sales.

Any source code or other supplementary material referenced by the author in this book is available to readers on GitHub via the book's product page, located at www.apress.com/9781484245453. For more detailed information, please visit http://www.apress.com/source-code.

Printed on acid-free paper

To Jennifer, Alex, David, Peter, and Katie.
Your unconditional love and support make
all things possible.

Table of Contents

About the Author

Dr. Aaron Engelsrud is a Senior PeopleSoft Systems Administrator at Strategic Education, Inc. With over 20 years of IT industry experience ranging from business intelligence, data warehousing, and analytics to system administration and marketing technologies, he brings a diverse background and wide range of relevant experience to the table. Dr. Engelsrud earned a Master of Science in Information Technology in 2006, an MBA in IT Management in 2011, and in 2017 completed Doctor of Business Administration with a specialization in Business Intelligence. Over the past decade, Dr. Engelsrud has presented on a variety of topics, including business intelligence and PeopleSoft administration at industry conferences throughout the United States. When away from the office, he stays active in his community by serving as firefighter/EMT and enjoys spending time at the hockey rink with his four kids.

About the Technical Reviewer

Judi Hotsinpiller has a master's degree in Computer Resource Management. Judi spent 5 years as a Computer Technology Instructor at Central Carolina Technical College. She spent years in the corporate world as a Senior Analyst before moving to the university and government setting. Judi developed the Oracle training program at the University of New Mexico, and she is a Certified Oracle Professional. Judi started working as a PeopleSoft Financial Developer in 2002 at the University of Utah, and then relocated to New Mexico at Sandia National Laboratories. Judi is the lead PeopleSoft Developer for the Department of Energy's pension system on the PeopleSoft Human Resources modules. Judi is the current Director of SIGs for IOUG (Independent Oracle Users Group).

Introduction

Managing PeopleSoft on the Oracle Cloud: Best Practices with PeopleSoft Cloud Manager explains how PeopleSoft customers can make the transition from hosting their PeopleSoft applications in a traditional, on-premise data center to hosting those same applications in the Oracle Cloud Infrastructure. Covering both functional and technical aspects of PeopleSoft Cloud Manager, this book will provide the reader with not only the knowledge to make the case to move their on-premise application to the Oracle Cloud Infrastructure but also the technical skills necessary to install and support PeopleSoft Cloud Manager and the knowledge necessary to run it.

A necessary resource for the functional analyst or IT manager who is looking to make a case for moving PeopleSoft to the Oracle Cloud Infrastructure as well as the PeopleSoft system administrator or developer tasked with making that move happen, this book provides multiple cloud use cases and explains how to correctly estimate costs incurred from running PeopleSoft instances in the Oracle Cloud. Additionally, PeopleSoft system configuration best practices are clearly defined, specific requirements for running PeopleSoft Cloud Manager on the Oracle Cloud are spelled out, and tips and tricks for running PeopleSoft instances in the cloud are outlined.

PART I

Managing PeopleSoft on the Oracle Cloud

CHAPTER 1

Getting Started with Oracle Cloud Services

Oracle Cloud Services provides you with a rich and diverse set of tools and services which you can leverage for a wide variety of purposes. In this chapter, you will get a brief introduction to Oracle Cloud Services including what the Cloud Services can be used for and the types of services offered. Next, you will use the step-by-step process for signing up with Oracle Cloud Services. Then you will use the detail to successfully navigate the Oracle Cloud web sites and related content. You will then come to better understand the various Oracle Cloud subscription options including both metered and nonmetered subscription offerings. Finally, this chapter will highlight the Oracle Cloud Service Trial program as well as the free cloud services promotions provided by Oracle and demonstrate how you can activate a trial subscription and verify that your trial subscription is running.

Oracle Cloud Services Offerings

Simply put, Oracle Cloud Services is an enterprise-ready cloud infrastructure designed specifically for businesses. Like cloud services offered by Amazon or Microsoft, Oracle provides cloud users with a wide variety of services designed to augment or replace an on-premises enterprise IT infrastructure. To build this broad infrastructure of cloud services Oracle has formed its cloud offerings around three key service groups: Software as a Service (SaaS), Platform as a Service (PaaS), and Infrastructure as a Service (IaaS).

© Aaron Engelsrud 2019
A. Engelsrud, *Managing PeopleSoft on the Oracle Cloud*, https://doi.org/10.1007/978-1-4842-4546-0_1

Software as a Service (SaaS)

From a generic perspective, Software as a Service (SaaS) is a methodology of software delivery and licensing in which the software itself is hosted centrally, typically in a cloud type infrastructure, and is licensed via a monthly or annual subscription model. Figure 1-1 illustrates, showing that customers interact with applications that are entirely managed on the provider side of the cloud.

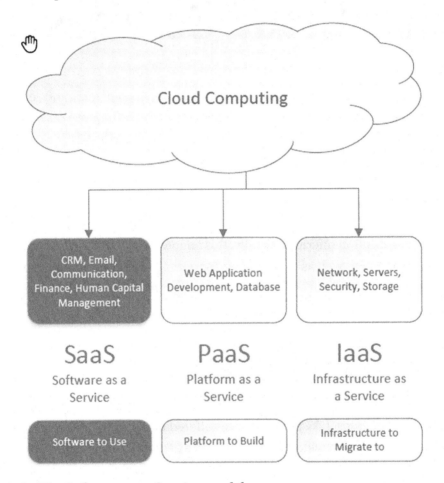

Figure 1-1. *The Software as a Service model*

Oracle Cloud Services offers a wide variety of SaaS offerings including human capital management, enterprise performance management, supply chain management, customer relationship management, and financials. This platform allows businesses the opportunity to grow their application stack as their business grows and provides business users with a consistent and integrated suite of software tools at their disposal.

Platform as a Service (PaaS)

Platform as a Service (PaaS) is best described as a cloud service offering that provides everything necessary for a customer to develop, run, and manage applications while not having to manage the infrastructure pieces that are generally necessary to build and run custom applications. Different than SaaS offerings, PaaS solutions do not provide actual applications but rather provide the servers, network, storage, database options, operating systems, and middleware (like Java, .NET, WebLogic, etc.) necessary to build and host applications. See Figure 1-2 for an illustration of the PaaS model.

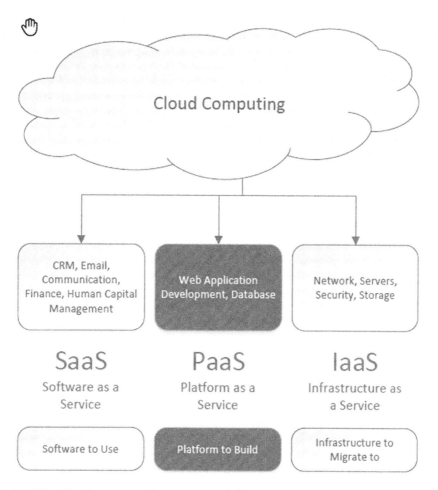

Figure 1-2. *The Platform as a Service model*

Here too Oracle Cloud Services provides a wide variety of PaaS solutions to customers including offerings in data management, application development, integration, business analytics, security, and systems management. Oracle PaaS solutions allow customers to build, deploy, and manage cloud-based applications in a variety of platforms and programming languages.

Infrastructure as a Service (IaaS)

From the perspective of PeopleSoft in the Cloud and PeopleSoft Cloud Manager, Infrastructure as a Service (IaaS) is the cloud space in which we will be spending the most time as Oracle's IaaS offerings provide the framework on which PeopleSoft Cloud Manager runs. IaaS offerings are typically thought of as one level lower than PaaS offerings. Where PaaS offers access to servers already configured and running operating systems along with development tools ready to go, IaaS offers customers the ability to build the infrastructure pieces they want, to the specifications they need. Oracle provides IaaS customers with multiple offerings including compute resources, network, storage, database, connectivity solutions, high availability solutions, and governance options. PeopleSoft Cloud Manager relies heavily on the Oracle Compute Cloud, the Oracle Storage Cloud, and, in some cases, Oracle's Database as a Service (DBaaS) offerings as well. Figure 1-3 provides an overview of what is typically included in the IaaS.

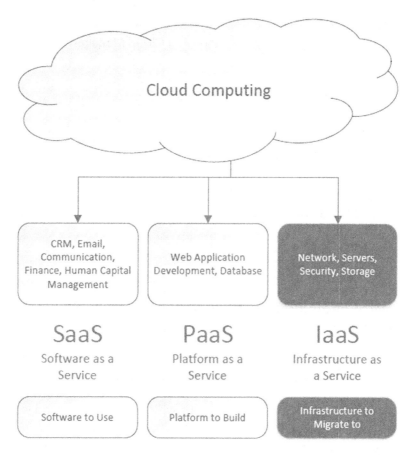

Figure 1-3. *Infrastructure as a Service*

The Oracle Cloud Marketplace

Before we move in to the details of working in Oracle Cloud Services, it is important
to understand some of the framework upon which Oracle Cloud Services operate.
One key component of this framework is the Oracle Cloud Marketplace (http://
cloudmarketplace.oracle.com). Much like the Apple Store allows you to find apps for
your iPhone and applications for your MacBook, the Oracle Cloud Marketplace allows
you to find business and development applications that run in the Oracle Cloud.

The Oracle Cloud Marketplace is an important part of running PeopleSoft applications
in the Cloud and a critical component in installing PeopleSoft Cloud Manager. The first steps
in installing PeopleSoft Cloud Manager involve navigating the Oracle Cloud Marketplace to
find specific Window and Linux images that are necessary to complete the PeopleSoft Cloud
Manager installation. Additionally, as you see in Figure 1-4, the Oracle Cloud Marketplace

can also provide a location for you to find current PeopleSoft Images across all PeopleSoft applications as well at the current image of PeopleSoft Cloud Manager.

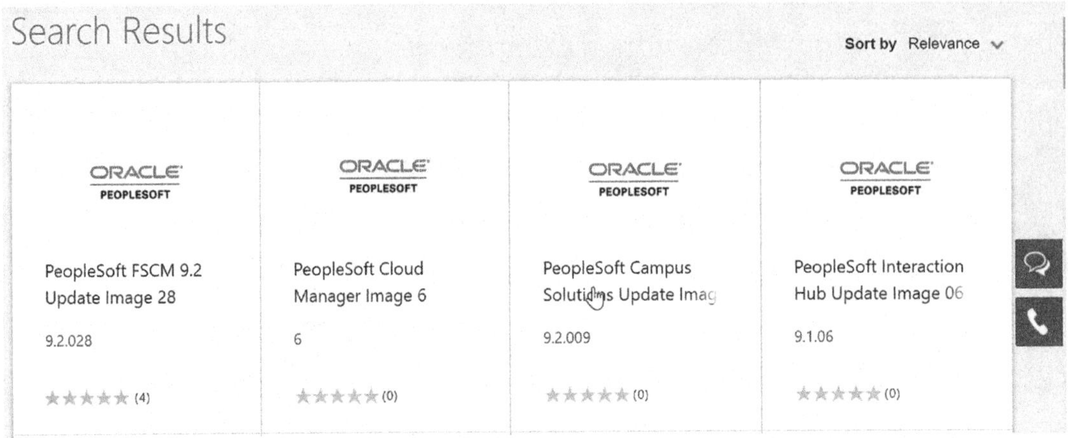

Figure 1-4. *Searching for the term "PeopleSoft" in the Oracle Cloud Marketplace provides you with all of the current PeopleSoft images*

Oracle Cloud Subscription Options

If you are new to Oracle Cloud Services, Oracle provides a free trial period which allows you to try the services, set up some proof-of-concept infrastructure, and even install PeopleSoft Cloud Manager, risk free. In addition to the free trial provided by Oracle, there are several Oracle Cloud subscription options that you can choose from once your free trial period expires. The various subscription options provided allow you and your business a variety of billing and payment choices to not only make your Cloud Services more affordable but also provide options that are better tailored to your business requirements. Subscription options provided by Oracle include Universal Credit Service and Bring Your Own License along with Traditional Metered and Traditional Nonmetered Service offerings. Universal Credits provide users with a flexible buying and usage model for Oracle Cloud Services including both Infrastructure as a Service and Platform as a Service services. Once your Oracle Cloud Services account is approved, you immediately have unlimited access to all PaaS and IaaS services and are governed by either a pay as you go or pay in advance model. From a cost perspective, the pay in advance model, typically paid in advance for a year of services based on an estimated monthly usage, is a better value than the pay as you go plan. An additional benefit of utilizing Universal Credits is that you have immediate access to new and improved service offerings as soon as they are released to the cloud infrastructure by Oracle.

Bring Your Own License (BYOL) allows you the opportunity to use your existing on-premises Oracle licenses in the Oracle Cloud. This includes offering in both Oracle's IaaS and PaaS infrastructures. A good example of how this option may benefit you is if you are already an Oracle Database customer and would like to move your Oracle Database license to the cloud. You can bring your already existing license to the cloud and save money on the initial implementation of your Oracle Database in the Oracle Cloud. Additionally, the BYOL subscription model also allows complete portability of your existing Oracle licenses, meaning this provides the opportunity for you to not only convert existing on-premises license to the cloud but also move them back again.

Note   Oracle customers must continue to pay their annual support fee for the on-premises licenses they have moved to the cloud. This will ensure that, as an Oracle customer, you will continue to get the same production level and non-production level support you have come to expect from your on-premises Oracle products in the Oracle Cloud.

The Oracle Free Cloud Trial Program

The free Oracle Cloud Promotion allows prospective Oracle Cloud customers the opportunity to kick the tires on the Oracle Cloud Infrastructure for free over the span of 30 days. Specifically, at the time of this writing, the Free Oracle Cloud Promotion includes $300 in free Oracle credits that can be used in both the IaaS and PaaS offerings during the 30-day trial period. Any credits not used at the end of the 30-day trial will expire, and Oracle will not offer the extension of the 30-day trial under any circumstances. You can sign up for the Oracle Cloud Promotion on the Free Oracle Cloud Promotion web site (https://cloud.oracle.com/en_US/tryit).

Note   During your trial period, you will pay only the IaaS rates for all the platform services which are normally billed at a higher rate. Examples of these services include Oracle Databases, MySQL, and Java Cloud Service. Before considering the final cost of Oracle Cloud Services, consider using the Oracle Cloud Cost Estimator (https://cloud.oracle.com/en_US/cost-estimator) to more closely determine your posttrial cloud costs.

A detailed explanation of the steps involved in signing up for the Free Oracle Cloud Promotion is included in the next section. This provides all the details necessary to both create your Oracle account and gain access to the $300 of free credit available through this promotion.

Account Creation with Oracle Cloud Services

The first step in moving your PeopleSoft applications, or anything else, to the Oracle Cloud requires you to create an Oracle.com user account if you don't already have one. This can be done quite simply and for free by going to www.oracle.com and finding the **Sign In** drop-down at the top of the page. In the **Sign In** drop-down window, select the **Create an account** link. Figure 1-5 shows where to find link.

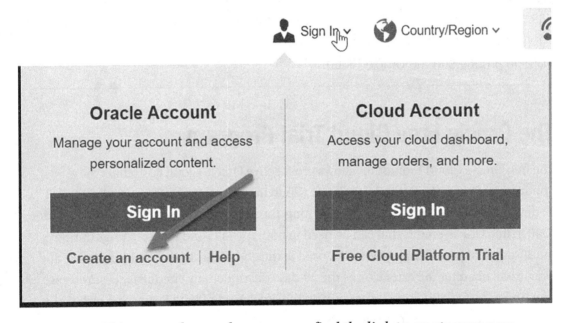

Figure 1-5. *This screen shows where you can find the link to create your new Oracle.com account to help you get started with Oracle Cloud Services*

Clicking this link will open a new page web page titled *Create Your Oracle Account.* This web page and the Oracle.com registration process require the following pieces of personal information to complete:

- **Valid Email Address:** A valid email address uses the standard email format: user-name@company-name.com. It's also important to note that you can only create one Oracle.com account per valid email address.

- **Password (enter twice for validation):** Oracle.com password requirements require that you include upper- and lowercase letters, at least one number, it cannot match any part of your email address, and the password must be at least eight characters long.

- **Your Country**

- **Your Name:** First and last

- **Your Job Title**

- **Work Phone Number:** It helps if this number can receive texts as Oracle will send validation codes to your phone at various points in the setup process.

- **Your Company Name**

- **Company Address:** Including street address, city, state, and zip code.

- **Marketing Materials Check Box:** You can also choose to accept being sent Oracle marking communications to the email address listed.

Once you have filled out all the appropriate information in the form, click the **Create Account** button at the bottom of the page. At this point, Oracle will create your account and send you a confirmation email to the email address you listed when you created the account.

You should receive the verification email from Oracle within a few minutes. If you don't see it right away, check your junk or spam email folder to ensure you don't miss it. Once you get the email, follow the directions included – largely it is just clicking the Verify Email Address button – and finish the Oracle.com registration process.

If all has gone well so far, you should now see a success message from Oracle.com indicating that your account is now ready to use. You can now use this Oracle.com account to help you through the Oracle Cloud Services registration process.

Signing Up for the Free Oracle Cloud Promotion

To get started with the Oracle Cloud Services registration process, the first thing you will need to do is sign in to your newly created Oracle.com. Again, the sign in link can be found in the upper right corner of the `www.oracle.com` web site.

Once signed in with your Oracle.com account, select the **Account** drop-down at the top of the page and then, from the account window, click the **Free Cloud Platform Trial** link as shown in Figure 1-6.

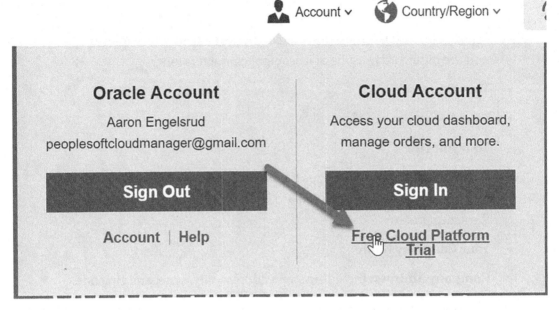

Figure 1-6. *Click the Free Cloud Platform Trial link to get started with the Oracle Cloud registration process*

Following these steps will take you to the Oracle Cloud home page which can also be found at `http://cloud.oracle.com`. While this page contains a lot of important information that you will eventually need to access, right now we only need to focus on continuing through the cloud services registration process. To do so, all you need to do is click the **Create a Free Account** link/button found in the middle of the home page. This will start the four-step cloud registration process.

Note   In order to complete this registration process, you will need to provide a verifiable phone number along with a valid credit card. While there is no charge for the free cloud services promotion, Oracle does require that you provide a valid credit card for verification and future use should you decide to pay for your Oracle Cloud Services usage.

Step 1 – Account Details

The first step in setting up your Oracle Cloud account and also securing the $300 credit toward cloud services involves inputting much of the same information included in setting up your Oracle.com user account. To complete this step in the process, you will need to provide Oracle with the following information as shown in Figure 1-7:

- **Account Type:** There are two options provided by Oracle, Business and Personal. This is a required field.

- **Cloud Account Name:** This needs to be a unique username, and Oracle will check to ensure what you choose is available prior to moving on to the next step. Oracle suggests that you use a recognizable name, such as your company, as this Cloud Account Name will be used in your account URLs. The URL will look something like this: `https://myservices-cloud_account_name.console.oraclecloud.com`. This is a required field and will validate as valid or invalid when you exit the field.

- **Default Data Region:** To ensure that you get the best possible performance out of your cloud infrastructure, you need to choose a region that is close to your users. You can find more information on the available data regions here: `https://cloud.oracle.com/data-regions`. This is a required drop-down selection.

- **Email Address:** This is your email address, preferably the same email address used to set up your Oracle.com account. This is a required field and will validate as valid or invalid when you exit the field.

- **First Name:** Your first name. This is a required field.

- **Last Name:** Your last name. This is a required field.

- **Country/Territory:** The country or territory within which you live or where your company is located. This is a required field.

- **Address:** Your physical address. This is a required field.

- **City:** The city associated with the address listed. This is a required field.

- **State:** The state associated with the address and city you have listed. This is a required field.

- **Zip/Postal Code:** Your zip or postal code. This is a required field.

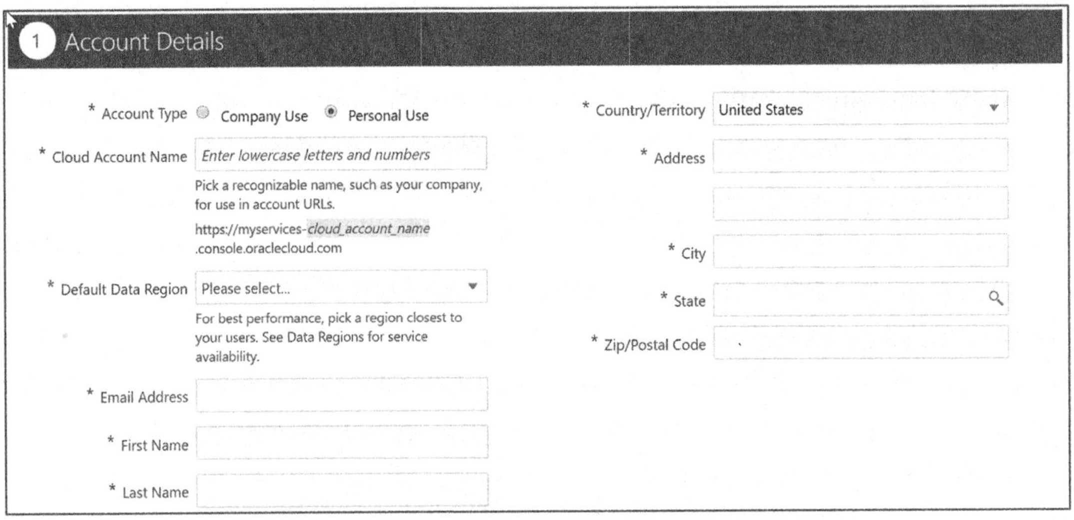

Figure 1-7. *This shows all the details necessary to complete Step 1 in the Cloud Services account setup process*

Completing the preceding information will satisfy the requirements of step 1 and allows you to move on to step 2 of the Cloud Services sign up process.

Step 2 – Verification Code

Once step 1 is complete and you have appropriately entered your Cloud Account Name and other relevant information, the next step involves verifying your personal phone number. Step 2 requires only two pieces of data to be entered, first your phone number and then second the verification code, received via a text message from Oracle. You can see the detail required for this screen in Figure 1-8.

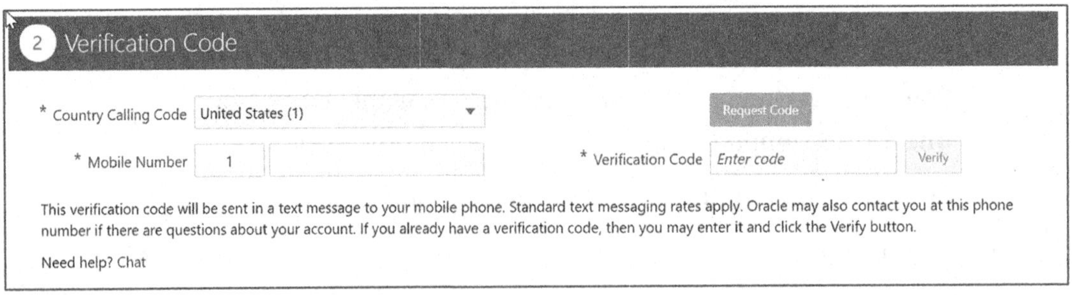

Figure 1-8. *This shows the detail necessary to complete the phone verification step in the Oracle Cloud account setup process*

This step requires that a text message be sent to the phone number you provide. Additionally, if you are charged for text messages with your phone plan, you will be charged for this text message. Also, as you progress through this step, keep in mind that Oracle may also use this phone number to contact you directly if there are any questions or issues around your cloud account. Finally, and perhaps most importantly, please note that the registration process will not allow you to continue to step 3 prior to the successful completion of this portion of the process.

Step 3 – Credit Card Details

Step 3 is a very straightforward process and is required as part of the Oracle Cloud Services registration process. While it is true that you are in the process of signing up to get free access to the Oracle Cloud Infrastructure and you will not be charged anything unless you elect to be charged after the trial period, Oracle still requires you to provide a valid credit card that they will keep on file. To get started entering your information, click the *Add Payment Method* button indicated in Figure 1-9.

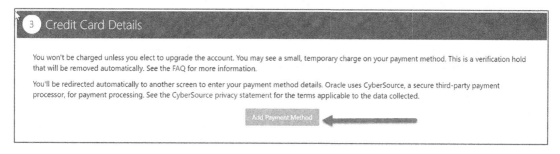

Figure 1-9. *Click the Add Payment Method button to add your credit card information to your Oracle Cloud Services account*

Clicking this button will open a new dialogue that will allow you to enter your personal information and verify that the credit card you enter is valid. This dialogue requires the typical payment information including your name, billing address, phone number, email address, card type, card number, card expiration date, and the card verification number. All these pieces of data are required and must be completed for verification. Like the previous phone number verification step, you will not be allowed to continue with the registration process until this step is successfully completed.

Step 4 – Terms and Conditions

This is the final step in the Cloud Services registration workflow. Simply check the check box located in the top left of the Terms and Conditions section and then click the *Complete* button located in the bottom right. Both points are indicated in Figure 1-10. The Complete button will not be activated and clickable until you accept the terms and conditions of the Oracle Cloud Services Agreement for Oracle America, Inc. This agreement will include language around the Free Oracle Cloud Promotion Universal Credits you are receiving.

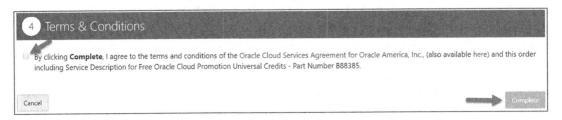

Figure 1-10. *Indicated by arrows are the check box stating that you agree to the Oracle terms and conditions and the Complete button, finishing the registration process*

Final Steps – Activation Steps

This technically completes the four-step registration process; there are a few more things that need to happen and additional pieces of information you will need to provide to continue to move this process forward. First, once you click complete, you will receive an email from Oracle welcoming you to the Oracle Cloud and indicating that your request will be reviewed, and more information will follow. It will look something like the email found in Figure 1-11.

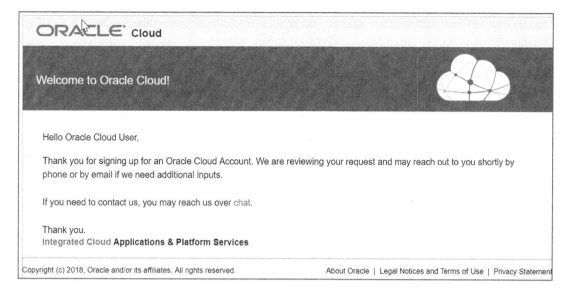

Figure 1-11. *Welcome to the Oracle Cloud email*

After you receive the welcome email, you will receive another email from Oracle Help (oraclehelp_ww@oracle.com) simply titled *Oracle Cloud Services.* This email will provide instructions on validating your payment information and is required prior to moving on with the Oracle Cloud Services account creation. Do not ignore this email. Without completing the steps required, your Oracle Cloud account provisioning will not continue. The content of this email can be seen in Figure 1-12.

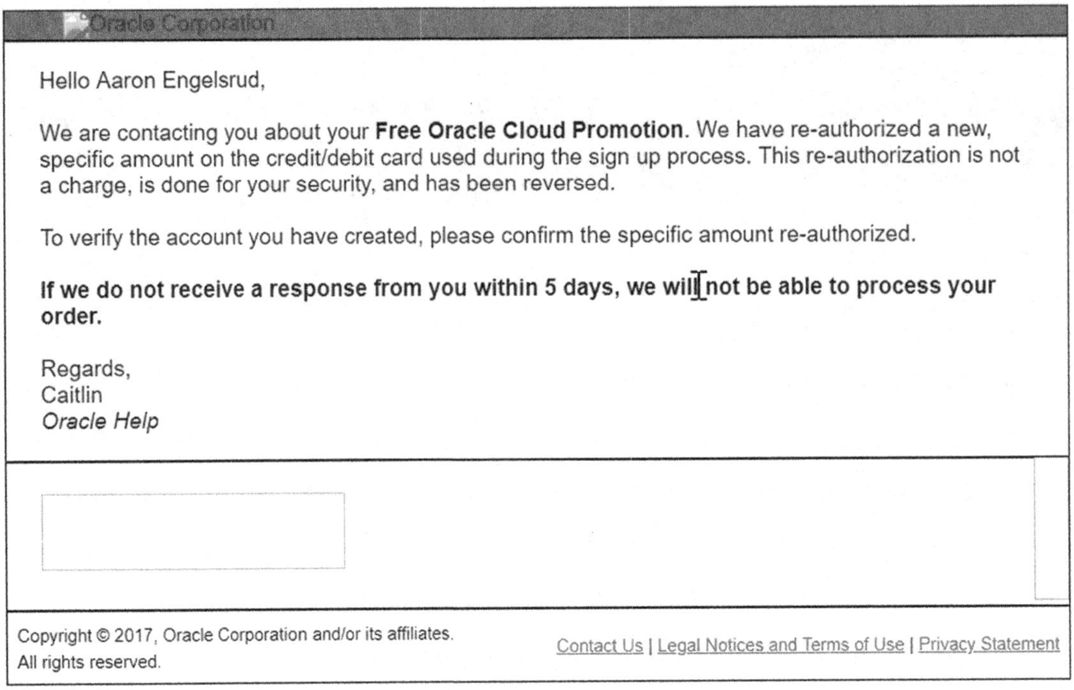
Oracle Corporation

Hello Aaron Engelsrud,

We are contacting you about your **Free Oracle Cloud Promotion**. We have re-authorized a new, specific amount on the credit/debit card used during the sign up process. This re-authorization is not a charge, is done for your security, and has been reversed.

To verify the account you have created, please confirm the specific amount re-authorized.

If we do not receive a response from you within 5 days, we will not be able to process your order.

Regards,
Caitlin
Oracle Help

Copyright © 2017, Oracle Corporation and/or its affiliates.
All rights reserved.

Contact Us | Legal Notices and Terms of Use | Privacy Statement

Figure 1-12. *Oracle payment method verification email*

(I didn't get a payment verification email—searched everywhere but my account created with no issue and my card was charged and reversed $1) While it is not immediately clear from the email you receive, Oracle is expecting you to reply directly back to oraclehelp_ww@oralce.com with the amount of the debit (charge) and reversal (credit) they have processed on your payment methodology. These two transactions result in a net zero transaction and fall off your account before they are ever posted. For example, in my case Oracle placed a charge of $56.11 on the card I used in the Credit Card Details step (step 3 of the cloud services account registration process) along with a corresponding reversal of $56.11. This equals a net zero transaction. To finish this step, you can simply reply back to this email and note the amount of the transaction Oracle posted to your account. You will be rewarded with a confirmation email stating that your order is processing and should be completed within the next 24 hours. You are now on your way to the cloud!

CHAPTER 2

PeopleSoft Cloud Manager Prerequisites

PeopleSoft Cloud Manager is the key software that allows you to quickly and easily deploy and manage PeopleSoft instances within the Oracle Cloud Infrastructure. PeopleSoft Cloud Manager can deploy PeopleSoft environments on both Linux and Windows virtual machines and provides you with environment management tools to make supporting those environments easier.

This chapter outlines the prerequisites necessary to install and set up PeopleSoft Cloud Manager. Completing the PeopleSoft Cloud Manager prerequisite steps includes the following components: collecting the required information for the installation, obtaining the proper Linux and Windows images for installation, setting up your SSH key within the Oracle Cloud, creating all the necessary security objects for the installation, and provisioning and updating a private Windows image for use by PeopleSoft Cloud Manager. Let's get started!

Collect Required Information for Installing PeopleSoft Cloud Manager

It is important that, as you go through the steps involved in the PeopleSoft Cloud Manager installation process including the Cloud Manager Instance Configuration Wizard, you have all the required input information easily available to you. Collecting and recording these details will help you move more easily through the process and also assist you should you find the need to work through the Configuration Wizard multiple times.

To help ensure you get all the required details recorded prior to starting your installation, I have provided a downloadable text document that is ready to go with spaces for you to record all the necessary information collected in the following steps.

© Aaron Engelsrud 2019
A. Engelsrud, *Managing PeopleSoft on the Oracle Cloud*, https://doi.org/10.1007/978-1-4842-4546-0_2

You can go download this document now, all you need is a simple text editor like notepad; to open it, use the template.

Here is the link: `https://drive.google.com/open?id=13i9VLJ-cOL6OWxzwGlExLKHR9gnxZJOw`

Accessing Your Services in the Oracle Cloud

In Chapter 1 we covered in detail how you go about creating the necessary Oracle accounts and gaining access to the free Oracle Cloud trial. You should have received all the required information from Oracle to allow you to log in to the Oracle Cloud.

There are two different account types within the Oracle Cloud, cloud accounts with Identity Cloud Service and Traditional Cloud Accounts. The majority of the services offered within the Oracle Cloud are designed to run in an Oracle account with Oracle Identity Cloud Service. However, there are still some services that rely on their own identity management systems or Oracle Identity and Access Management for the same purposes. For our purposes, we will be relying on services which are all managed with Identity Cloud Service, but it is important, as you move forward with deploying PeopleSoft in the Oracle Cloud, that you understand the difference between these account types and understand what services are offered in which account type.

When we created our Oracle Cloud accounts, we were given a Cloud Account with Identity Cloud Service (IDCS). Oracle Identity Cloud Service provides a wide range of both user management and cloud security features that are all specifically designed within the Oracle Cloud Infrastructure, and a version of this service is delivered with every cloud account. The Identity Cloud Service is a unified security service that allows you, as the Cloud Administrator, the ability to create and manage users and control access to services within the Oracle Cloud. In an enterprise environment, Identity Cloud Service is the key service that will allow you to meet the security requirements of your organization.

Traditional Cloud Accounts do not leverage the security users and roles configured within the Identity Cloud Service and instead rely on traditional access and identity management software. When you sign up for the Oracle Cloud free credit promotion, a Traditional Cloud Account is automatically set up for you. The services that require the use of the Traditional Cloud Account are the Exadata Cloud Services, Messaging Cloud Service, Big Data Cloud Service, and the Data Visualization Cloud Service.

While at some point you may need access to one of the Traditional Cloud Account services within your organization, they are all outside the scope of this book. Given this, you can expect that the following examples will be focused on services and procedures within the Oracle Identity Cloud Service.

Setting Up the Oracle Cloud Dashboard

The Oracle Cloud Dashboard is your portal into everything you have configured and deployed within the Oracle Cloud. Given this and given that the Oracle Cloud Dashboard is highly configurable, it is important that you learn how to configure and use the dashboard to meet your needs and provide the important information in once consolidated view. There are a few key components that will help you as you walk through the installation of PeopleSoft Cloud Manager:

1. Log in to the Oracle Cloud My Services application with your Oracle Cloud IDCS Account by going to `https://cloud.oracle.com/sign-in` and selecting **Cloud Account with Identity Cloud Service** from the drop-down (Figure 2-1).

Figure 2-1. *Logging in with Identity Cloud Service*

2. Enter the Cloud Account Name provided in your Oracle Welcome email, and click **Next**.

Note   If you have lost any of your Oracle Cloud Information, you can easily have Oracle resend your account details by clicking the **Account Details** button on the right of the sign in page and providing your cloud account email address.

---

3. Provide your username and password, and then click the **Sign In** button (Figure 2-2).

Figure 2-2. *Oracle Cloud Account Sign In*

4. You should now see your Oracle Cloud My Services Dashboard.

5. To customize your dashboard, click the **Customize Dashboard** tile found near the center of the dashboard. Figure 2-3 highlights this tile.

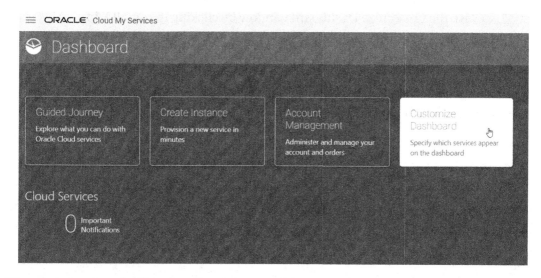

Figure 2-3. *Oracle Cloud My Services Dashboard*

6. In the Customize Dashboard window, change Compute Classic, Storage Classic, and Database Classic to Show rather than the default, Automatic (Figure 2-4).

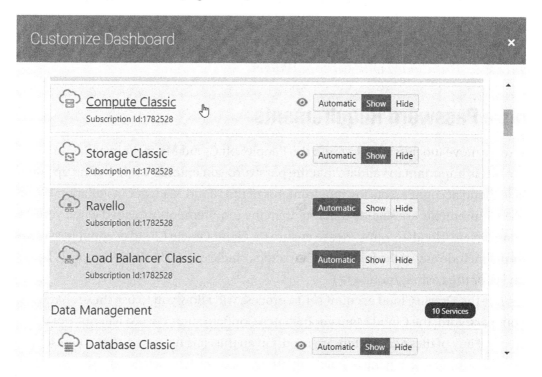

Figure 2-4. *Customize the Oracle Cloud My Services Dashboard*

7. Close the Customize Dashboard window by clicking the small X in the top right corner of the window.

8. Back on the dashboard, you will now see tiles for Compute Classic, Storage Classic, and Database Classic at the bottom of the page. Figure 2-5 shows the updated dashboard view.

Figure 2-5. *Dashboard with Custom Widgets*

Oracle Password Requirements

Before we move too much further into the PeopleSoft Cloud Manager installation process, it is important to validate that the password you entered while setting up your Oracle Cloud account meets the requirements of the Cloud Manager Installation Wizard. These requirements are slightly different than the requirements provided when you set up your Oracle Cloud account. Please ensure that your Oracle Cloud account password does not include any of the following characters: single quote ('), double quote ("), slash (\), or the hashtag/pound (#).

While the Oracle Cloud account setup process will allow you to use these characters in your password, the Cloud Manager Instance Configuration Wizard will not work correctly if any of these characters are used. Given this, it is necessary that you reset you password prior to starting the installation process if these characters exist within your password.

To change your Cloud Account password, complete the following steps:

1. From the Oracle Cloud My Service Dashboard, Click the User
   Preferences icon on the top right corner of the dashboard.
   Figure 2-6 provides a view of the Preferences options.

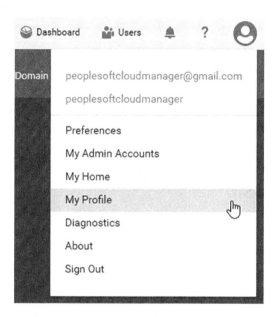

Figure 2-6. *Finding the My Profile menu option*

2. Select **My Profile** from the menu options.

3. On the User Management/My Profile window, click the **Change
   Password** tab.

4. Enter your Old Password, New Password, and Confirm New
   Password details. Figure 2-7 shows the change password dialogue.

Figure 2-7. *Change Password detail*

5. Click **Save**. All done.

Validating Account Access to Compute Classic and Storage Classic

For you to successfully complete the installation of PeopleSoft Cloud Manager in the Oracle Cloud, you need to first validate that you have access to the two essential services used in the installation process, the Compute Classic and Storage Classic services. Completing the following steps successfully will ensure you have the access necessary to move on. If you find that you do not have the access noted in these steps, you may need to contact your Cloud Administrator to open things up for you and provide access to the required services:

1. If you are no longer logged in to the Oracle Cloud My Services Dashboard, log in to the Oracle Cloud My Services application with your Oracle Cloud IDCS Account by going to `https://cloud.oracle.com/sign-in`. Follow the steps outlined in the previous section.

2. Once you have accessed your dashbaord, click the menu icon on the right side of the Compute Classic widget, and select **Open Service Console** (Figure 2-8). If the Service Console opens successfully, you have access.

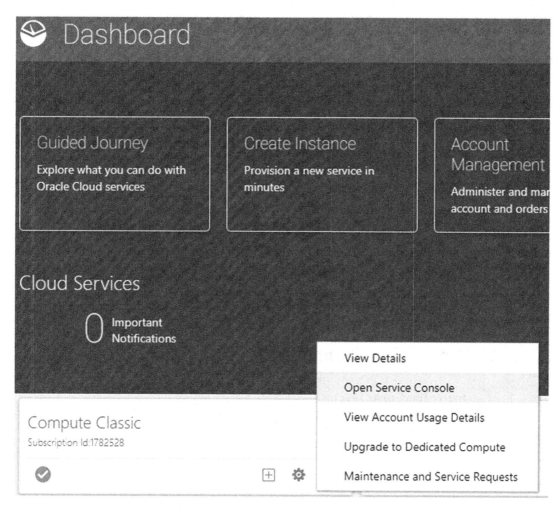

Figure 2-8. Opening the Compute Classic Service Console

3. Repeat these steps for the Storage Classic service to determine
    access to that service as well.

Note   If you do not see the Compute Classic or Storage Classic widgets on your
dashboard, you may need to go back and make sure you completed the steps in
the section titled **Setting Up the Oracle Cloud Dashboard**.

Find and Record REST Endpoint URLs

If you are new to cloud services or just new to web services in general, you may be wondering what exactly a REST endpoint is and, more to the point of this installation, how these endpoints are used to help leverage the various cloud services we will be interreacting with. REST is an acronym for representational state transfer which provides standards for communication between computer systems on the Web, making it easier for the computers to both talk to and understand each other. REST endpoints are the URLs (web addresses) where the RESTful services you are going to use can be accessed over the Internet.

In order to provide the PeopleSoft Cloud Manager configuration wizard the information it requires, we need to collect REST endpoints (the URL where we can talk to the services over the Internet) for our Compute Classic, Storage Classic, and Database services. To complete this task, you will need three pieces of information: your username and password for Oracle Cloud, the correct data center, and your Oracle Cloud identity domain.

Compute Classic REST Endpoint

1. Log in to `cloud.oracle.com`.

2. On your dashboard, click the small menu icon on the left of the Compute Classic widget, and select **Open Service Console** (Figure 2-9).

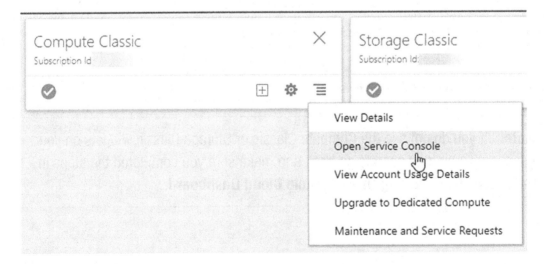

Figure 2-9. *Compute Classic Service Console*

3. Within the Compute Classic Service Console, find the site name at the top of the page and click it. Figure 2-10 highlights the site name.

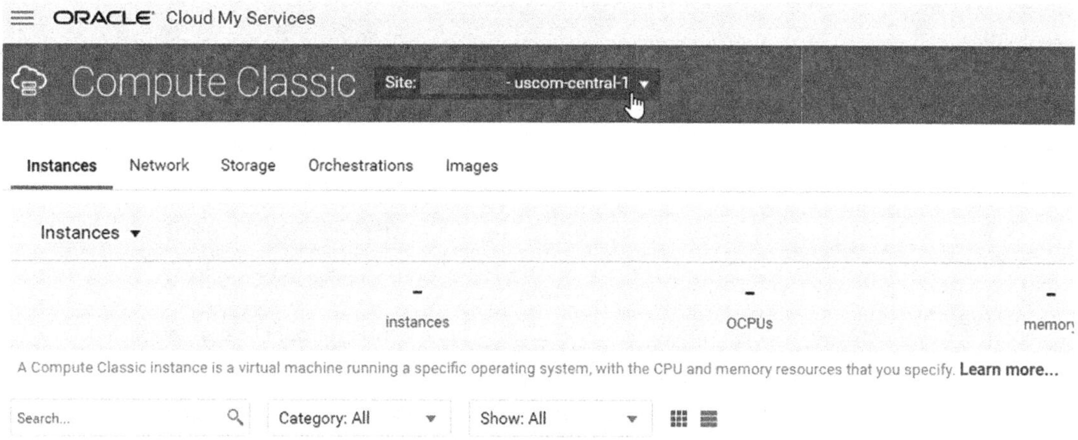

Figure 2-10. *Location of Site Selector Information*

4. Within the Site Selector dialogue box, copy the REST endpoint listed for your Service Instance ID. Add this value to the list of information you are recording for your installation process. Figure 2-11 indicates the location of the REST endpoint.

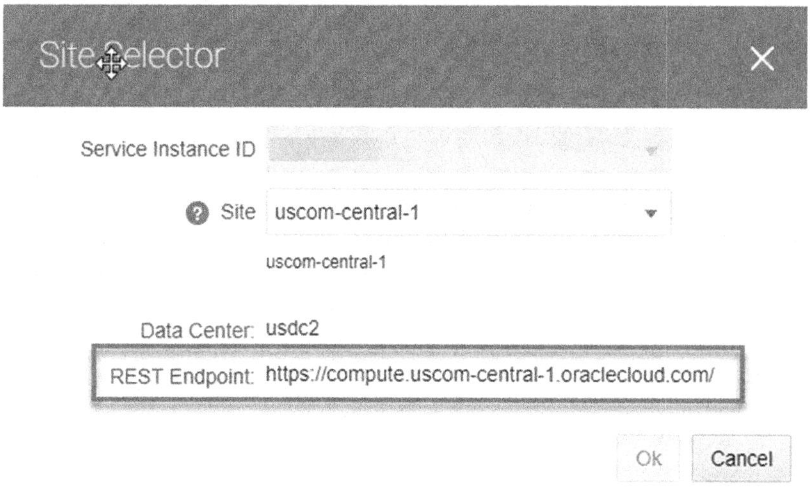

Figure 2-11. *Compute Classic REST Endpoint*

Storage Classic REST Endpoint

Starting from the Oracle Cloud Dashboard, click the small menu icon on the left corner of the Storage Classic widget, and select **View Details** (Figure 2-12).

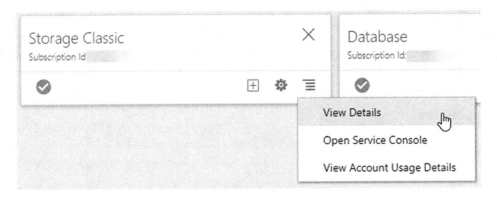

Figure 2-12. *View Details for the Storage Classic Service*

1. On the Storage Classic details page on the Overview tab, you will find the REST details you are looking for. Record the REST endpoint and the Auth V1 endpoint, and add them to the list of information you are collecting for your installation. The REST and Auth V1 endpoint locations are shown in Figure 2-13.

Service: Oracle Cloud Infrastructure Object Storage Classic

Overview   Billing Metrics   Billing Alerts   Monitoring Metrics   Business Metrics   Documents

Overview Information

Category	Oracle IaaS and PaaS Cloud Services
Cloud Account Name	
Cloud Account Id	
Subscription	Pay As You Go

Additional Information

Plan	Oracle Cloud Infrastructure Object Storage Classic	Identity Service Id	
Service Start Date	10-Aug-2018	Status	Active
Subscription ID		Buyer	
Service Instance ID		REST Endpoint (Permanent)	https://Storage-33fec22189e24bb9929d8ad36aaf90da.us.storage.oracle
Customer Account		REST Endpoint	https://peoplesoftcloudmanager.us.storage.oraclecloud.com/v1/Storage
CSI Number		Auth V1 Endpoint	https://peoplesoftcloudmanager.us.storage.oraclecloud.com/auth/v1.0

Figure 2-13. *REST Endpoints for Storage Classic*

Database REST Endpoint

1. Starting from the Oracle Cloud Dashboard, click the small menu icon on the left corner of the Database Classic widget, and select **View Details** (Figure 2-14).

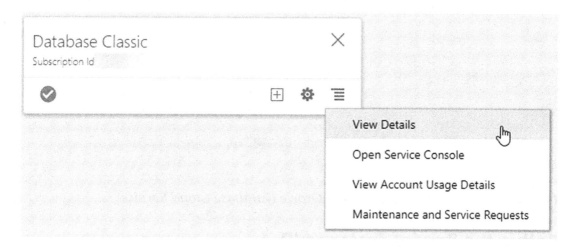

Figure 2-14. *View Details on the Database Classic Service*

2. On the View Details page for the Oracle Database Classic service, you will find the REST endpoint information you need. Record this information in your text document and move on. The Oracle Database Cloud Service REST endpoint location is shown in Figure 2-15.

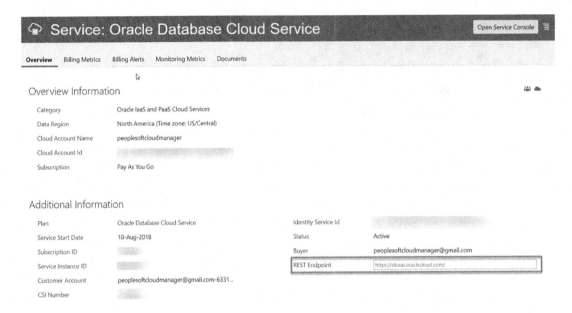

Figure 2-15. *REST Endpoint for the Oracle Database Cloud Service*

Gather the Service Instance ID

An additional input that is required in the Cloud Manager Instance Configuration Wizard is the Service Instance ID. Complete the following steps to collect your Service Instance ID:

1. Starting from the Oracle Cloud Dashboard, click the small menu icon on the left corner of the Compute Classic widget, and select **View Details** (Figure 2-16).

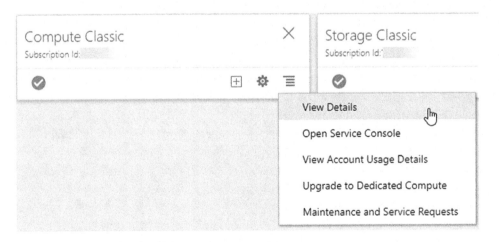

Figure 2-16. *View Details on Compute Classic*

2. On the Overview tab of the Compute Classic details page, find and
    record the Service Instance ID.

Secure Shell Requirements and Upload for PeopleSoft Cloud Manager

Before you start to create your Compute Classic instance, you need to upload a secure shell (SSH) public key to Oracle Cloud. There are two basic methods for generating the SSH public/private key pair; you will need to access your Compute Classic instance in the Oracle Cloud.

Generate SSH Key Pair on Unix/Linux with ssh-keygen

If you are generating a SSH key pair on a Linux, Unix, or Mac environment, you can use the ssh-keygen command to complete the process. Thankfully, the ssh-keygen command works the same way regardless of the host computer operating system you are running the command on, so the following instructions should work on any Unix or Unix-like system:

1. Open a command window on the computer on which you are
    planning on generating the SSH key pair.

2. Run the ssh-keygen -b 2048 -t rsa command from the
    command prompt (Figure 2-17).

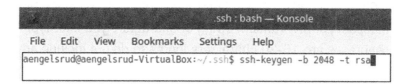

Figure 2-17. *ssh-keygen command*

Note   The -b flag (bits) specifies the specific number of bits in the key that will be created. The minimum number of bits is 768, but 2048 is the default and generally considered to be sufficiently sized. The -t flag (type) allows the user to specify the type of ssh key that will be generated. The type options include rsa1 (protocol version 1), rsa, and dsa (protocol version 2). This installation requires a rsa type key pair.

---

3. The command will now prompt you either to accept the default
    file and file path (directory) for the key or to enter a different
    specific file and file path in which you would like to save your key
    pair. The default file is suggested in parentheses and is typically
    something resembling /home/user/.ssh/id_rsa. You can accept
    the default file and file path by simply hitting enter, or you can
    manually enter a file name and file path of your choosing, and
    then press enter (Figure 2-18).

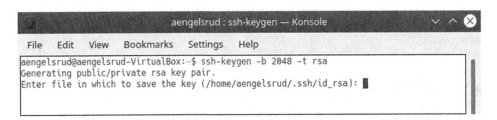

Figure 2-18. *ssh-keygen file path prompt*

4. You will next be prompted for a passphrase. You will not see the
    passphrase as you type it in, and it is important to remember the
    passphrase as it is not recoverable if forgotten.

Note   You can either leave the passphrase empty to indicate no passphrase or
the passphrase can be a string of any length. Keep in mind, a passphrase is like a
password, except that it allows you to enter a combination or words, punctuation,
numbers, whitespace, or any random string of characters you like. Typically
adequate passphrases are 10-30 characters long and do not include anything that
would be easily guessable.

---

5. Confirm your passphrase (Figure 2-19).

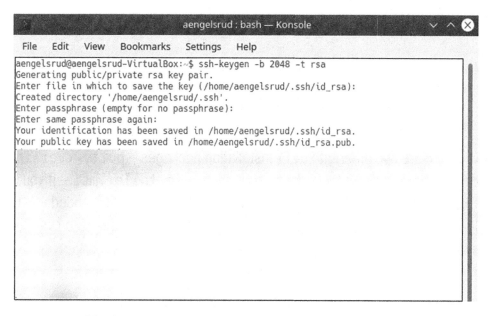

Figure 2-19. *Public key generation*

6. The command will now generate the ssh key pair which includes both a public and private key. If you name your private key cloudkey, the name of the corresponding public key will be cloudkey.pub (Figure 2-20).

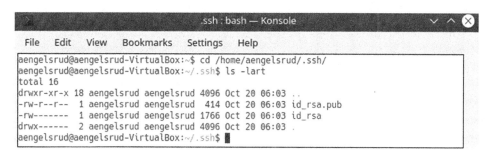

Figure 2-20. *Public and private key files*

7. In the text document where you are recording all your installation information, make a note of the file path and key name for later use.

Generate SSH Key Pair on Windows with PuTTYGEN

1. Download and install the PuTTY installation package (`www.ssh.com/ssh/putty/download`). This package will install `putty.exe`, `puttygen.exe`, `psftp.exe`, `pscp.exe`, and `pagent.ext`.

Note   There are two different PuTTY installation packages – `putty-<version>-installer.msi` and `putty-64bit-<version>-installer.msi` – if you have a 64-bit computer (most PCs bought after 2015), it is recommended you use the 64-bit version. However, if you are unsure, it is safe to use the 32-bit version on any Windows PC.

---

2. After your installation is complete, run PuTTYgen. You will find the program by going Windows Start Menu ➤ All Programs ➤ PuTTY ➤ PuTTYgen.

3. Once the program opens, select the type of key to generate – in this case we will be using an rsa type key – along with the number of bits used in the key – 2048-bit key size is appropriate.

4. Click **Generate** (Figure 2-21).

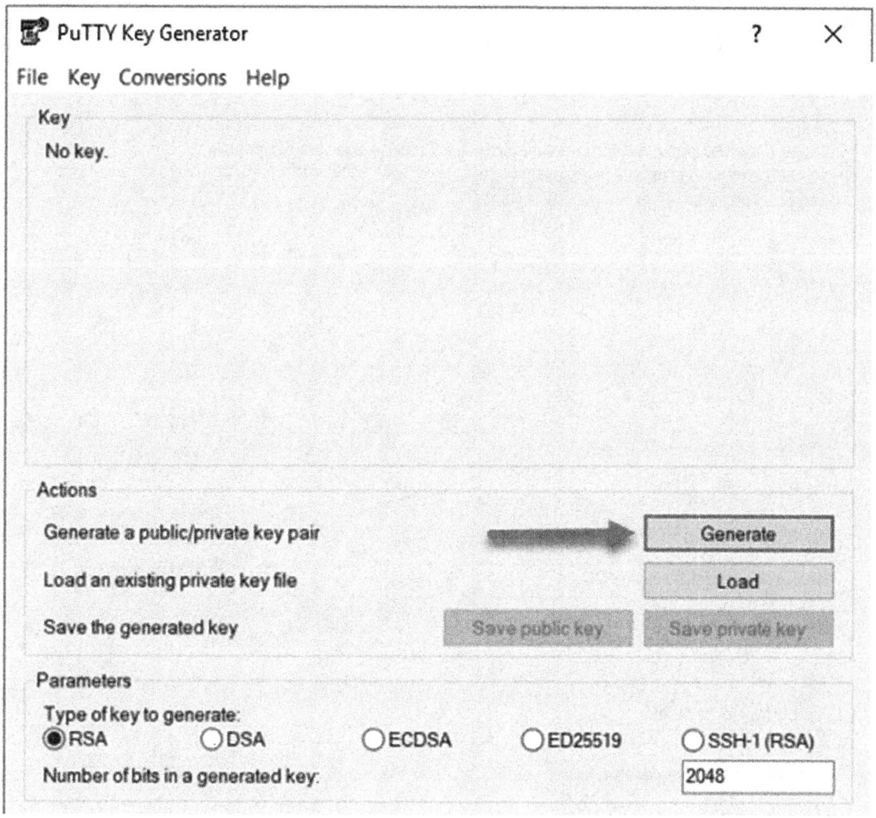

Figure 2-21. *PuTTY Key Generator*

5. After you click **Generate**, you will need to move your mouse
    pointer around the PuTTYgen window. This movement is used by
    the application to generate randomness. As you move the mouse,
    the green progress bar should advance. Figure 2-22 highlights this
    progress bar.

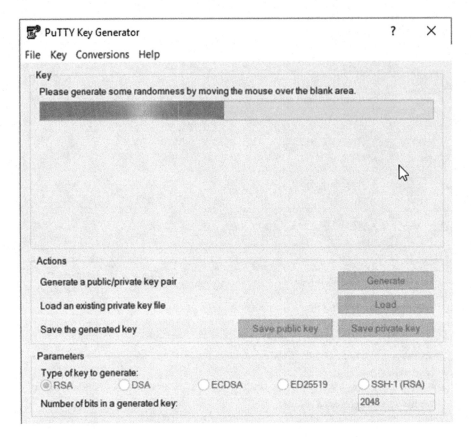

Figure 2-22. *Generating randomness*

6. Once the progress bar completes, the key is generated.

7. Next you can enter a Key passphrase of your choosing including words, whitespace, characters, numbers, as well as lower- and uppercase letters.

8. Finally, you can click **Save public key** and **Save private key.** In each case you will need to point PuTTYgen to the directory where you would like to save the key files and provide a key file name (Figure 2-23).

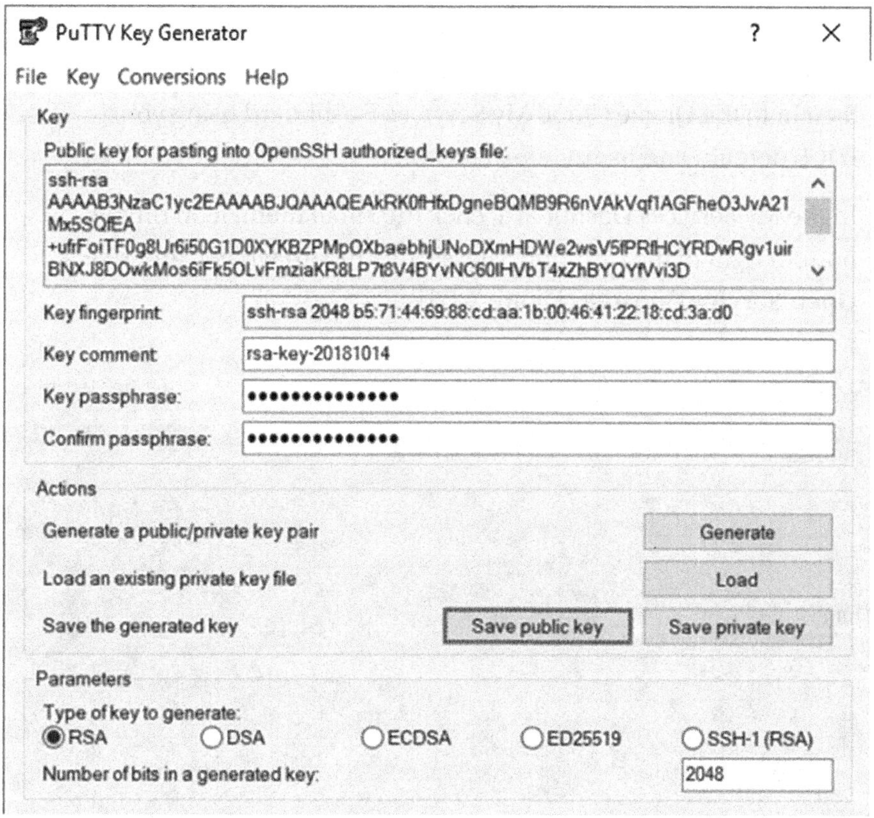

Figure 2-23. *Saving the public and private key files*

9. Once complete, you will find that you have two key files, one public and one private. These two files are shown in Figure 2-24.

Figure 2-24. *Key files in Windows*

Upload SSH Public Key to Compute Classic

Now that you have successfully generated an SSH key pair to use with the Oracle Cloud, you will need to upload the public key you generated to the Compute Classic Oracle Cloud Service. When you start creating instances in the Oracle Cloud, this public key will be used for security of the instance. When you remotely access one of your cloud instances, you will need to provide the path to the corresponding private key for validation:

1. Sign in to the Oracle Cloud My Services Dashboard using your IDCS domain and username/password.

2. In the My Services Dashboard, click the small menu icon on the bottom right of the Compute Classic dashboard widget, and select **Open Service Console** (Figure 2-25).

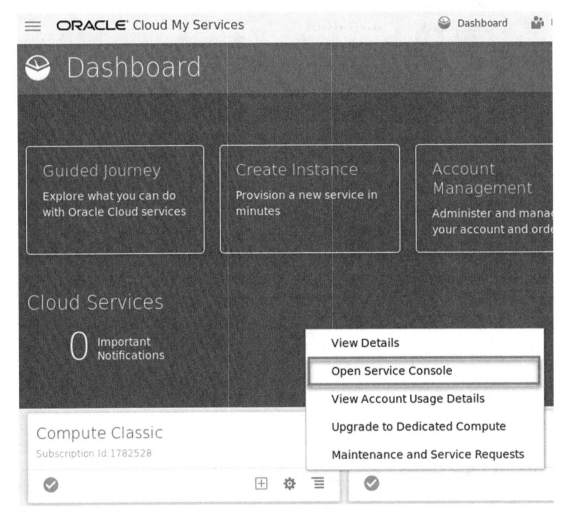

Figure 2-25. *Open Compute Classic Service Console*

3. Within the Compute Classic Service Console, click the Network
    tab (Figure 2-26).

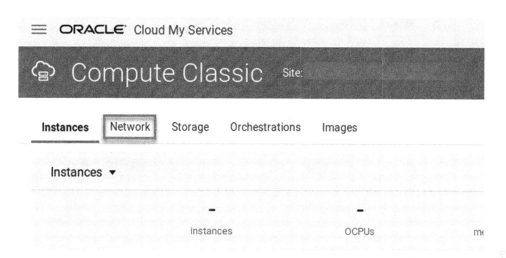

Figure 2-26. *Navigating to the Network tab in the Service Console*

4. Within the Network tab, find and click **SSH Public Key** in the
    left-hand navigation (Figure 2-27).

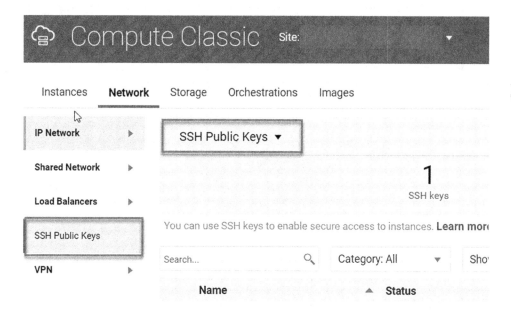

Figure 2-27. *Compute Classic SSH Public Keys*

5. Click the **Add SSH Public Key** button on the right side of the page
    (Figure 2-28).

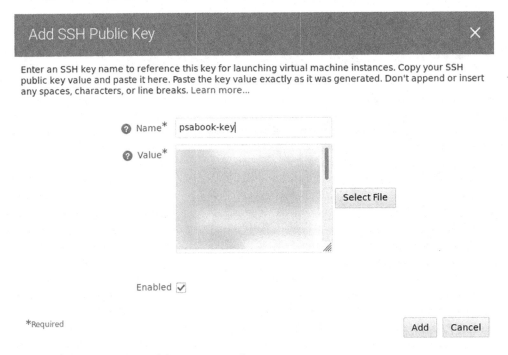

Figure 2-28. *Add SSH Public Key*

6. Within the Add SSH Public Key dialog box, give your SSH Public
    Key a name, and also input the value of the SSH Public Key you
    generated (Figure 2-29).

Figure 2-29. *Add SSH Public Key window*

Note   You can input the SSH Public Key value one of two ways: First, simply copy and paste the text within the .pub file you generated to the text box, or second, click **Select File**, browse to your public key file location and select it.

7. Click **Add**.

8. This key will now show up in the list of SSH Public Keys in your Compute Classic Service Console Network tab. Figure 2-30 shows the newly added key.

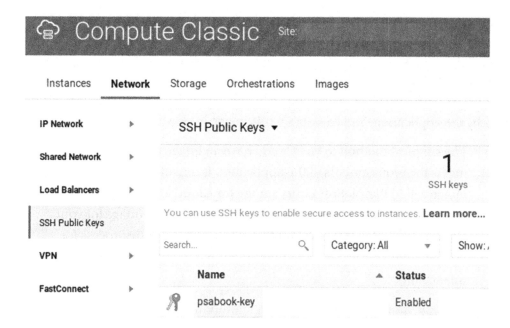

Figure 2-30. *Verification of public key addition*

Congratulations! Adding this public key will allow you to access the instances you create securely and easily.

Oracle Linux and Microsoft Windows Images for PeopleSoft Cloud Manager

The installation and ongoing use of PeopleSoft Cloud Manager requires that you have both a Linux 6 image and an updated Microsoft Windows image available in your Compute Classic Image tab. These images are used for the installation of PeopleSoft Cloud Manager itself, file storage for People Soft Cloud Manger, and for PeopleSoft instance creation. It is very important that you have images available that meet the requirements necessary for the intended purpose.

Linux Image Options for PeopleSoft Cloud Manager

PeopleSoft Cloud Manager requires an Oracle Linux 6 image to be used to complete the installation of the application in the Oracle Cloud. Once PeopleSoft Cloud Manager is installed, you will use this Oracle Linux 6 image to create a file server that is used for storage by the application. You can obtain this image in one of the three ways:

- The simplest method to ensure you have an image available that meets the requirements of the application is download a Linux image called **PeopleSoft Linux Image for Cloud Manager** from the Oracle Cloud Marketplace. I recommend you use this image for your initial installation of PeopleSoft Cloud Manager, and the process for downloading this image from the Oracle Cloud Marketplace follows this section.

- If you or your company has specific requirements, security or otherwise, that this Linux image needs to meet, you can create a custom image that is based on the PeopleSoft Linux Image for Cloud Manager reference image.

- Finally, you can also create a custom Linux image using a base Oracle Linux Image. However, it is important to note that if you do go down this road, you will need to ensure that you take the necessary steps to properly configure the image to work with PeopleSoft Cloud Manager.

How to Get the PeopleSoft Linux Image for Cloud Manager from the Oracle Cloud Marketplace

The Oracle Cloud Marketplace enables you, as an Oracle Cloud customer, to browse, evaluate, and purchase hundreds of different business applications including PeopleSoft application, Linux images, and Microsoft Windows Server images. These applications and images are easily deployable to the Oracle Cloud directly from the marketplace and makes getting the tools you need to be successful in the Oracle Cloud fast and easy.

The first step required in getting applications from the Oracle Cloud Marketplace to the Oracle Cloud involves a simple process to create a link and permissions between your Oracle.com account user account and your Oracle Cloud account. To complete linking your Oracle Cloud user account and your Oracle.com (Oracle Support) user account and to allow the Oracle Cloud Marketplace access to your Oracle Cloud Services, the following steps need to be completed to update your permission settings within Oracle My Services Dashboard:

1. Sign in to the My Services Application (`http://cloud.oracle.com`).

2. Click your user icon at the top of the page, and click the **Preferences** menu option (Figure 2-31).

Figure 2-31. *Setting cloud preferences*

3. On the Preferences window, check the Permission Setting check box (Figure 2-32).

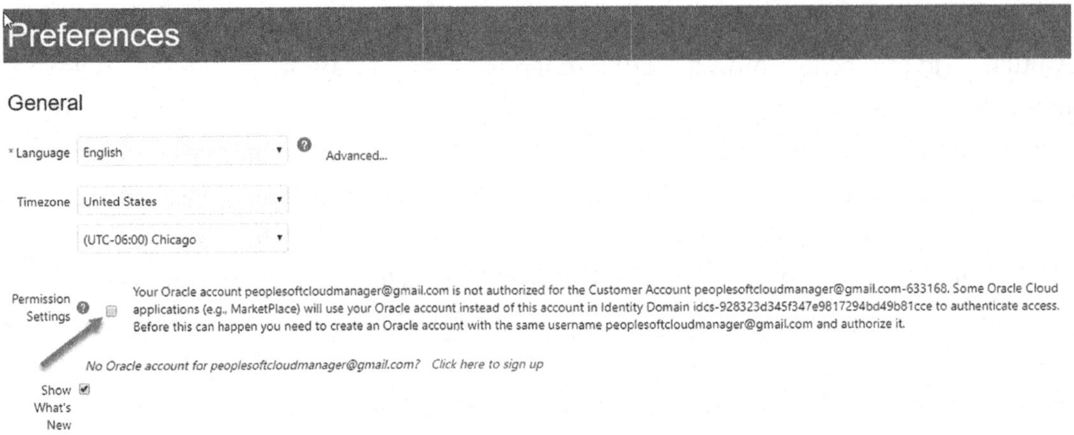

Figure 2-32. *Update Cloud Marketplace permission settings*

4. Click **Save** at the bottom of the page.

5. Once the web page shows a success message at the top of the page, you are all done!

Now that your Oracle Cloud user account and your Oracle.com user account are correctly configured, you can start getting applications and images from the Oracle Cloud Marketplace installed to your Oracle Cloud instance. To obtain the Oracle Linux Image for Cloud Manager, complete the following steps:

1. Browse to the Oracle Cloud Marketplace (`https://cloudmarketplace.oracle.com/marketplace/en_US/homePage`).

2. Sign in using the Sign In link at this top right of the page. This will require the login you created when setting up your Oracle.com user account, not your cloud account (Figure 2-33).

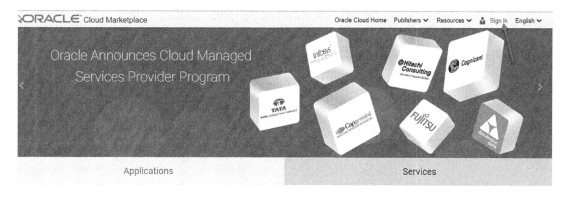

Figure 2-33. *Oracle Cloud Marketplace*

3. Enter your username and password, and click **Sign In**.

4. To locate the required Oracle Linux Image, type "peoplesoft linux image" into the search window, and click **Go** (Figure 2-34).

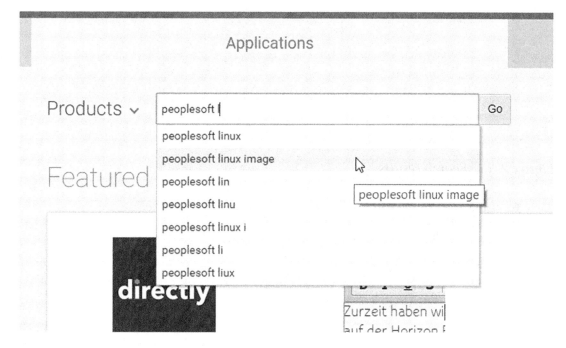

Figure 2-34. *Searching the Cloud Marketplace*

5. This search should bring back multiple PeopleSoft images, but the one you are looking for, PeopleSoft Linux Image for Cloud Manager (version 6.6_02 at the time of this writing), should be first in the list. Figure 2-35 provides a view of the PeopleSoft Linux Image for Cloud Manager.

Figure 2-35. *Search results*

6. Click the **PeopleSoft Linux Image for Cloud Manager** tile.

7. The PeopleSoft Linux Image for Cloud Manager details page provides you information specific to this image including the version, release, and kernel. In the upper right corner of the page, click **Get App** (Figure 2-36).

Figure 2-36. *Get App button in Oracle Cloud Marketplace*

8. This will start the Install Application workflow within the Oracle
    Cloud Marketplace.

9. Select the Compute Account you want the image installed to, and
    check the check box to accept the Oracle Standard Terms and
    Restrictions (Figure 2-37).

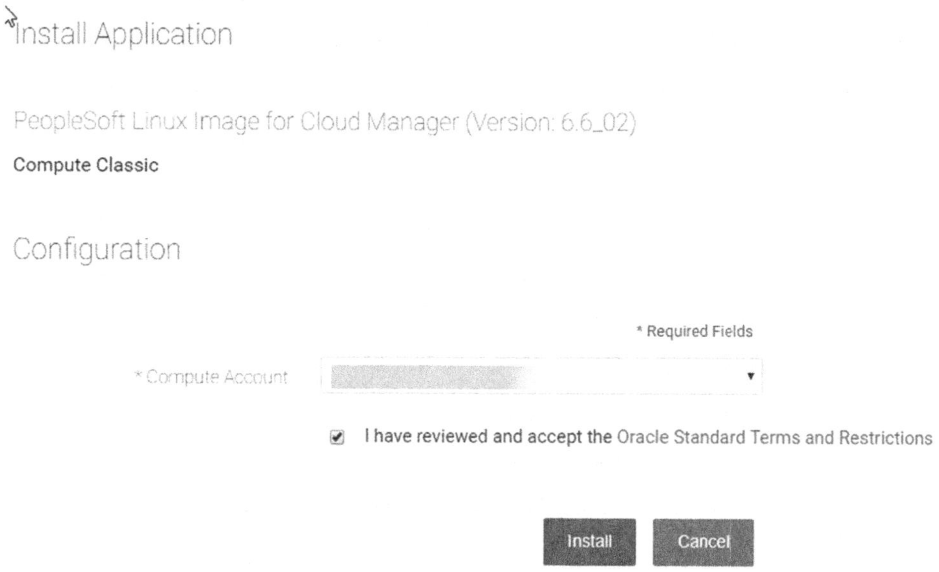

Install Application

PeopleSoft Linux Image for Cloud Manager (Version: 6.6_02)
Compute Classic

Configuration

* Required Fields

* Compute Account   [▼]

☑ I have reviewed and accept the Oracle Standard Terms and Restrictions

[Install]   [Cancel]

Figure 2-37. *Cloud Marketplace install dialogue*

10. Click **Install**.

11. Wait for the **Processing ...** dialogue to complete.

12. Success! Figure 2-38 provides a view of the success page.

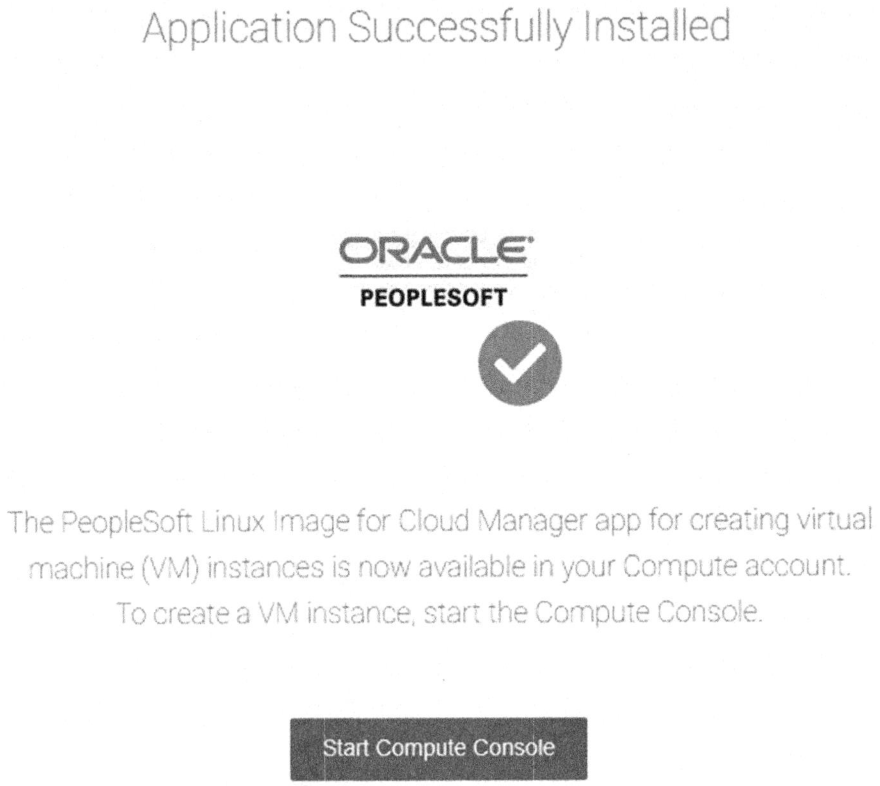
Application Successfully Installed
ORACLE
PEOPLESOFT
The PeopleSoft Linux Image for Cloud Manager app for creating virtual machine (VM) instances is now available in your Compute account.
To create a VM instance, start the Compute Console.
Start Compute Console

Figure 2-38. *PeopleSoft Cloud Marketplace Installation success*

13. Click **Start Compute Console**.

14. Do not provision this instance yet! Instead, go to your Compute Classic Service Console, and click the **Image** tab. You should now see the PeopleSoft Linux Image for Cloud Manager in your Image repository (Figure 2-39).

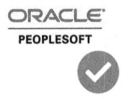

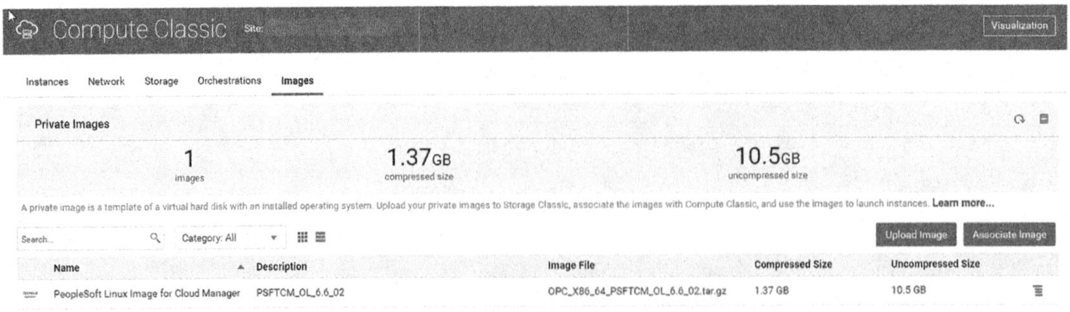
Compute Classic
Visualization
Instances
Network
Storage
Orchestrations
Images
Private Images
1
images
1.37GB
compressed size
10.5GB
uncompressed size
Upload Image
Associate Image
Name
Description
Image File
Compressed Size
Uncompressed Size
PeopleSoft Linux Image for Cloud Manager
PSFTCM_OL_6.6_02
OPC_X86_64_PSFTCM_OL_6.6_02.tar.gz
1.37 GB
10.5 GB

Figure 2-39. *PeopleSoft Linux image in the Compute Classic Service Console*

15. You will need the fully qualified name of this image later in the Cloud Manager installation process, so while you are here, you should record the image name. If you place your cursor over the image name you will see the fully qualified image name in a pop-up box. The fully qualified image name will follow the following format: `Compute-<service_instance_id>/<user_name>/<imagename>`, for example, `/Compute-XXXXXXXXX/peoplesoftcloudmanager@gmail.com/PSFTCM_OL_6.6_02`.

Save this name to your install-information.txt document under the heading PeopleSoft Linux Image.

Microsoft Windows Image for PeopleSoft Cloud Manager

Along with the Oracle Linux 6 Image, PeopleSoft Cloud Manager also uses a Microsoft Windows image to install various PeopleSoft components such as PeopleSoft Client tools like Application Designer, Datamover, and Change Assistant. To get a Windows image that is up to date, secure, and ready to be used by PeopleSoft Cloud Manager, you will need to create a new private Windows image for cloud use. This is a multistep process that requires you to get the base Windows image from the Oracle Cloud Marketplace, provision the image, update the image with Windows updates and Oracle Cloud security requirements, and finally create a snapshot and use that image to create a Private Image. The steps to complete this task follow.

Obtain the Window Image from the Oracle Cloud Marketplace

Much like the Oracle Linux Image in the previous section, you will need to go the Oracle Cloud Marketplace to obtain a working Windows image to start from:

1. Sign in to the Oracle Cloud Marketplace (`https://cloudmarketplace.oracle.com/marketplace/en_US/homePage.jspx`) with your Oracle.com username and password.

2. Search for "Windows Server 2012" in the Oracle Cloud Marketplace search box.

3. This search will return quite a few different options, but the image we are looking for is called **Microsoft Windows Server 2012 R2** (Figure 2-40).

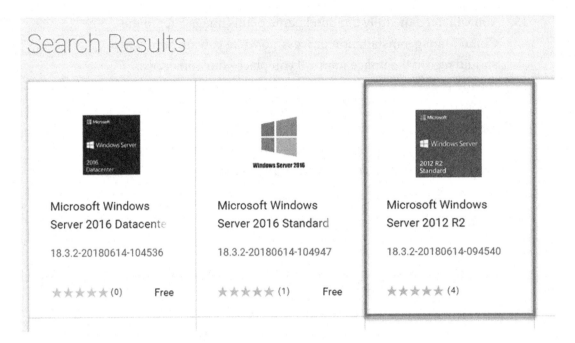

Figure 2-40. *Microsoft Windows search result*

4. Click the Microsoft Windows Server 2012 R2 tile.

5. On the Microsoft Windows Server 2012 R2 details page, click the
    Get App button at the top of the page.

6. From the Install Application page, select your Compute Account
    from the drop-down in the center of the page, check the Oracle
    and Microsoft Windows Terms of Use check box, and then click
    the **Install** button.

7. Once the cloud installation process complete, click the **Start
    Compute Console** button to start the provisioning process.

Provision the Windows VM in Compute Classic

Now that you have the Microsoft Windows Server 2012 R2 image available for use in
your Compute Classic Service, you need to take steps to ensure that the image is both
updated with current Microsoft updates and has proper security in place. To get started
completing these tasks, you much first provision the installed image:

1. Sign in to the Oracle Cloud My Services Dashboard.

2. Click **Open Service Console** on the menu from the Compute
    Classic widget.

3. On the Compute Classic Service Console, go to the **Images** tab.

4. If you've followed the steps so far, you should see two images
    in the images tab, a PeopleSoft Linux Image for Cloud Manager
    Image and the Microsoft Windows Server R2 Standard Image.

    On the far-right side of the row labeled Microsoft Windows Server
    R2 Standard Image, you will see a small menu icon, select it and
    click **Create Instance** (Figure 2-41).

Figure 2-41. *Create Instance from Compute Classic*

5. This will open a six-step Create Instance wizard. The first step in
    the wizard is **Image**. Click the **Select** button to the right of the
    Microsoft Window image description, and then click the small
    arrow to move to the next step (Figure 2-42).

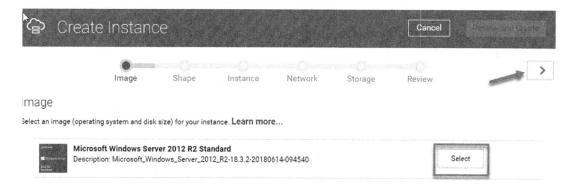

Figure 2-42. *Step 1, Image, in the Create Instance process*

6. Step 2 of the Create Instance wizard allows you to select the shape, the number of CPUs, and memory that will be allocated to the image. There are many options based on your needs.

    For the purpose of this exercise, you can select the base General Purpose shape with 1 OCPU (an OCPU is the CPU capacity equivalent of one physical core of an Intel Xeon processor with hyper-threading enabled) and 7.5 GB of memory. Once you've selected the shape for your image, click the next arrow at the top of the page. Figure 2-43 provides a view of some of the shape options available.

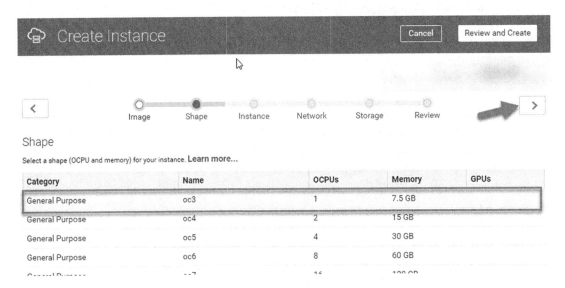

Figure 2-43. *Step 2, Shape*

Next is the Instance page. On this page, complete the following information, and then click the next page button at the top of the page:

Persistent: False.

Placement: Auto.

Name: Microsoft_Windows_Seerver_2012_R2 (or your choice).

Label: Microsoft_Windows_Seerver_2012_R2 (or your choice).

Description: Custom Windows Image for Cloud Manager.

Tags: PeopleSoft (tags can be used to organize images).

SSH Keys: Select the public key we uploaded earlier in this process (psabook-key).

RDP: Enabled.

Administrator Password: Your choice – it will appear unmasked in this window. Record this password somewhere as you will need it later to access the running virtual machine.

Custom Attributes: The password you entered will automatically populate in clear text here also (Figure 2-44).

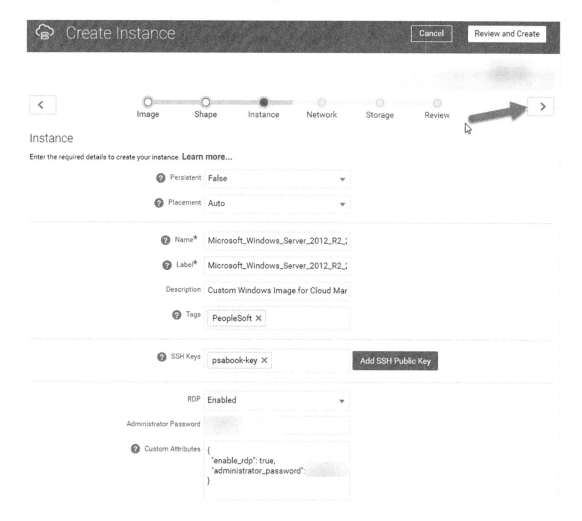

Figure 2-44. *Step 3, Instance*

7. On the Network step, check the **Shared Network** check box, and
    make sure that the default security list is in place in the Security
    List row. Click the next button at the top of the page when
    complete.

Note   You can specify a DNS Hostname Prefix in this step. This allows you to
enter a custom hostname prefix that will be used to reference this virtual machine
instance internally on Compute Classic (Figure 2-45).

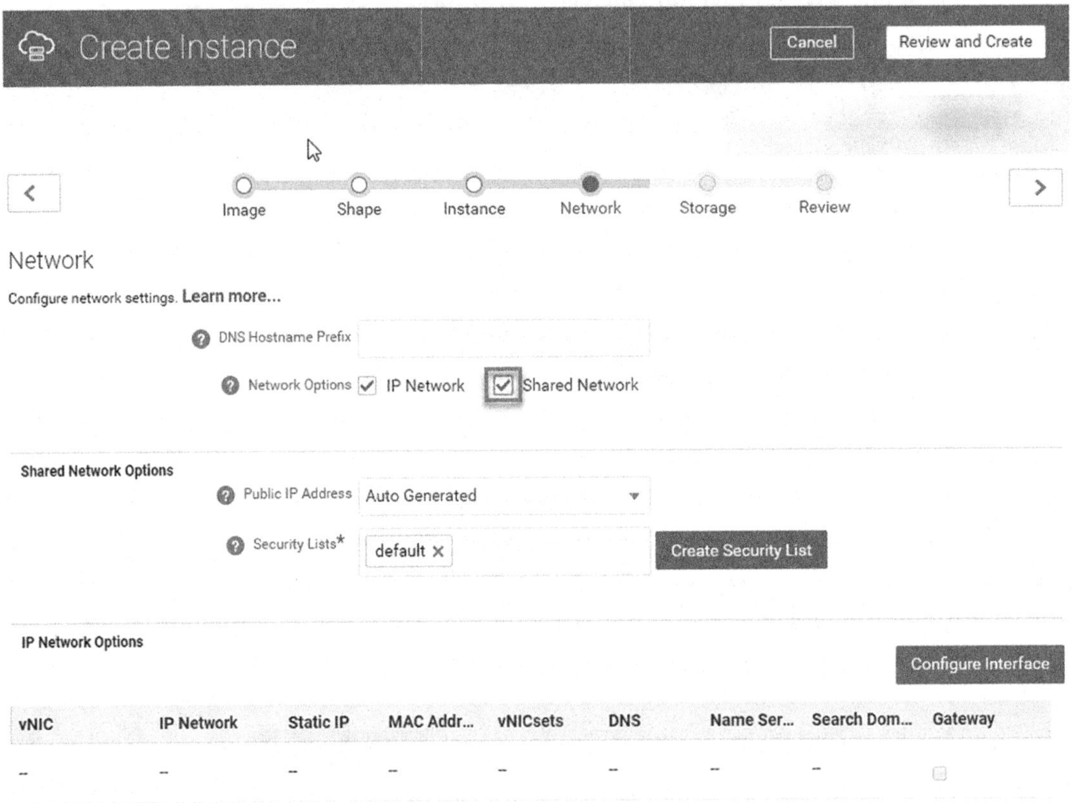

Figure 2-45. *Step 4, Network*

8. The next step in the wizard is the Storage step. Here, click the small menu icon to the right of the storage description, and select **Remove** from the menu options. This will create a nonpersistent boot drive for this instance – this means that the boot disk will be deleted on the termination of the instance rather than created and mounted as part of the instance. Figure 2-46 highlights the Remove menu option.

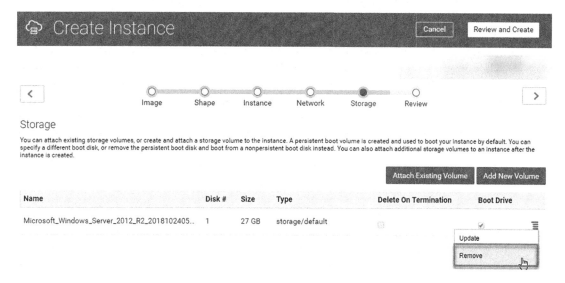

Figure 2-46. *Step 5, Storage*

9. Review all your instance settings on the Review step. Once you are satisfied that you have everything as needed, click the **Create** button at the top of the page (Figure 2-47).

Figure 2-47. *Step 6, Review*

10. Once you have started the instance provisioning process, you
can check the status of this Windows instance in the Instance tab
within the Compute Classic Service Console. It is ready to use
when the instance status is set to Running (Figure 2-48).

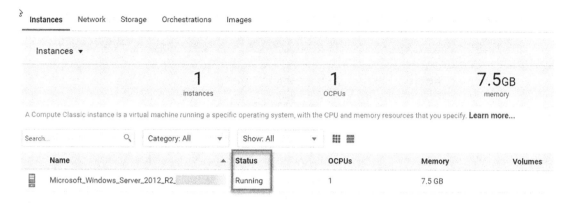

Figure 2-48. *A running instance in the Oracle Cloud Compute Classic Service*

Creating Security for the Windows VM

To allow access from a local Microsoft Windows host to the Windows virtual machine we just created, you will need to create a Security List and a Security Rule which enable that access. We will first create the security list, and then we will use that security list to create a Security Rule.

Creating a Security List

1. Assuming you've not left the Compute Classic My Services Console, navigate to the Network tab.

2. On the Navigation tab, from either the left-hand navigation menu or the drop-down menu at the top of the page, select **Security Lists**, which is found under the **Shared Network** menu group (Figure 2-49).

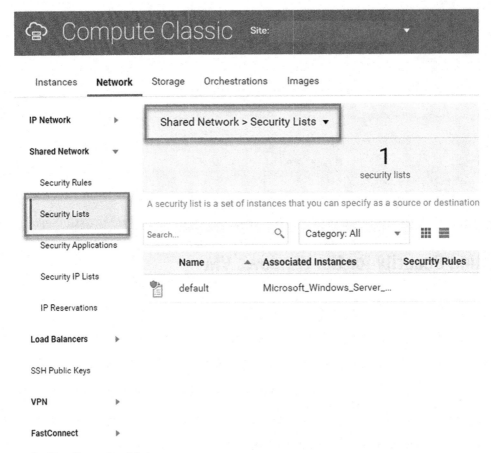

Figure 2-49. *Security Lists*

3. From the Security Lists page, click the **Create Security List** button
    in the upper right-hand corner (Figure 2-50).

Figure 2-50. *Create a Security List*

4.   In the Create Access Control List window, you will need to enter
     a few points of information to correctly create the security list
     (Figure 2-51).

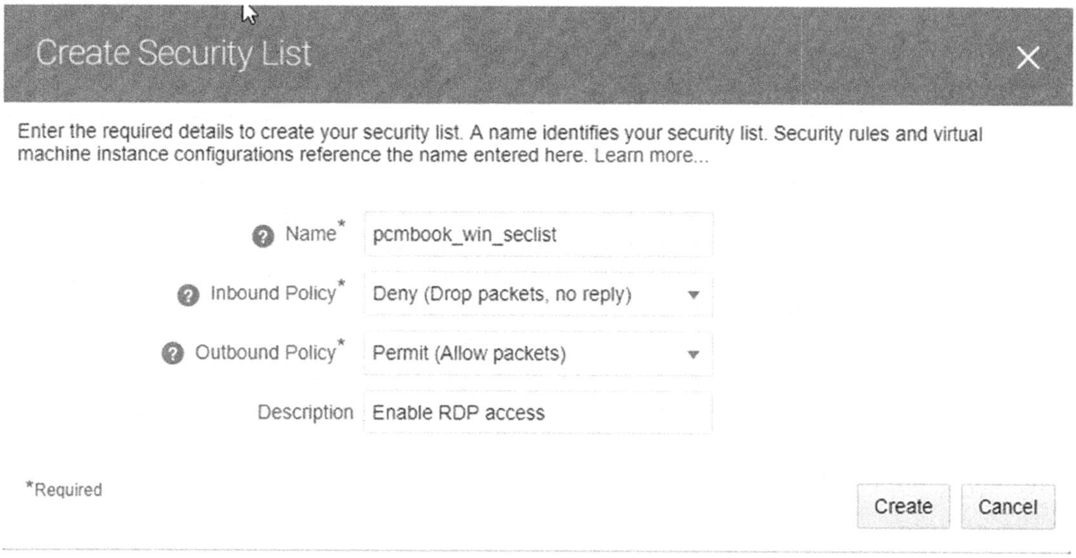

Figure 2-51. *Create Security List dialogue*

- **Name:** Provide a name for the new security list. For this instance,
  I will be using **pcmbook_win_ACL,** but within your company
  or for your purposes, you may choose to use a more appropriate
  name to indicate what this security list is for.

- **Inbound Policy:** Leave it as the default, **Deny (Drop packets,
  no reply).**

- **Outbound Policy:** Select the **Permit (Allow packets)** option
  from the drop-down menu.

- **Description:** Here you can provide any description of the Access
  Control List you find necessary. For our example an adequate
  description is **Enable RDP access**.

5.   Once this information is entered, click the **Create** button in the
     bottom right corner of the Create Security List window.

6. You will now see your security list listed on the main Security List
    page. You will notice, however, that this security list does not have
    any associated images listed – we will do that next. Figure 2-52
    indicates a completed security list.

Figure 2-52. *Completed Security List*

7. From the **Instances** tab, select the **View** menu option from the
    menu icon on the far-right side of the running Windows instance
    (Figure 2-53).

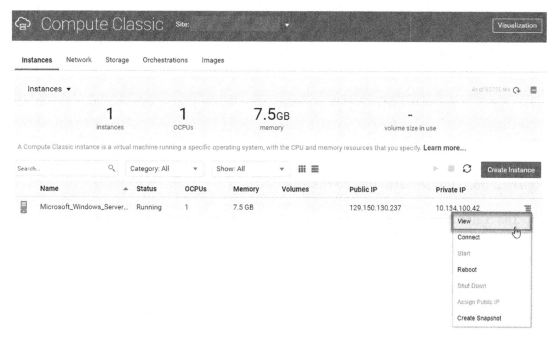

Figure 2-53. *Getting to the Instance Details page*

8. This will open an Instance Details page for your Microsoft Windows
    Server 2012 R2 instance. Under the Security Lists section of this
    details page, click the **Add to Security List** button (Figure 2-54).

Figure 2-54. *Add to Security List*

9. In the **Add to Security List** window, select the security list you just
    created from the drop-down menu (Figure 2-55).

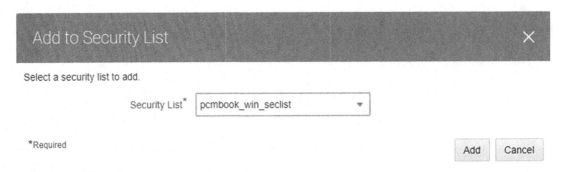

Figure 2-55. *Add to Security List dialogue box*

10.   Click **Add**.

11.   Your new security list will now show up in the Security List section
      on your Instance Details page for the Microsoft Windows Server
      2012 R2 instance (Figure 2-56).

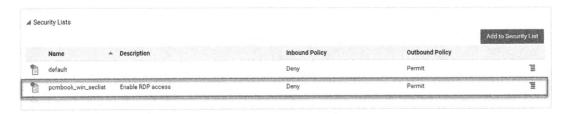

Figure 2-56. *Newly added Security List*

Creating a Security Rule

1.   Next, we will continue to add security to our Windows Server
     image by creating a new Security Rule. Start by navigating to the
     Network tab and selecting the **Security Rules** option in the Shared
     Network group (Figure 2-57).

Figure 2-57. *Navigation to Security Rules*

2. Click the **Create Security Rule** button in the bottom right corner
    of the page (Figure 2-58).

Figure 2-58. *Create Security Rule*

3. In the Create Security Rule window, enter the following
    information:

    *   **Name:** Like the Security List, use the proper naming convention
        for your organization or purpose. For our purpose, this Security
        Rule will be named **pcmbook_win_secrule**.

    *   **Status:** Leave as the default, **Enabled**.

    *   **Security Application:** Select **rpd** from the drop-down menu.

    *   **Source:** Select the **Security IP List** radio button and then, from
        the drop-down menu, select the **public-internet** option.

    *   **Destination:** Select the **Security List** radio button and then, from
        the drop-down menu, select the **pcmbook_win_seclist** Security
        List.

- **Description:** Like any of the description fields, feel free to add as
  much detail as you like to help you better know what this Security
  Rule is for. In this case, **Enable rdp access** should be sufficient
  (Figure 2-59).

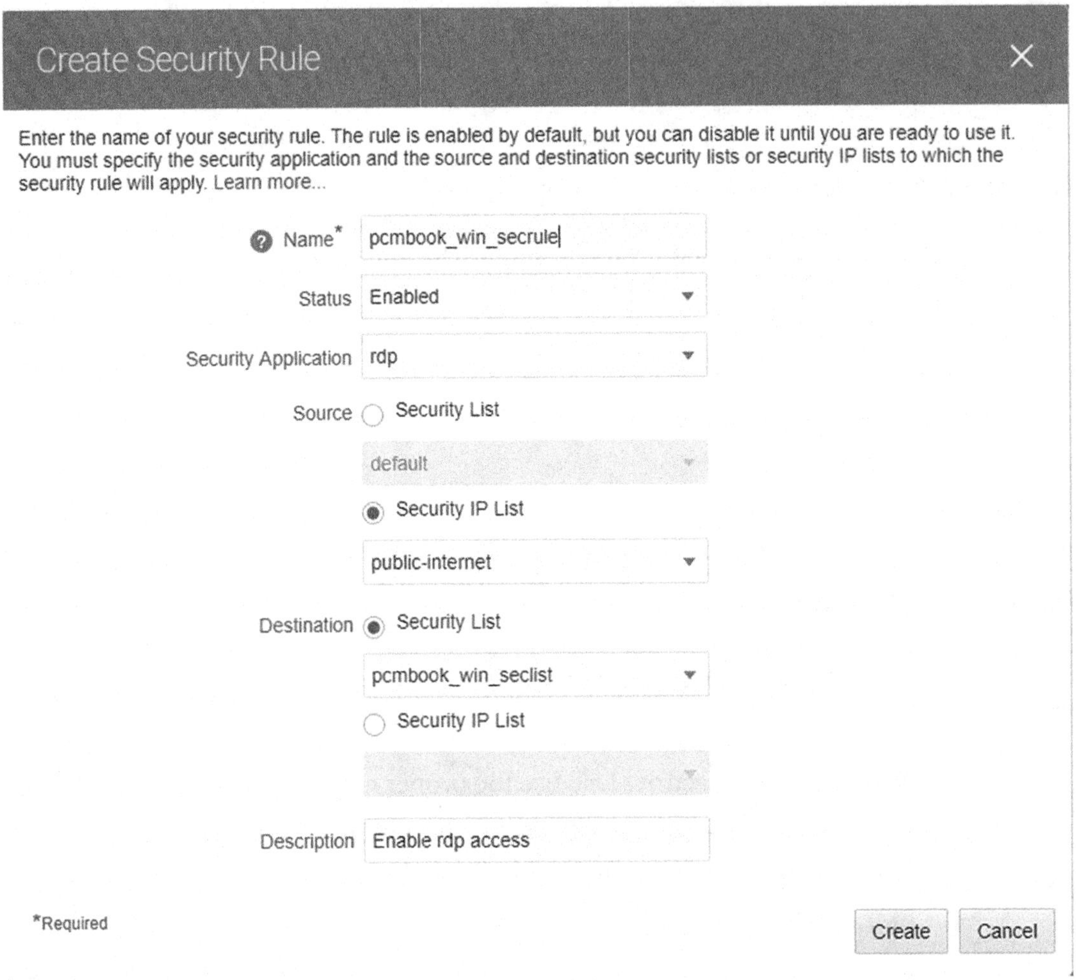

Figure 2-59. *Create Security Rule dialogue box*

4. Click **Create**.

5. This Security Rule will now be listed in your Shared Network
    Security Rules (Figure 2-60).

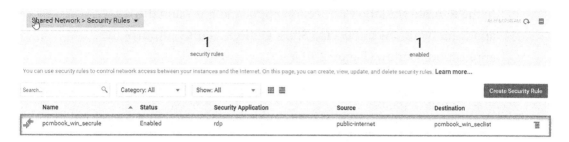

Figure 2-60. *Completed Security Rule*

Apply Windows Updates

Now that we have a Security List and a Security Rule in place, we can take a few additional steps to make sure that our Windows Server 2012 R2 instance is up to date with all the current security updates and patches. To do this, we will need to connect to the Windows instance using the remote desktop protocol (RDP). To connect to your Windows virtual machine from a local Windows host, you can use Remote Desktop Connection, which is Windows default RDP client.

To properly connect to your Windows Server 2012 R2 instance in the Oracle Cloud, you will need two pieces of information. First, from the Compute Classic Service Console, you need to get the public IP address for the instance you are going to connect to via RDP. The public IP address can be found on the Instances tab in the Compute Classic Service Console in a column to the right of the instance name. Second, you need the administrator password you supplied to the provisioning wizard when you configured this machine. Once you have these two pieces of information, you are ready to update your Windows instance.

Connecting to a Windows VM from a Windows Host

1. From your Windows host, launch the Remote Desktop Connection application. From Window 10, opening the Windows menu and typing Remote can easily accomplish this. The Windows default RDP client, Remote Desktop Connection, should be at the top of the list.

2. In the Remote Desktop Connection application, expand the
    application options by clicking Show Options at the bottom of the
    application window (Figure 2-61).

Figure 2-61. *Windows Remote Desktop Connection Client*

3. To connect to your Windows VM in the Oracle Cloud, enter the
    public IP address for the VM you are connecting to, and enter the
    username Administrator (Figure 2-62).

Figure 2-62. *Windows Remote Desktop Connection computer and username options*

4. Click **Connect** in the bottom right of the application window.

5. A security message/window will open indicating that the identity of the remote computer cannot be verified. Click **Yes** on this security message (Figure 2-63).

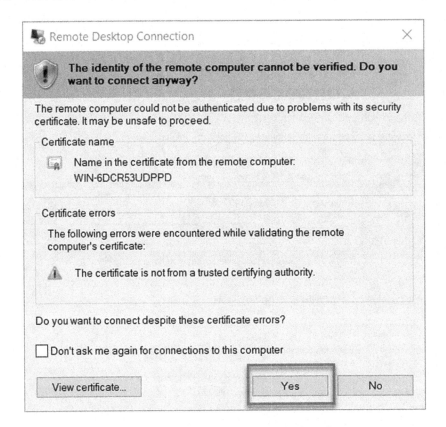

Figure 2-63. *Remote Desktop Connection Security Warning*

6. The Windows VM should now open.

Connecting to a Windows VM from a Linux Host

1. From your Linux host, launch the RDP client. In my case I am running Kubuntu, which comes ready to go with the KRDC KDE Remote Desktop Client. If you are running a different flavor of Linux or a different remote desktop connection manager, your steps may be slightly different than this.

2. Once the Remote Desktop Client opens, select RDP from the **Connect to** drop-down at the top of the application window. Enter the public IP address for your Windows Server 2012 R2 instance, and click the next arrow on the right of the application window (Figure 2-64).

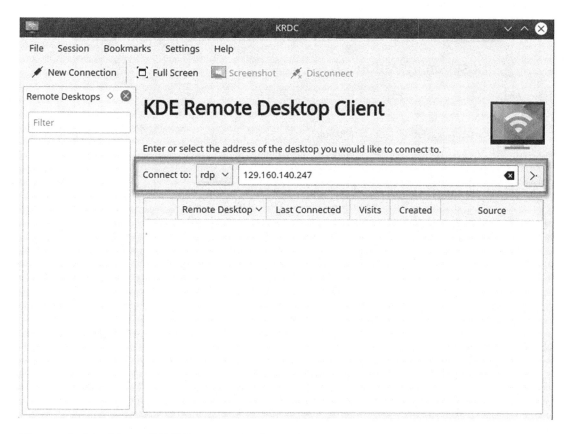

Figure 2-64. *Linux KDE Remote Desktop Connection*

3. Make any changes to the Host Configuration window you deem necessary, and click **OK** (Figure 2-65).

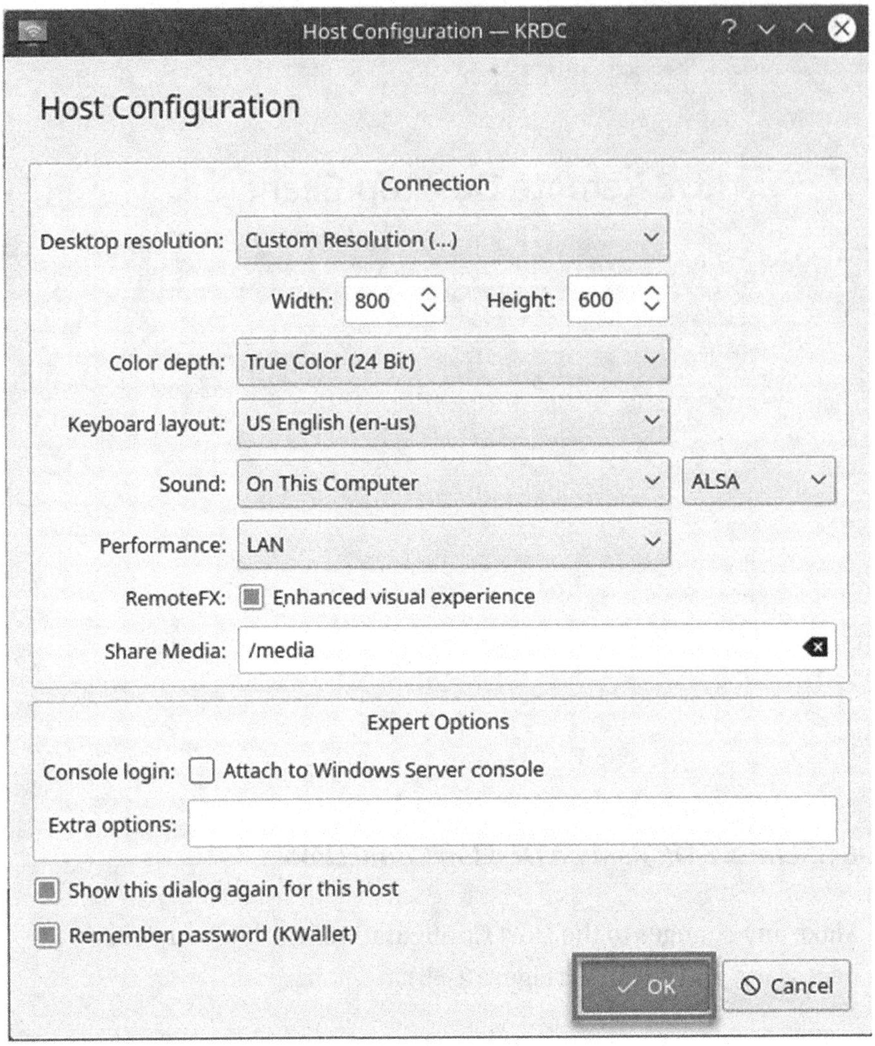

Figure 2-65. *KDE Remote Desktop Connection Host Configuration Window*

4. In the Enter Username window, type in **Administrator,** and click
    OK (Figure 2-66).

Figure 2-66. *KDE Remote Desktop Connection Administrator user*

5. Enter the password your supplied for the virtual machine when you provisioned it, and click **OK** (Figure 2-67).

Figure 2-67. *KDE Remote Desktop Connection password*

6. You should now be remotely connected to your Windows Server 2012 R2 instance in the Oracle Compute Cloud.

Installing Windows Updates

Once you have successfully connected to the Windows Server 2012 R2 host, you need to update the OS on that host. This will ensure that all proper security and other important updates are applied to your virtual machine:

1. From the desktop of the Windows VM, open the Windows menu; select Control Panel, Systems and Security, and finally Windows Update.

2. Click **Change Settings**.

3. Allow Windows to install important updates automatically.
    This is the default setting. You can also allow Windows to treat
    recommended updates in the same way. Once your setting is
    updated, click the **OK** button at the bottom of the window to start
    checking for updates. Figure 2-68 shows the Windows dialogue
    detail for installing updates automatically.

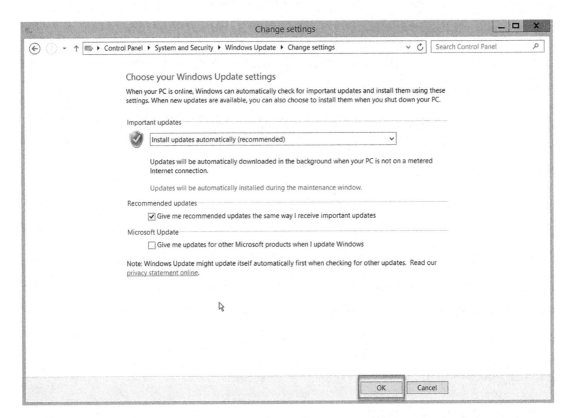

Figure 2-68.   *Windows Update Settings*

4. Once Windows returns the number of important and
    recommended updates that are required to update your Windows
    Server 2012 R2 instance, click the link in the window for the
    important updates.

5. The next window allows you the opportunity to select which important and recommended updates you'd like to install. Select all updates by clicking the check box at the top of the window. Do the same thing for the recommended updates tab. Once all necessary updates are selected, click the **Install** button in the bottom corner of the window (Figure 2-69).

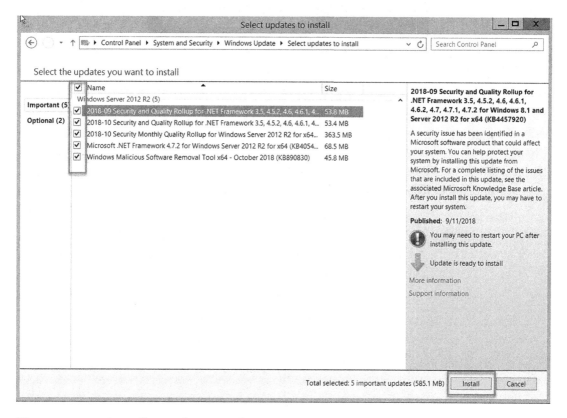

Figure 2-69. *Install Windows Updates*

6. Windows will first download the necessary updates and then install them.

7. When the install and update is complete, do not reboot the Windows VM from Windows; rather close the Windows Update window and Disconnect from the Remote Desktop Connection setting (Figure 2-70).

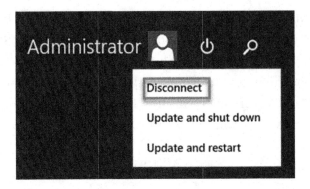

Figure 2-70. *Disconnect from the virtual machine*

8. Now that the updates are in place, you need to reboot the virtual machine. In the Compute Classic Services Console, go to the **Instances** tab.

9. Find the Windows Server 2012 R2 instance that you just updated, and select **Reboot** from the menu for that instance (Figure 2-71).

Figure 2-71. *Reboot the virtual machine from the Compute Classic Service Console*

10. Confirm the reboot by clicking the **Yes** button in the Reboot Instance window (Figure 2-72).

Figure 2-72. *Confirm the reboot*

11. The virtual machine will reboot and will once again show as Running in the Service Console.

Save a Snapshot of the Instance

Once you have successfully rebooted the Windows Server 2012 R2 instance, the virtual machine is back online and running; you can create a snapshot and associate that snapshot to a new private image. Later in the PeopleSoft Cloud Manger installation process, you will use this private image to provide a Windows image to be used by PCM for various purposes such as deploying PeopleTools Client instances and Change Assistant:

1. If you have closed your login to the Oracle Cloud, log back in and make your way back to the Compute Classic Services Console Instances tab.

2. From the Instances tab, select **Create Snapshot** by clicking the small menu icon found at the end of the row for our Microsoft Windows 2012 R2 instance (Figure 2-73).

Figure 2-73. *Create Snapshot*

3. In the Create Instance Snapshot window, provide a name for the snapshot you are creating. For our purposes here, we can call this snapshot **pcmbook_winsnapshot.** Make sure the **Deferred Snapshot** check box is unchecked, and then click **Create** (Figure 2-74).

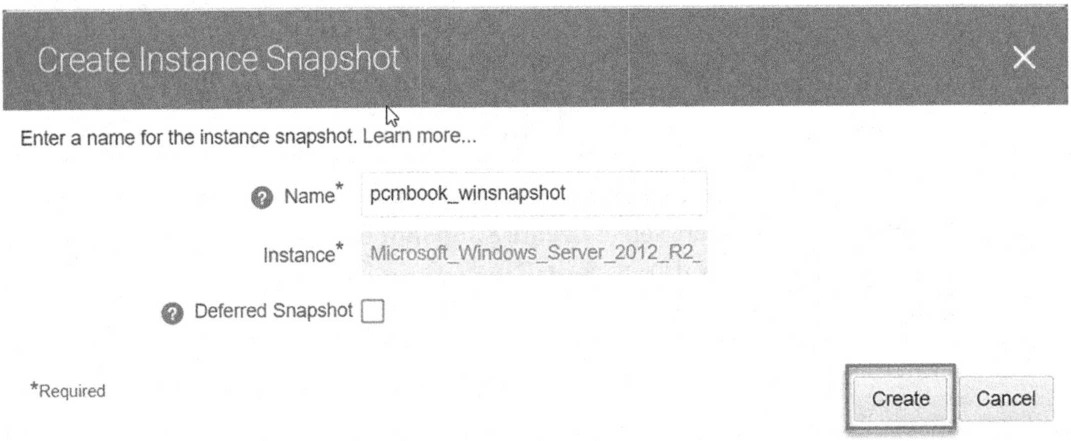

Create Instance Snapshot   ✕

Enter a name for the instance snapshot. Learn more...

        ❓ Name*   pcmbook_winsnapshot

       Instance*   Microsoft_Windows_Server_2012_R2_

    ❓ Deferred Snapshot ☐

*Required   Create   Cancel

Figure 2-74. *Create Instance Snapshot*

4. Select Instance Snapshot from the Instance drop-down (Figure 2-75).

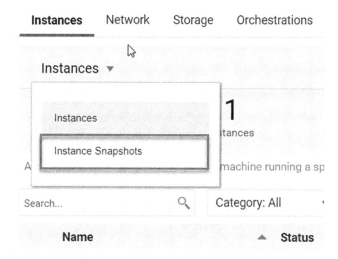

Figure 2-75. *View the Instance Snapshots*

5. Verify that the new snapshot you just created is now in an Active status. When the snapshot is ready, the status will change to Complete (Figure 2-76).

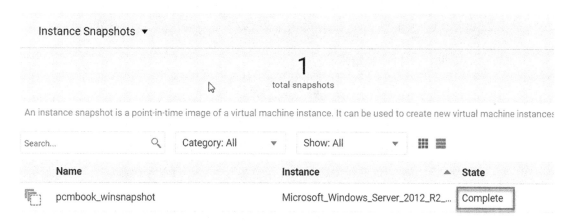

Figure 2-76. *Wait for the snapshot creation to complete*

6. Once the instance snapshot status is Complete, click the menu icon on the right side of the instance snapshot, and select **Associate Image** (Figure 2-77).

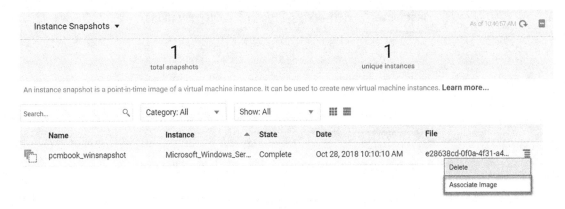

Figure 2-77. *Associate Image drop-down*

7. In the Associate Image window, provide a description for the
    image. For this instance, a description of **Private Windows image
    for Cloud Manager** is perfect. Once the description is entered,
    click **OK** (Figure 2-78).

Figure 2-78. *Associate Image dialogue*

8. Congratulations! You have successfully created and appropriately
    associated a private Windows image to be used by Cloud Manager.
    To save yourself some time and effort later in the PeopleSoft Cloud
    Manager installation process, go to the **Images** tab and hold your
    cursor over the private Windows image you just created. Make a
    note of the full path and name of this image in your text document
    – you will need it later.

Note   Once the private image is created, you can safely delete the instance you used to create the snapshot. To do this, go to the Orchestrations tab in the Compute Classic Service Console, find the orchestration that was used to create the Windows Server 2012 R2 instance that is running. For this orchestration, click **Suspend** from the drop-down menu, and then click **OK** in the Suspend Orchestration window.

Fulfilling Oracle Cloud Security Requirements

In Chapter 3, we will be installing the PeopleSoft Cloud Manager application within the Oracle Cloud. This application contains a web server instance that is, by default, configured to listen on port 8000 for HTTP requests and port 8443 for HTTPS requests. Your environment, infrastructure, or corporate standards may require that you use listening port values that are different from those. While the steps that follow will stick to the examples of using ports 8000 and 8443, if you do use other ports, you can configure them by following the corresponding steps and then supplying the specific values you used when you are running the Cloud Manager Instance Configuration Wizard.

There are three main components that are required by the Oracle Cloud Infrastructure to properly secure PeopleSoft Cloud Manager. The three components are the Security List, the Security Application, and the Security Rule. Each of these will be explained in more detail in subsequent sections, but these three components work together to control the traffic in and out of your Oracle Cloud applications.

Create Security List

The Security List is used by the Compute Classic Service as a means to restrict traffic and provide a set of rules for the inbound and outbound data traffic for your Compute Classic instances within the Oracle Cloud. The Security List is enforced at the instance level; however, the Security List is configured at the subnet level, meaning all instances within the same subnet are subject to the same set of traffic rules.

To create the required security list:

1. If you have logged out of the Oracle Cloud, log back in and navigate to the Compute Cloud Service Console.

2. Select the **Network** tab on the Compute Classic Service Console.

3. From the Network tab, select the **Security Lists** menu option under the **Shared Network** heading (Figure 2-79).

Figure 2-79. *Security Lists navigation*

4. Click **Create Security List** in the upper right corner of the page.

5. In the **Create Security List** window, there are four pieces of information you need to provide: the security list name, the inbound data policy, the outbound data policy, and a description of the security list.

   - **Name:** This can be unique to your organization and needs. For our purposes, we will use **pcmbook_seclist.**

   - **Inbound Policy:** Deny (Drop packets, no reply).

   - **Outbound Policy:** Permit (Allow packets).

   - **Description:** PeopleSoft Cloud Manager security list (Figure 2-80).

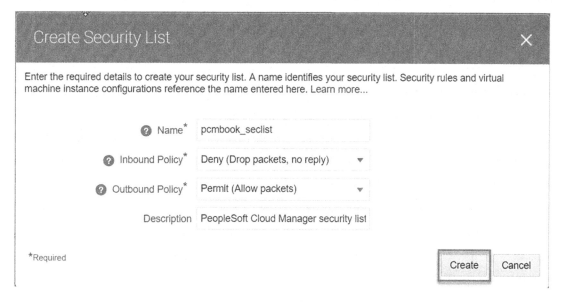

Figure 2-80.   *Create Security List dialogue box*

6.   Click **Create**.

7.   At this point, per your business requirements, you can add additional security lists as needed.

Create Security Application

A Security Application allows you to specify what type of traffic (like TCP, UDP, or ICMP) is allowed on specific ports within your Compute Classic instance. Within our context, we will be setting up a Security Application to allow TCP traffic on port 8000. In your environment you may need to allow some specific traffic on some other port, for example, you may need to allow TCP traffic on port 16100 as this is your company standard for HTTP traffic. This can be accomplished by setting up a Service Application:

1.   From the Network tab of the Compute Classic Service Console, select **Security Applications** under the **Shared Network** submenu (Figure 2-81).

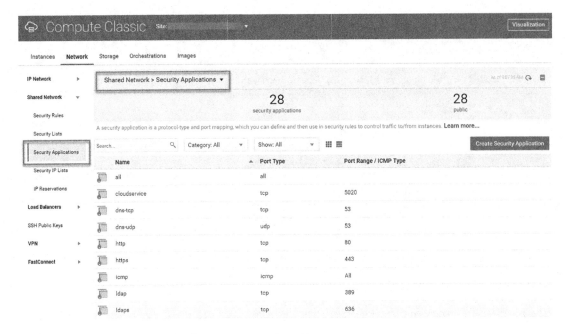

Figure 2-81. *Security Applications navigation*

2.   Click the **Create Security Application** button in the top right
     corner of the page.

3.   In the Create Security Application pop-up window, you will need
     to provide the following information:

     •   **Name:** Use whatever naming convention your enterprise
         requires, but for our purposes, this Security Application will be
         named **pcmbook_tcp8000**.

     •   **Port Type:** Select **TCP** from the drop-down list.

     •   **Port Range Start:** 8000 – However, if your organization
         requires different ports for TCP traffic, say 16100 or some
         other port between 0 and 65535, you can use that port here as
         well. Remember to make a note of the port you are using, and
         configure PeopleSoft Cloud Manager accordingly.

     •   **Port Range End:** Leave this blank; this will open only the single
         port specified in the Port Range Start field, in our case port 8000.

- • **Description:** Allow TCP traffic on port 8000 – or list the specific
  port you have specified in setting up this Service Application
  (Figure 2-82).

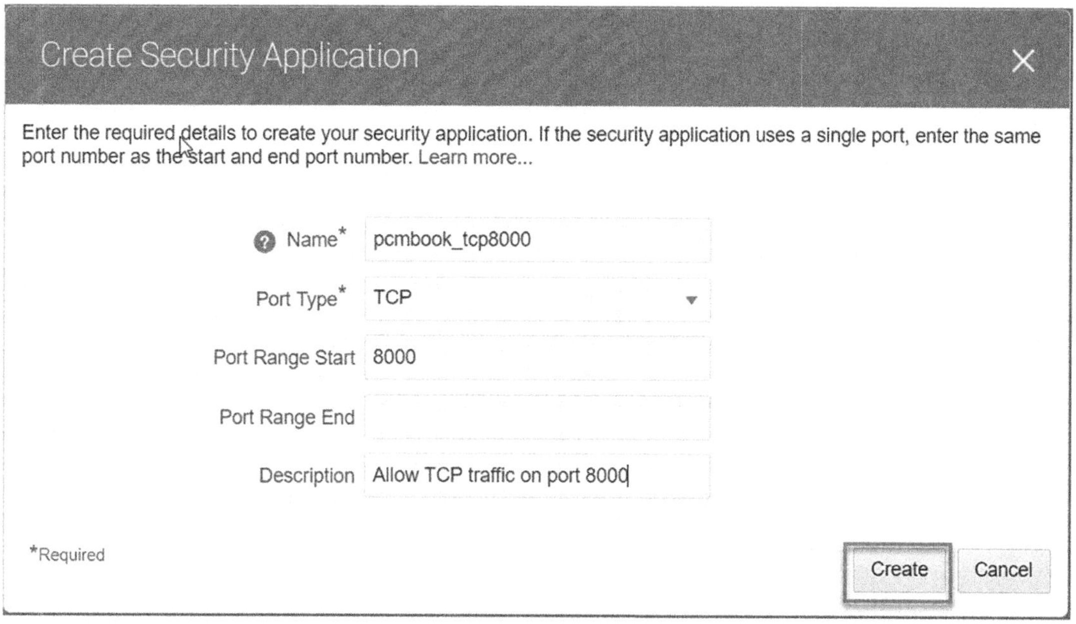

Figure 2-82. *Create Security Application dialogue*

    4.   Click the **Create** button.

Note   You can add as many Security Applications as you like. Do notice however that Oracle provides several common, or default, Security Applications for your use. You will find HTTP for port 80, HTTPS for port 443, and mysql for port 3306 already set up and configured within the Service Applications page.

Create Security Rule

To create a Security Rule:

    1.   From the Network tab of the Compute Classic Service Console,
select **Security Rules** under the **Shared Network** submenu
(Figure 2-83).

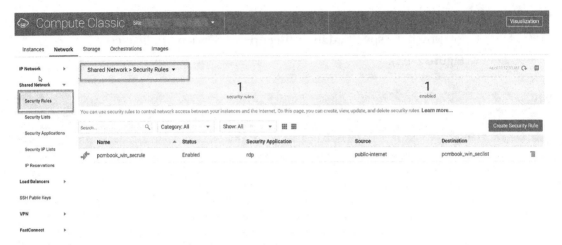

Figure 2-83. *Security Rules navigation*

2. Click the **Create Security Rule** button in the top right corner of the page.

3. In the Create Security Rule pop-up window, you will need to provide the following information:

    - **Name:** Provide a name of your choice for this Security Rule, I have used **pcmbook_secrule8000**.

    - **Status: Enabled**.

    - **Security Application:** Select the Security Application we created in the previous step, **pcmbook_tcp8000**.

    - **Source:** Select the **Security IP List** radio button option, and then select **public-internet** from the corresponding drop-down menu.

    - **Destination:** Select the **Security List** radio button option, and then select **pcmbook_seclist** (the Security List we previously created) from the corresponding drop-down menu.

    - **Description:** Provide a description of your choice; I have used **PeopleSoft Cloud Manager security rule** in this example (Figure 2-84).

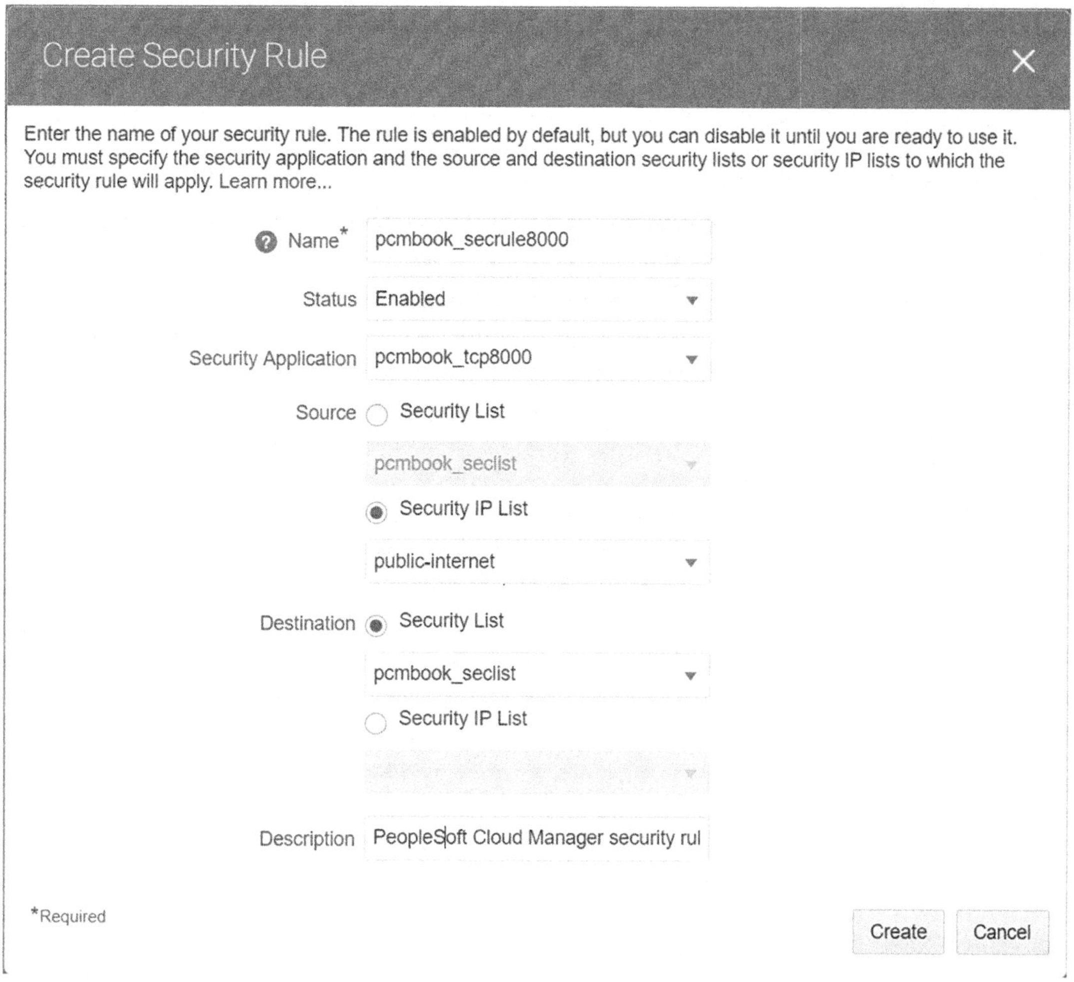

Create Security Rule   ✕

Enter the name of your security rule. The rule is enabled by default, but you can disable it until you are ready to use it.
You must specify the security application and the source and destination security lists or security IP lists to which the
security rule will apply. Learn more...

❓ Name*	pcmbook_secrule8000
Status	Enabled ▼
Security Application	pcmbook_tcp8000 ▼
Source ○	Security List
	pcmbook_seclist ▼
◉	Security IP List
	public-internet ▼
Destination ◉	Security List
	pcmbook_seclist ▼
○	Security IP List
	▼
Description	PeopleSoft Cloud Manager security rul

*Required   Create   Cancel

Figure 2-84. *Create Security Rule dialogue box*

4. Click the **Create** button.

Note   You may want to create additional Security Rules based on the needs of
your organization and the Security Lists and Applications you set up to meet those
organizational needs. If you do not, see a **default**.

Allowing SSH Access to Compute Classic Instances

You will need SSH access to the Compute Classic instance you create in the Oracle Cloud. To grant this access for all instances, we need to create a Security Rule that uses the default security list to broadly grant SSH access. To do this properly, you need to first determine that you have the **default** security list created. **Default** is an Oracle created security list, and, if it is not present, you will need to contact Oracle Support to get assistance in getting this issue resolved. Figure 2-85 shows the default security list.

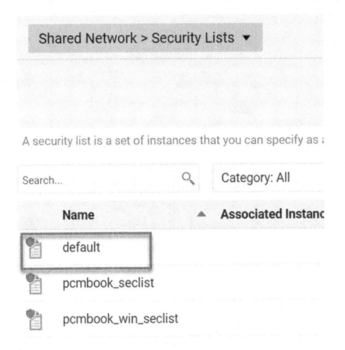

Figure 2-85. *Default Security List*

To allow SSH access to Compute Classic instances:

1. Go to the **Network** tab in the Compute Classic Service Console.

2. On the **Network** tab, select **Security Rules** under the **Shared Network** submenu.

3. Click the **Create Security Rule** button in the top right corner of the page.

4. In the Create Security Rule pop-up window, you will need to provide the following information:

    •   **Name: DefaultPublicSSHAccess**

    •   **Status: Enabled**.

    •   **Security Application: SSH**.

    •   **Source:** Select the **Security IP List** radio button option, and then select **public-internet** from the corresponding drop-down menu.

    •   **Destination:** Select the **Security List** radio button option, and then select **default** from the corresponding drop-down menu.

    •   **Description:** Provide a description of your choice; I have used **Default Security Rule for public SSH access** in this example (Figure 2-86).

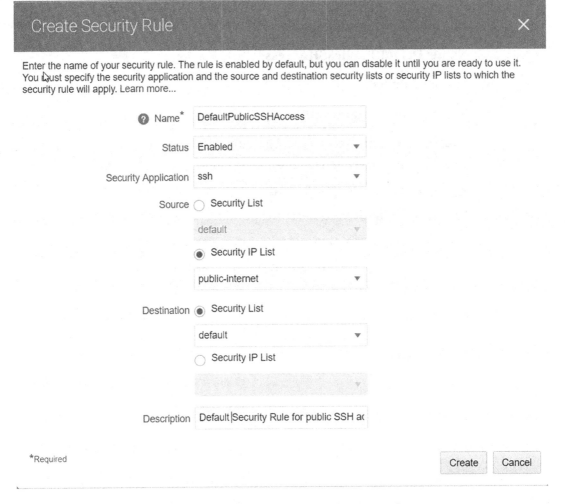

Figure 2-86. *Create Default Public SSH Access Security Rule*

5. Click the **Create** button.

CHAPTER 3

Installing PeopleSoft Cloud Manager on Compute Classic

You should now have all the bits and pieces you need to move forward with your PeopleSoft Cloud Manger application installation. This chapter will walk you through the steps necessary to obtain the PeopleSoft Cloud Manager Image (currently image 7) from the Oracle Cloud Marketplace, provision that image in the Compute Classic Service, and fully install PeopleSoft Cloud Manager in the Oracle Cloud.

Deploy PeopleSoft Cloud Manager Application from Oracle Cloud Marketplace

Like we previously went to the Oracle Cloud Marketplace and found both a suitable Linux and Windows image to use in our PeopleSoft Cloud, we now need to go to the Oracle Cloud Marketplace to obtain the current PeopleSoft Cloud Manager image. At the time this book was written, People Soft Cloud Manager Image 7 was the most current image available and will be used throughout the remainder of the book. Given that Oracle releases images rather regularly, you may find that a new image is now available for you to deploy.

91

© Aaron Engelsrud 2019
A. Engelsrud, *Managing PeopleSoft on the Oracle Cloud*, https://doi.org/10.1007/978-1-4842-4546-0_3

1. Go to the Oracle Cloud Marketplace (`https://cloudmarketplace.oracle.com`) and sign in. The sign in link is in the top right corner of the marketplace.

2. In the main search window, type in "PeopleSoft Cloud Manager," you should get an option to search for image 7. Select it and click **Go** (Figure 3-1).

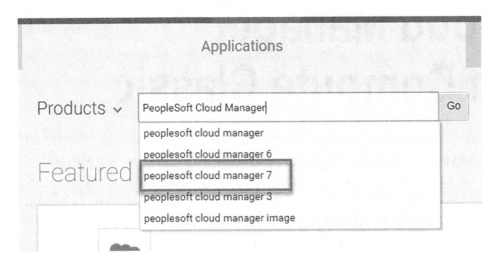

Figure 3-1. *Search for Cloud Manager Image from the Oracle Cloud Marketplace*

3. From the search results, select the PeopleSoft Cloud Manager for Image 07 application from the tiles that are provided. Since you are installing on Compute Classic, make sure you do not choose Image 07 for OCI (Figure 3-2).

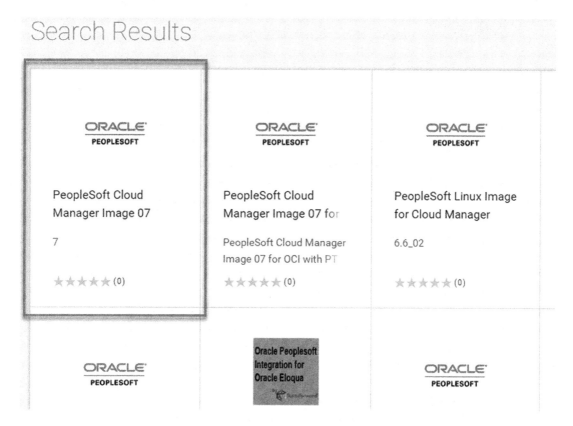

Figure 3-2. *Select the Current Image*

4. On the PeopleSoft Cloud Manager Image 07 page, click the green
    Get App ➤ button in the upper right-hand corner (Figure 3-3).

Figure 3-3. *Get PeopleSoft Cloud Manager from the marketplace*

5. Next the Install Application page will open. From this page, select
    the Compute Account you would like to deploy this application
    to, check the box to agree to Oracle's Standard Terms and
    Restrictions, and then click the blue **Install** button in the bottom
    center of the page (Figure 3-4).

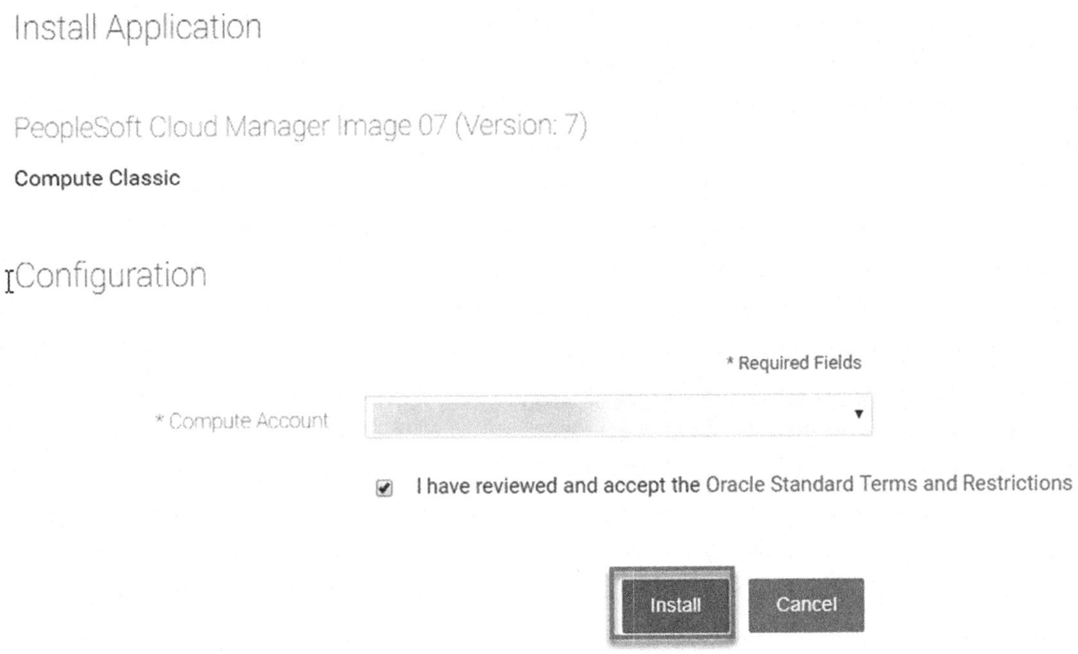

Install Application

PeopleSoft Cloud Manager Image 07 (Version: 7)

Compute Classic

ᵢConfiguration

* Required Fields

* Compute Account

☑ I have reviewed and accept the Oracle Standard Terms and Restrictions

Install   Cancel

Figure 3-4. *Install the image*

6. The deploy process should now start, and you should see a progress bar on the screen.

7. Once the deployment is complete, you should see a Application Successfully Installed message on the screen. Click the blue **Start Compute Console** button at the bottom of the page to start provisioning the Linux image.

Provision a Linux Image Using the PeopleSoft Cloud Manager Image

Now that you have successfully deployed the PeopleSoft Cloud Manager Image from the Oracle Cloud Marketplace, you now need to get the Linux VM that will get PeopleSoft Cloud Manager up and running. This will take you through the Create Instance wizard once again, just like you did with the Windows image earlier. Your choices here will be a little bit different, so make sure you make note of what is required for provisioning this image:

1. If you clicked the Start Compute Console button after you deployed the application, you should now see the Create Instance wizard. If you are not on the Create Instance wizard for PeopleSoft Cloud Manager Image 07, go to your Compute Classic Service Console, click the Images tab, and then select **Create Instance** from the menu icon for the PeopleSoft Cloud Manager Image 07 image.

2. In step 1 of the wizard, you simply select the image you are creating, in our case PeopleSoft Cloud Manager Image 07. You select this image by clicking the **Select** button on the right-hand side of the page, and then click the next arrow in the top corner (Figure 3-5).

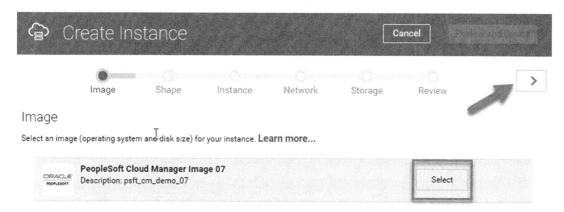

Figure 3-5. *Step 1 of the instance provisioning process*

3. Step 2 is the Shape option for the Linux image. Per Oracle's documentation, the minimum requirements are oc1m, which a high memory image with 1 OCPU and 15 GB of memory allocated. Select that option (or greater if you think you'll need a more powerful instance to support your needs), and click the next arrow (Figure 3-6).

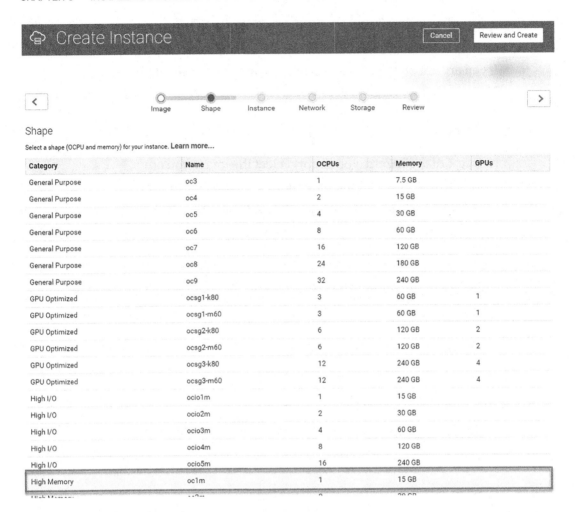

Figure 3-6. Step 2, Image Shape

4. In step 3, you will need to provide some details about the instance image. Provide this information as follows:

    - **Placement:** Auto (unless there is a specific domain you would like to select).

    - **Name:** You can choose any name you like or that fits with your needs. For our purposes here, I am using **CloudManager_ pcmbook.**

    - **Label:** Here too, use what works best for you and your needs. I am using **CloudManager_pcmbook.**

- **Description:** Enter a short description of the image. I provided **Cloud Manager Instance for pcmbook**.

- **Tags:** This is totally optional. I've been consistent in tagging everything with **PeopleSoft**, so I am continuing that standard.

- **SSH Keys:** Select the key you uploaded to the Oracle Cloud previously. I named this key **psabook-key.**

- **Custom Attributes:** You do not need to add anything further in this section. It should contain "cloud_manager_image":"true" by default.

Once this information is provided, click the next arrow at the top of the page as shown in Figure 3-7.

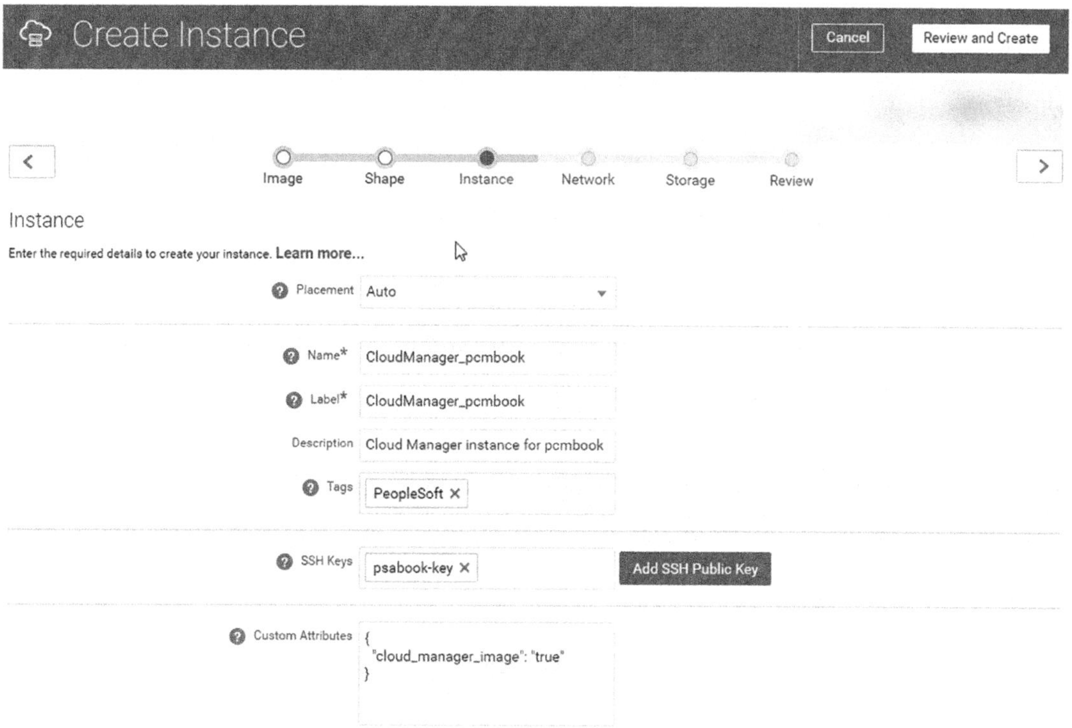

Figure 3-7. *Step 3, Instance detail*

5. Step 4 provides the image the required network details. Start by making sure that the **default** security list is in place in the Security Lists box. Once this is done, provide the following details:

a. **DNS Hostname Prefix:** Provide a useful DNS prefix; this prefix will be used to reference your image internally on Compute Classic. I am providing **pcmbook** as my DNS Hostname Prefix.

b. **Network Options:** Check both the **IP Network** and **Shared Network** check boxes.

c. **Public IP Address:** Select **Persistent Public IP Reservation** from the drop-down. This will then provide an additional blank drop-down menu. Click the **Create IP Reservation** button now (Figure 3-8).

Figure 3-8. *IP Reservation detail*

d. In the **Create Public IP Reservation** pop-up window, provide a name for your IP reservation. I am using **pcmbook_publicip.** Once this is entered, click the **Create** button (Figure 3-9).

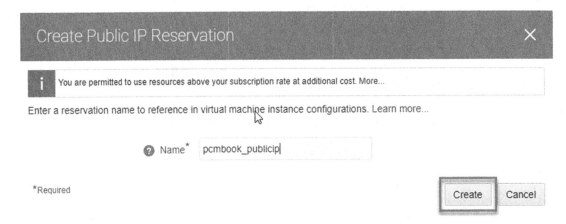

Figure 3-9. *Create Public IP Reservation*

e. Now the second drop-down should be populated. Make sure the Public IP
Reservation you just created is selected (Figure 3-10).

Figure 3-10. *Finalizing the Public IP Information*

f. Once all necessary information is provided, click the next arrow at the top
of the page. Note: If your instance creation is automatically creating an
entry for a vNIC, click the small menu icon on the right of the vNIC entry,
and click delete (Figure 3-11).

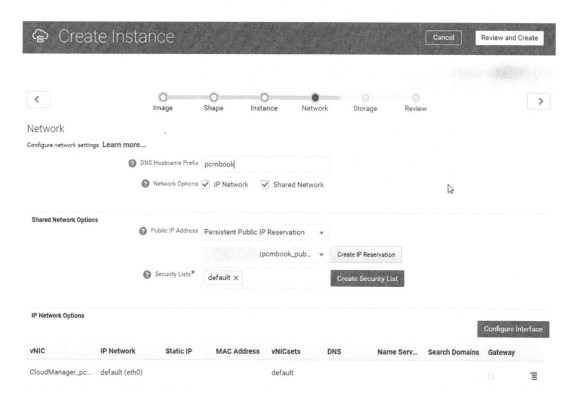

Figure 3-11. *Step 4, Network detail*

6. On step 5, the Storage step, simply allow all the defaults, and click
    the next arrow at the top of the page (Figure 3-12).

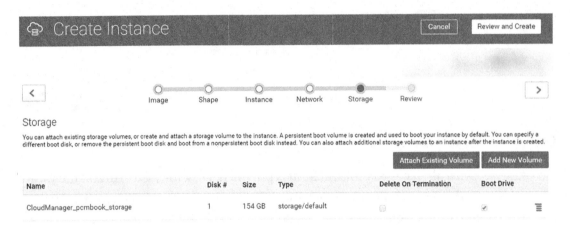

Figure 3-12. *Step 5, Storage detail*

7. Step 6 allows you to review all your inputs before moving on. If
    you are happy with the inputs you have provided, click the **Create**
    button at the top of the page. If you are not happy, use the back
    arrow to fix anything you have incorrect (Figure 3-13).

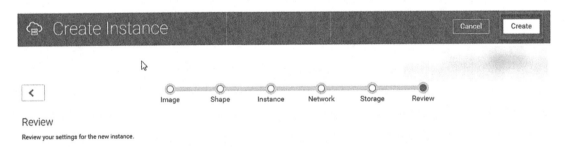

Figure 3-13. *Step 6, Review details*

Your new PeopleSoft Cloud Manager Image will now be provisioned, and you should
see it in your list of running instances on your Compute Classic Service Console.

PeopleSoft Cloud Manager Instance Configuration Wizard

While Oracle provides the Linux image with PeopleSoft Cloud Manager installed, after provisioning the image, you still need to go through a process to properly configure the application on the image and get things up and running. To do this, Oracle provides a setup script called the Cloud Manager Instance Configuration Wizard that will walk you through this process. The configuration wizard will prompt you for multiple pieces of input, specifically, all the information we gathered in Chapter 2 and documented in the text document. Before starting this process, make sure that you have that information handy and ready to go.

Accessing Your Linux VM from a Linux or Unix System

To connect to the Linux virtual machine you just provisioned in the previous section, you will need three pieces of information. First, you will need the public IP address for the virtual box you are connecting to. Second, you need the directory path and name of your private key you created. Third, you need to provide the Linux console with a correctly formatted SSH connection string.

To get started connecting to your Linux virtual machine, you will need the public IP of the virtual machine you are connecting to. To gather the public IP address for your Linux virtual machine, first log in to your Oracle Cloud account, and go to your Compute Classic Service Console. On the Instances tab of the Service Console, you should see the Linux virtual machine you provisioned listed and running (if your instance is not in a Running status, you should start it now). To the right of the instance name, you will see both the public and private IP addresses. Record the public IP address in your prerequisite text document as you will need it later to connect to the instance. Figure 3-14 shows the location of the public IP address.

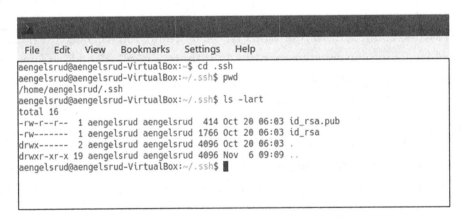

Figure 3-14. *Public IP*

Once you have obtained the public IP address from the Compute Classic Service Console, you will next need to determine the directory path and file name for the private key match to the public key you uploaded to the Oracle Cloud earlier in the installation process. We specifically created this SSH key in Chapter 2. This information is one of the bits of information you were encouraged to record in your text file. If you did not record that, then you will need to go out and find where the private key is sitting now. Typically, you will be able to find this key in the /home/<user>/.ssh directory. Along with the file path and file name, you will also need to know the passphrase you created (Figure 3-15).

```
aengelsrud@aengelsrud-VirtualBox:~$ cd .ssh
aengelsrud@aengelsrud-VirtualBox:~/.ssh$ pwd
/home/aengelsrud/.ssh
aengelsrud@aengelsrud-VirtualBox:~/.ssh$ ls -lart
total 16
-rw-r--r--  1 aengelsrud aengelsrud  414 Oct 20 06:03 id_rsa.pub
-rw-------  1 aengelsrud aengelsrud 1766 Oct 20 06:03 id_rsa
drwx------  2 aengelsrud aengelsrud 4096 Oct 20 06:03 .
drwxr-xr-x 19 aengelsrud aengelsrud 4096 Nov  6 09:09 ..
aengelsrud@aengelsrud-VirtualBox:~/.ssh$ 
```

Figure 3-15. *SSH key*

Finally, we need to take all these pieces of information and string together the correct command to make a secure connection via the SSH command to the Linux virtual machine in the Oracle Cloud. To help you, Oracle has provided a SSH connect string template that will get you started. The template connection string looks like this:

```
ssh -i <path_to_private_key_file>/<private_key_name> -o
ServerAliveInterval=5 -o ServerAliveCountMax=1 opc@<public_ip_address_of_
instance>
```

You can see the pieces of information that are missing: <path_to_private_key_file>, <private_key_name>, and <public_ip_address_of_instance>. For reference, this connection string is also setting the Server Keep Alive Interval (ServerAliveInterval) equal to five and the Server Keep Alive Count Max equal to one. These settings will force the server to send a null packet to the other side every 5 seconds and give up if it doesn't receive a response after one try. Fill those missing values in, and your connection string should look something like this:

```
ssh -i /home/aengelsrud/.ssh/id_rsa -o ServerAliveInterval=5 -o
ServerAliveCountMax=1 opc@129.150.113.214
```

Accessing Your Linux VM from a Windows System

If you are accessing your newly provisioned Linux virtual machine from a computer running the Windows operating system, you will need to ensure you have PuTTY installed for SSH access. The process for installing the PuTTY Windows client was covered in detail in the Chapter 2 section detailing the process to generate an SSH key pair on a Windows machine. If you did not install PuTTY as part of that process, go back to Chapter 2 and review the installation process for PuTTY. You can find the PuTTY application download here: www.ssh.com/ssh/putty/download.

Once you have PuTTY installed, you will need two pieces of information to supply the PuTTY application to properly connect to the Linux virtual machine from your Windows workstation. First, you will need to have the public IP address of the Linux VM you are connecting to. Second, you will need the location on the Windows workstation of the private key that corresponds to the public key you generated and uploaded to your Oracle Cloud Compute Classic Service Console.

To get started connecting to your Linux virtual machine, you will need the public IP of the virtual machine you are connecting to. To gather the public IP address for your Linux virtual machine, first log in to your Oracle Cloud account, and go to your Compute Classic Service Console. On the Instances tab of the Service Console, you should see the Linux virtual machine you provisioned listed and running (if your instance is not in a Running status, you should start it now). To the right of the instance name, you will see both the public and private IP addresses. Record the public IP address in your prerequisite text document as you will need it later to connect to the instance. Figure 3-16 shows the location of the public IP address.

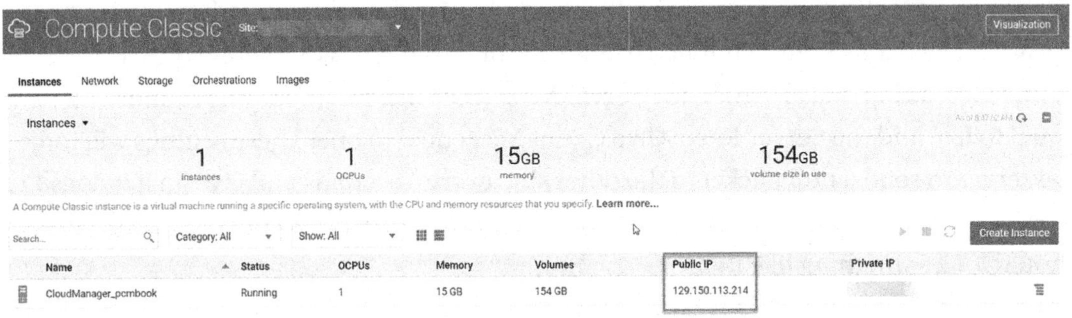

Figure 3-16. *Public IP address*

Next, you need to locate the private key that was generated when you created the public key that was uploaded to your Compute Classic Service. You have a couple of options available to get the private key you need. First, if you did not generate a private key when you created the public key, you can do so now within the PuTTYgen application. You will need to provide PuTTYgen with the public key and passphrase (if there is one), and then PuTTYgen will generate a corresponding private key for you. You can then save that private key locally. Second, if you don't have the private key you need on your Windows workstation, you can grab a copy of the private key from any location where it is stored, say a Linux or Mac workstation, and copy it to a file and directory on your Windows workstation. You will still need the passphrase to connect to the Linux virtual machine in the Oracle Cloud. Finally, if you did save the private key when you generated the public key, you can simply point PuTTY to the file directory location where you saved the key.

Note   In any of these options, you will need the key passphrase when you attempt to connect to the Linux VM. In my case, I saved a copy of my private key to my C:\Temp\ directory as shown in Figure 3-17.

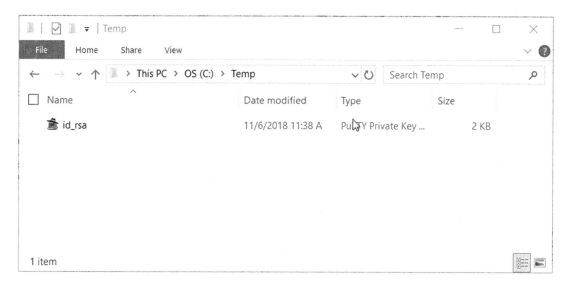

Figure 3-17. *Private Key file*

Now that you have collected all the relevant information you need to connect to the Linux VM, open the PuTTY application to start an SSH connection:

1. Open PuTTY from the Windows start menu.

2. In the PuTTY application, provide the public IP address for the Linux VM you are connecting to in the **Host Name (or IP address)** box, and make sure the SSH radio button is selected (Figure 3-18).

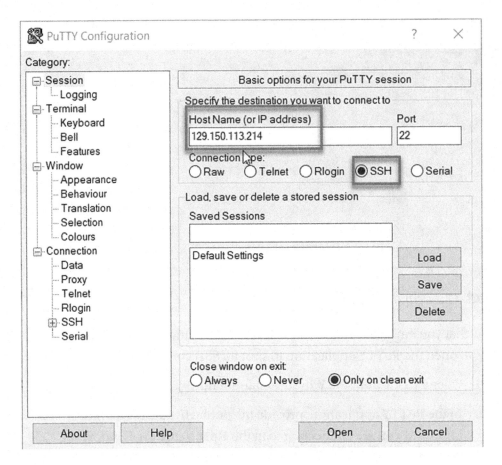

Figure 3-18. *PuTTY Input*

3. In the Category pane on the left side of the PuTTY application, select **Connection** and enter 5 in the **Seconds between keepalives (0 to turn off)** box (Figure 3-19).

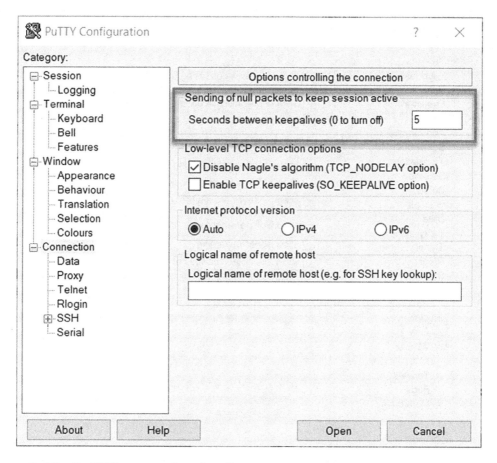

Figure 3-19. *PuTTY connection detail*

4. Next, in the Category pane, click the + next to **SSH** under
   Connection, and select **Auth**. Provide the path and file name (or
   click the **Browse...** button to select the location and file) for the
   private key (Figure 3-20).

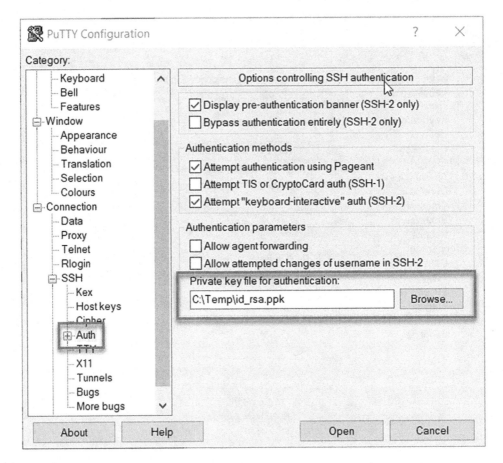

Figure 3-20. *PuTTY Private Key file detail*

5. Once you have provided the required information, click the **Open**
    button.

Changing the opc User Password

Once you are successful in connecting to the PeopleSoft Cloud Manager Linux image for
the first time, you will need to take the necessary steps to change the password for the
delivered opc user. The delivered, one-time password for the opc user is *OracleCloud*.
This password must be changed before you will be allowed any further access to the
virtual machine, and the new password must meet a stringent set of requirements as set
by Oracle. The new password you provide must comply with the following requirements:

- The password must be alphanumeric (contain both letters and numbers).

- Must be a minimum of eight characters long.

- Must contain at least one uppercase letter.

- Must contain at least one numeric character.

- Must contain at least one special character (@,#,$,%,&,etc.).

- It cannot closely resemble a dictionary word. For example, Cloud#Manager123 will not work even though it meets all the other requirements.

When you initially connect to your PeopleSoft Cloud Manager instance, you will first need to provide the ssh key passphrase. Figure 3-21 shows the passphrase input detail.

```
Authorized uses only. All activity may be monitored and reported.
Enter passphrase for key '/home/aengelsrud/.ssh/id_rsa':
```

Figure 3-21. *Passphrase detail*

Once you successfully enter the ssh key passphrase, you will see a warning stating that your password is expired and that you need to change your password and log in again. Enter the default Oracle provided password at the **(current) UNIX password** prompt and then your new password (following the preceding guidelines) at the **New password** prompt. Once you validate your new password a second time, the password will be updated, and the connection to your virtual machine will be closed (Figure 3-22).

```
You are required to change your password immediately (root enforced)
Authorized uses only. All activity may be monitored and reported.
WARNING: Your password has expired.
You must change your password now and login again!
Changing password for user opc.
Changing password for opc.
(current) UNIX password:
New password:
Retype new password:
passwd: all authentication tokens updated successfully.
Connection to 129.150.113.214 closed.
```

Figure 3-22. *Initial access detail*

Now that the password change is complete, you can log back in to the virtual machine, using your new password, and continue with the PeopleSoft Cloud Manager installation process.

PeopleSoft Cloud Manager Instance Configuration Wizard

Before moving forward with the PeopleSoft Cloud Manager Installation Wizard, it is very important that you have obtained all the prerequisite information detailed in Chapter 2 of this book. If you followed the process outlined there, you will now have everything you need to move forward successfully. If you skipped over the prerequisite steps and information gathering process, go back to Chapter 2 and work through those steps; your installation will fail without all the proper details.

In addition to the information gathered in Chapter 2, you will also need to provide some instance specific information for the installation to work properly. This information is listed in the text doc download and highlighted in Chapter 2; it should be given some consideration before moving forward. The data required by the PeopleSoft Cloud Manager Instance Configuration Wizard includes the following:

- HTTP Port

- HTTPS Port

- JOLT Port

- WSL Port

- CLADM password (Domain Boot password for the Cloud Administrator)

- people (CONNECT ID) password

- SYSADM password

- SYS/SYSTEM password

- WebLogic (system) password

- PTWEBSERVER password

- Integration Gateway user password

Once you have all this detail collected, you are ready to get started running the wizard to help you through the PeopleSoft Cloud Manager installation process:

1. Start the instance configuration wizard by logging back in to the PeopleSoft Cloud Manager virtual machine using the same methodology you used previously.

2. Once you supply the passphrase (if you created one when you instantiated your private key), you will get your first instance configuration wizard prompt.

3. Enter your PeopleSoft Cloud account user id and password. This is the user id and password you use to sign in to `http://cloud.oracle.com` (Figure 3-23).

```
*****************************************************************
*     Welcome to Cloud Manager Instance Configuration Wizard    *
*****************************************************************


Enter the Oracle Cloud user id: peoplesoftcloudmanager@gmail.com

Enter the Oracle Cloud user password :
Re-Enter the Oracle Cloud user password :
```

Figure 3-23. *Instance Configuration Wizard*

4. Next enter your Oracle Cloud domain name or Service ID. You should have recorded your Service ID in the prerequisite steps – now is the time to put that list to work! The menu input is shown in Figure 3-24.

```
Enter the Oracle Cloud domain name or Service ID (IDCS):
```

Figure 3-24. *Oracle Cloud Domain Name*

5. The configuration wizard will now prompt you for your Oracle Cloud Compute REST endpoint. Supply the proper URL and hit enter (Figure 3-25).

```
Enter the Oracle Cloud Compute REST end point: https://compute.uscom-central-1.oraclecloud.com/
```

Figure 3-25. *Compute REST endpoint entry*

6. You will now be prompted to enter your My Oracle Support user id and password. This is the user id and password you use to sign on to http://support.oracle.com (Figure 3-26).

```
Enter the My Oracle Support user id: peoplesoftcloudmanager@gmail.com

Enter the My Oracle Support user password :
Re-Enter the My Oracle Support user password :
```

Figure 3-26. *Support user id and password entry*

7. Once you successfully entered the My Oracle Support user id and password, you will be prompted to enter the new Domain Boot user password for the Cloud Administrator user CLADM. IMPORTANT: Do NOT follow the password requirements shown on the screen. The **password** should be no more than eight characters and contain only alphanumeric characters (Figure 3-27).

```
Enter the new Domain Boot user password for user CLADM.
Ensure that the password contains only alphanumeric characters
and is no more than 32 characters in length:
Re-Enter the new Domain Boot user password for user CLADM:
```

Figure 3-27. *CLADM password entry*

8. Enter the PeopleSoft Connect ID password for the people user (Figure 3-28).

```
Enter the new PeopleSoft Connect ID password for user people. Ensure that
the password does not contain any spaces ( ), dashes (-) percentage (%), slash (/) and
quote characters (",') and is at least 6 and no more than 30 characters in length:
Re-Enter the new PeopleSoft Connect ID password for user people:
```

Figure 3-28. *PeopleSoft Connect ID Password*

9. Next, you have a choice to either supply a new PeopleSoft Access ID or accept the default SYSADM user and then supply a password. This password can be no more than eight characters and contain only alphanumeric characters (Figure 3-29).

```
Enter the PeopleSoft Access ID [SYSADM]:

Enter the new PeopleSoft Access password for user SYSADM.
Ensure that the password contains only alphanumeric characters and
is no more than 8 characters in length:
Re-Enter the new PeopleSoft Access password for user SYSADM:
```

Figure 3-29. *Sysadm password entry*

10. Enter a password for the SYS/SYSTEM user; this password needs to be 8–30 characters in length with at least one uppercase letter, one lowercase letter, one number, and one special character (_, -, #) (Figure 3-30).

```
Enter a new PeopleSoft database admin users [SYS/SYSTEM] password.
Ensure that the password is between 8 and 30 characters in length
with at least one lowercase letter, one uppercase letter, one number
and one special character (_,-,#):
Re-Enter the new Database Admin Password:
```

Figure 3-30. *SYS/SYSTEM password entry*

11. Enter a password for the Oracle WebLogic Administrator user, system. This password must be between 8 and 30 characters and contain one uppercase letter, one lowercase letter, and at least one number or special character (!, @, #, $, %, ^, &) (Figure 3-31).

```
Enter a new WebLogic Server Admin user [system] password. Ensure that
the password is between 8 and 30 characters in length with at least
one lowercase letter, one uppercase letter, one number or one
one special character (!@#$%^&):
Re-Enter a new WebLogic Server Admin user [system] password:
```

Figure 3-31. *WebLogic user password entry*

12. Provide a password for the PeopleSoft Web Profile user, PTWEBSERVER. This password can contain only alphanumeric characters and must be between 8 and 30 characters in length (Figure 3-32).

```
Enter the new password for Web Profile user PTWEBSERVER.
Ensure he password contains only alphanumeric characters and
is between 8 and 30 characters in length:
Re-Enter the password for Web Profile user PTWEBSERVER:
```

Figure 3-32. *PTWEBSERVER password entry*

13. Now enter the password for the Integration Gateway user (administrator). The prompt provided by the Instance Configuration Wizard indicates that this password needs to be between 8 and 30 characters in length and contain only alphanumeric characters (Figure 3-33).

```
Enter the new password for Integration Gateway user administrator.
Ensure the password contains only alphanumeric characters and
is between 8 and 30 characters in length:
Re-Enter the new password for Integration Gateway user administrator:
```

Figure 3-33. *Integration Gateway password entry*

14. Next, the Instance Configuration Wizard prompt allows you to choose if you would like access to the advanced configuration options. Generally, if you want to do things like change the Cloud Manager database name or supply custom HTTP, HTTPS, JOLT, or WLS port numbers, you should answer y (yes). If you are fine with the default database name and port numbers, answer n (no).

15. If you choose, change the Cloud Manager database name. In this case, I am changing the DB name to PCMBOOK (Figure 3-34).

```
Enter the name of the database. Please ensure that the database
name starts with a letter and includes only uppercase alphabets
and numbers and is no more than 8 characters in length [CMPSDB]: PCMBOOK
```

Figure 3-34. *Database name entry*

16. Next set the HTTP, HTTPS, JOLT, and WLS ports, or leave the defaults (Figure 3-35).

```
Enter the HTTP port. Please ensure that port value is between 1024 and 65535 [8000]:

Enter the HTTPS port. Please ensure that port value is between 1024 and 65535 [8443]:

Enter the JOLT port. Please ensure that port value is between 1024 and 65535 [9033]:

Enter the WSL port. Please ensure that port value is between 1024 and 65535 [7000]:
```

Figure 3-35. *Alternate Port entry*

17. The final set of prompts for PeopleSoft Cloud Manager Instance
    Configuration Wizard starts with requiring your Oracle Cloud
    Storage account name (Figure 3-36).

```
Enter the Oracle Cloud Storage account name: peoplesoftcloudmanager
```

Figure 3-36. *Cloud Storage Account entry*

18. Provide the Oracle Cloud Infrastructure Object Storage Classic
    REST endpoint.

19. Provide the Oracle Cloud Infrastructure Object Storage Classic
    authentication endpoint.

20. If you have access to the Oracle Database Cloud services, provide
    the Oracle Database Cloud REST endpoint (Figure 3-37).

```
Enter the Oracle Cloud Storage REST end point [https://peoplesoftcloudmanager.storage.oraclecloud.com/v1/Storag
e-peoplesoftcloudmanager]: https://peoplesoftcloudmanager.us.storage.oraclecloud.com/v1/Storage-peoplesoftcloud
manager

Enter the Oracle Cloud Storage Auth end point [https://peoplesoftcloudmanager.storage.oraclecloud.com/auth/v1.0
]: https://peoplesoftcloudmanager.us.storage.oraclecloud.com/auth/v1.0

Enter the Oracle Cloud DBAAS REST end point [https://dbaas.oraclecloud.com/]: https://dbaas.oraclecloud.com/
Validating the Cloud Manager Bootstrap input values ....
```

Figure 3-37. *Storage and Database REST endpoint entry*

21. Review all entered information. Answer y (yes) if you like the result and, perhaps most importantly, all four answers in the Cloud Manager Input Bootstrap Validation Summary are **SUCCESS**. If any of the validation responses are FAILURE or you don't like one of your answers, enter n (no) and go back through the Instance Configuration Wizard and correct your input. The next section outlines a few common issues for each of the four validation checks (Figure 3-38).

```
*************************************************************************************
                Cloud Manager Instance Configuration Summary
*************************************************************************************
Oracle Cloud user id                              : peoplesoftcloudmanager@gmail.com
Oracle Cloud user password                        : ********
Oracle Cloud domain name                          : 606724173
Oracle Cloud Compute REST end point               : https://compute.uscom-central-1.oraclecloud.com/
Oracle Cloud Storage account name                 : peoplesoftcloudmanager
Oracle Cloud Storage REST end point               : https://peoplesoftcloudmanager.us.storage.oraclecloud.com/v1
/Storage-peoplesoftcloudmanager
Oracle Cloud Storage Auth end point               : https://peoplesoftcloudmanager.us.storage.oraclecloud.com/au
th/v1.0
Oracle Cloud DBAAS REST end point                 : https://dbaas.oraclecloud.com/
My Oracle Support user id                         : peoplesoftcloudmanager@gmail.com
My Oracle Support user password                   : ********
Domain Boot user password for user CLADM          : ********
PeopleSoft Connect ID password for user people    : ********
PeopleSoft Access password for user SYSADM        : ********
Database Admin password                           : ********
WebLogic Server Admin password                    : ********
Web Profile user PTWEBSERVER password             : ********
Integration Gateway user administrator password   : ********
Name of the database                              : CMPSDB
HTTP port                                         : 8000
HTTPS port                                        : 8443
JOLT port                                         : 9033
WSL port                                          : 7000
Cloud Manager public ip                           : 129.150.113.214


*************************************************************************************
                Cloud Manager Bootstrap Input Validation Summary
*************************************************************************************

Oracle Cloud Authentication                  : SUCCESS
Cloud Manager IP validation                  : SUCCESS
Default sec-list validation                  : SUCCESS
[Sec-list name: /Compute-606724173/default/default]
Oracle Storage Cloud Access                  : SUCCESS
*************************************************************************************
Are you happy with your answers? [y|n|q]: █
```

Figure 3-38. *Instance Configuration Summary*

Once you are successful and select y, you can monitor the configuration process by tailing the Cloud Manager Status log file. This can be accomplished by entering the following command at a command prompt: `tail -f /opt/oracle/psft/dpk/scripts/CloudManagerStatus.log`.

This process can take several minutes to run to completion. In the end, the CloudManagerStatus.log file will provide you with the appropriate URL to access your newly instantiated PeopleSoft Cloud Manager instance.

There are several log files in addition to the Cloud Manager Status log that may be of interest as your instance is created. These log files include

- /opt/oracle/psft/dpk/scripts/psft_opc_setup.log

  This log includes detail around the Cloud Manager provisioning process.

- /home/psadm2/psft/data/cloud/cmlogs/BOOTSTRAP_LOGS/*

  These logs provide the administrator insight into PeopleSoft Cloud Manager processes such as file server creation.

- /home/psadm2/psft/data/cloud/cmlogs/envs/CLOUD_MANAGER_INSTANCE/*

  The logs included in this directory provide detail around instance creation specific to updating Cloud Manager.

Cloud Manager Instance Configuration Wizard Input Validation

The final validation step in the Instance Configuration Wizard provides you with four validation checks on your input data. The four checks are Oracle Cloud Authentication, Cloud Manager IP Validation, Default sec-list Validation, and Oracle Cloud Storage Access. If any of these validations result in failure, you should not go forward, and you should troubleshoot what may be causing the validation failures:

- **Oracle Cloud Authentication Failure:** This can be caused by incorrectly entering your Oracle Cloud user id, password, domain name, or Compute REST endpoint incorrectly. There is a possibility that errors here will cause other errors downstream.

- **Cloud Manager IP Validation Failure:** This validation failure can be caused by providing an incorrect Compute Classic REST endpoint. Along with this you may also see this validation failure when the Oracle Cloud Authentication validation fails.

- **Default sec-list Validation Failure:** This validation checks specifically to see if the default sec-list is associated with the Cloud Manager virtual machine. If the default sec-list does not exist, you may need Oracle support to help resolve this issue.

- **Oracle Storage Cloud Access Validation Failure:** This validation can fail if the provided user has never accessed the Cloud Storage console and never specified the geographic data jurisdiction. The user provided the Instance Configuration Wizard needs to be able to access the Oracle Cloud Storage for the provided domain.

Security to Access Cloud Manager PIA

Earlier in the installation process, we created a new security list for use by Cloud Manager, and now we need to make sure we add the Cloud Manager instance to that Security List. Doing this will allow access to the Cloud Manager PeopleSoft Internet Architecture from the public-internet security IP list. Additionally, adding this instance to the security list will allow it to communicate with any other instances in that same security list. There are a few steps that are required to complete this process:

1. Log in to cloud.oracle.com and navigate to the Compute Classic Service Console.

2. Select the Instances tab.

3. Find the row for the Cloud Manager instance, and click the menu icon on the right side of the page (Figure 3-39).

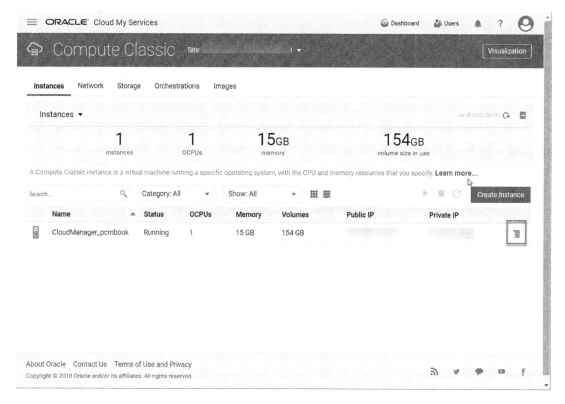

Figure 3-39. *Instance menu icon*

4. From this drop-down menu, select View (Figure 3-40).

Figure 3-40. *Select View*

5. On the Instance View page, click Add to Security List in the
    Security List section (Figure 3-41).

Figure 3-41. *Add to Security List*

6.   Select the appropriate Security List from the drop-down, in our
     case pcmbook-seclist, and then click Add (Figure 3-42).

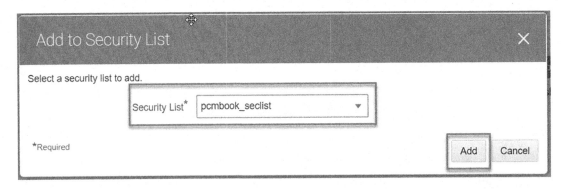

Figure 3-42. *Add to Security List dialogue box*

7.   IF you've created other security lists for specific purposes, add
     them to the instance in the same manner.

That's it. You should now have an installed, though not yet fully operational,
PeopleSoft Cloud Manager instance in the Oracle Cloud. In the next chapter, we will
learn how to access your Cloud Instance, set up a file server, manage user permissions,
and fully configure PeopleSoft Cloud Manager for use.

CHAPTER 4

Configuring PeopleSoft Cloud Manager

Now that you have the PeopleSoft Cloud Manager web application up and running in the Oracle Cloud, we need to make sure that we have everything in place to both have the space to store our PeopleSoft images and have a secure system with proper user access permissions. This chapter will first cover how to find the correct URL for your PeopleSoft Cloud Manager instance. Next, you will learn how to log in to web application along with some of the basic Cloud Manager Settings. Finally you will be given some tips and instructions on creating a file server for your Cloud Manager instance and a look into the roles and permissions included with PeopleSoft Cloud Manager. When you are done with this, you will have a fully functional, secure, PeopleSoft Cloud Manager instance.

Your First Login to PeopleSoft Cloud Manager

The first thing you'll need to access your newly created PeopleSoft Cloud Manager instance is the correct URL to link to or copy and paste in your browser window. You can either look this value up in the log file output from the Cloud Manager installation, or you can create the URL based on a typical format.

To find the correct URL in the Cloud Manager Status log, view the file using the following command from your SSH login to the Cloud Manager instance:

```
view /opt/oracle/psft/dpk/scripts/CloudManagerStatus.log
```

Once you are in the log, go to the bottom of the log output. You can either scroll to the bottom of the page using the down arrow, or simply hit shift-G on your keyboard. The last input in the log file is the Cloud Manager PIA URL, including both the HTTP and HTTPS addresses. These addresses are shown in Figure 4-1.

© Aaron Engelsrud 2019

A. Engelsrud, *Managing PeopleSoft on the Oracle Cloud*, https://doi.org/10.1007/978-1-4842-4546-0_4

```
The PeopleSoft Environment Setup Process Ended.

[  OK  ]^M
 Cloud Manager PIA URL: http://              .compute.oraclecloud.com:8000
 Cloud Manager PIA SSL URL: https://              .oraclecloud.com:8443
```

Figure 4-1. *PeopleSoft Cloud Manager URL*

You can also simply create this URL using the following format: `http://oc-<public-IP-address-separated-by-hyphens-rather-than-periods>.compute.oraclecloud.com:<htttp_port>/ps/signon.html`.

The HTTPS URL can be created similarly by inputting the HTTPS port in place of the of the standard HTTP port.

Paste this URL into a browser, click the "Please click here to PeopleSoft logon page" hyperlink, and log in to your PeopelSoft Cloud Manager instance using the CLADM user ID and password you set up during installation. The PeopleSoft Cloud Manager login page is shown in Figure 4-2.

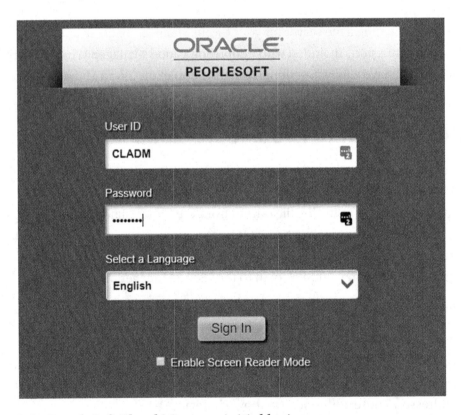

Figure 4-2. *PeopleSoft Cloud Manager initial login*

Create a New Admin Account

Before we move forward and start to actively set up and manage the settings and functions within PeopleSoft Cloud Manager, the first thing we are going to do is create a new administrator user to use when logging in to the application. This will enhance security, allow you to customize user security moving forward as you add other users to the system, and provide better auditability for changes and updates to the system as you move forward.

Once you have successfully logged in to the application with the CLADM user, complete the following steps to successfully create a new administrator user to use moving forward:

1. In the right-hand menu navigation, find the small compass icon and click this icon to open the PeopleSoft Cloud Manager NavBar and select Navigator (Figure 4-3).

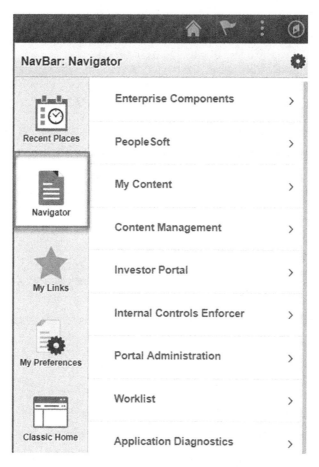

Figure 4-3. *NavBar Navigator menu*

2. Select **PeopleTools ➤ Security ➤ User Profiles ➤ Copy User Profiles** from the Navigator Menu (Figure 4-4).

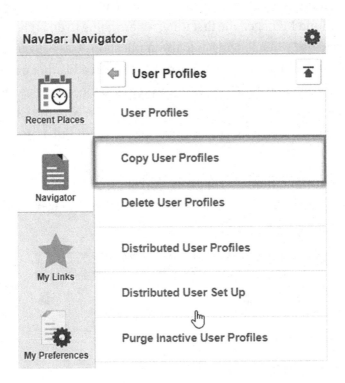

Figure 4-4. *Copy User Profile menu option*

3. Enter CLADM in the search window and click the Search button (Figure 4-5).

Copy User Profiles

Enter any information you have and click Search. Leave fields blank for a list of all values.

Find an Existing Value

▼ Search Criteria

Search by: [User ID ▼] begins with [CLADM]

| Search | Advanced Search

Figure 4-5. *Copy User Profile search window*

4. Enter the following information into the Copy User Profiles
    window:

    - **New User ID:** <Enter an ID of your Choice (I am using PCMADMIN)>

    - **Description:** PCM Admin Account

    - **New Password:** Password of your choice

    - **Confirm Password:** Same password of your choice (Figure 4-6)

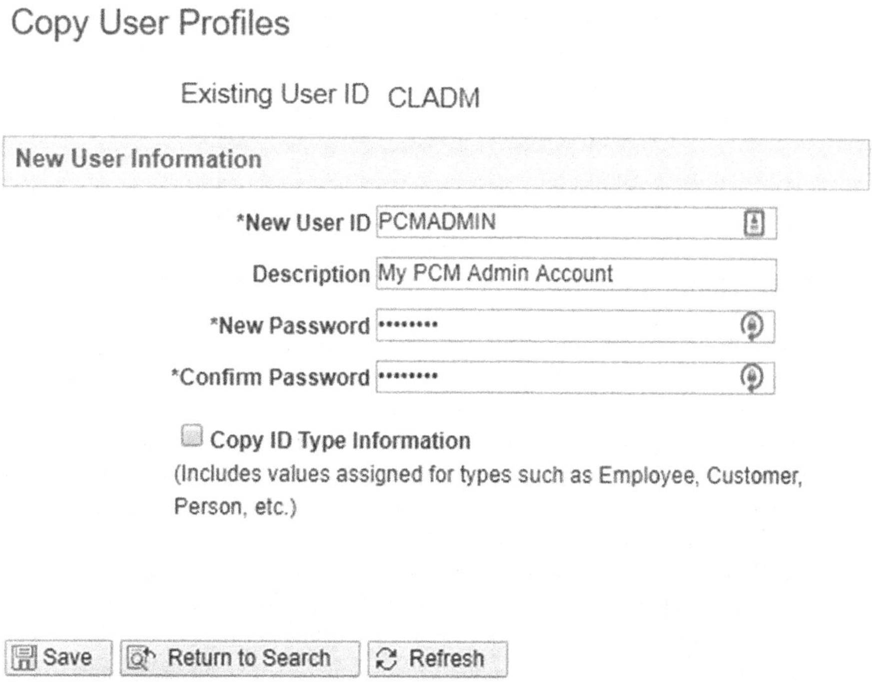

Copy User Profiles

Existing User ID CLADM

New User Information

*New User ID PCMADMIN

Description My PCM Admin Account

*New Password ••••••••

*Confirm Password ••••••••

☐ Copy ID Type Information
(Includes values assigned for types such as Employee, Customer,
Person, etc.)

🖫 Save |🔍ᵗ Return to Search |ℭ Refresh

Figure 4-6. *Copy User Profile dialogue window*

5. Click Save at the bottom of the window.

6. Sign out of the PeopleSoft Cloud Manager application using the
    menu in the upper right (Figure 4-7).

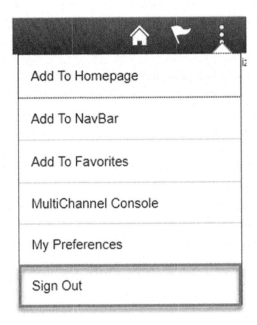

Figure 4-7. *Sign Out menu option*

7. Sign back in to the PeopleSoft Cloud Manager using your newly created Admin account (Figure 4-8).

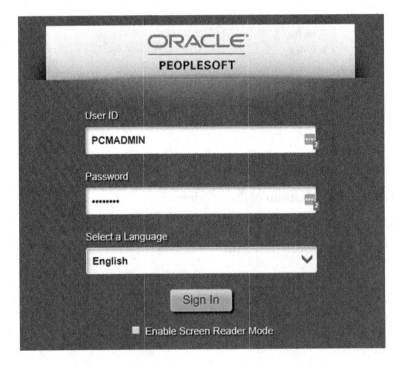

Figure 4-8. *Log in with new admin account*

Cloud Manager Settings

If you have been in a 9.2 PeopleSoft Application, the fluid, tile-based home page should be very familiar to you. The next several sections of this book will walk you through the content within the Cloud Manager Settings tile in order to complete the process of properly setting up and configuring your PeopleSoft Cloud Manager application. These settings include Oracle Cloud Service Detail, My Oracle Support (MOS) Credentials Input, PeopleSoft Credentials for REST Services Input, Lift & Shift Container Detail, COBOL License Input, Operating System Image Input, and File Server details. Each of these sections contains valuable and important information that you need to be familiar with to properly manage and administer your PeopleSoft Cloud Manager instance and the PeopleSoft instances that are created via PeopleSoft Cloud Manager. Figure 4-9 highlights the Cloud Manager Setting tile on the PeopleSoft Cloud Manager home page.

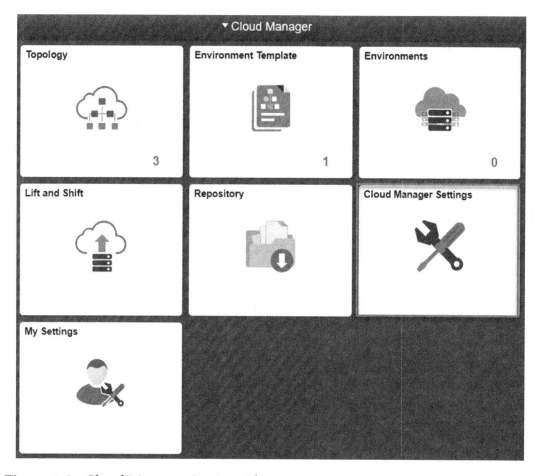

Figure 4-9. *Cloud Manager Settings tile*

Oracle Cloud Service Detail

It is important to verify that the information you entered while going through the Cloud Manager Instance Configuration Wizard is correct and complete now that the application is up and running. To verify the information you have provided, click the Cloud Manger Setting tile on the PeopleSoft Cloud Manager home page. The first section you will find is the Oracle Cloud Service section. This section contains the following fields and should already have the appropriate values included:

- **Domain Name:** This is your Compute Classic Identity Domain. It is important that you DO NOT change this value.

- **Username:** This field displays your Compute Classic account ID. Typically this is the email account that was used to set up PeopleSoft Cloud Manager. Here too, do not change this value from what is provided.

- **Password:** This is encrypted value of your Compute Classic account password.

- **Storage Account Name:** Here you will need to provide the name for your Storage Classic account. You can find this information on the View Detail Overview page of your Storage Classic account (Figure 4-10).

Overview Information

Category	Oracle IaaS and PaaS Cloud Services
Cloud Account Name	
Cloud Account Id	
Subscription	Pay As You Go

Figure 4-10. Storage Classic Cloud Account Name

- **Compute REST Endpoint:** This field contains the URL necessary to access Compute Classic. You found this value during the process of gathering information for the initial installation of PeopleSoft Cloud Manager in Chapter 2. If this is value is not provided for you, you will need to enter it now.

- **DBaaS REST Endpoint:** If you have an Oracle Database Cloud service account, the URL to access the service will be found here.

- **IDCS Storage REST Endpoint:** This is Storage Classic REST endpoint URL. You will need to provide this value.

- **IDCS Storage Auth REST Endpoint:** This is the Storage Classic Auth V1 REST Endpoint. You will need to provide this value as well (Figure 4-11).

Oracle Cloud Service

Domain Name	▓▓▓▓
User Name	peoplesoftcloudmanager@gmail.com
Password	••••••••••••••••••••••••••
Storage Account name	▓▓▓▓▓▓▓
Compute REST Endpoint	https://compute.uscom-central-1.oracleclouc
DBaaS REST Endpoint	https://dbaas.oraclecloud.com/
IDCS Storage REST Endpoint	https://uscom-central-1b.storage.oracleclouc
IDCS Storage Auth REST Endpoint	https://peoplesoftcloudmanager.us.storage.c

Figure 4-11. *Oracle Cloud Service detail*

My Oracle Support (MOS) Credentials Input

For PeopleSoft Cloud Manager to access My Oracle Support and download PeopleSoft Application Maintenance and PeopleTools Patches, the Cloud Manager application must have a valid My Oracle Support user id, password, and MOS URL available. This information was provided during the Instance Configuration Wizard setup process, but it is important that you validate that the information recorded here matches what you input. Additionally, it may be necessary to update this information if the user ID or password changes at some time in the future. Figure 4-12 shows the input for MOS credentials in PeopleSoft Cloud Manager.

My Oracle Support(MOS) Credentials

PeopleSoft Cloud Manager enables you to download PeopleSoft Application Maintenance and PeopleTools Patches directly from MOS.
To use MOS, you must create an Oracle Single SignOn (SSO) account and register at least one support identifier(SI) with MOS. Please ensure to enter the
credentials of the registered account in this page.
Use of MOS is subject to its terms of use and Oracle Private Policy. See MOS Terms of use and Oracle Privacy Policy

User ID	peoplesoftcloudmanager@gmail.com
Password	••••
Url	https://updates.oracle.com

Figure 4-12. *My Oracle Support (MOS) Credentials detail*

PeopleSoft Credentials for REST Services Input

The section titled PeopleSoft Credentials for REST Services contains the username and
password that are used by PeopleSoft Cloud Manager to access the standard Integration
Broker REST services. These values are initially provided by the Instance Configuration
Wizard and should contain the CLADM username and password. This dialogue is
editable, and you can put in a user of your choice to run the REST services. For example,
you could create new user specifically for this task and update this detail. It is important
to note that the new user would need to have the appropriate PeopleSoft security
required to access and run the Integration Broker REST services (Figure 4-13).

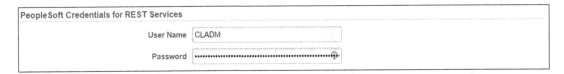

PeopleSoft Credentials for REST Services

User Name	CLADM
Password	••

Figure 4-13. *PeopleSoft Credentials for REST Services detail*

Lift & Shift Container Detail

In Lift & Shift Container section of the Cloud Manger Settings window, the only
information provided is the Container Name detail. This information is provided for
informational purposes only and cannot be edited or updated form this menu option
(Figure 4-14).

Lift & Shift Container

Container Name	psft_las

Figure 4-14. *Lift & Shift Container detail*

COBOL License Input

Your company or organization may have purchased a license for a COBOL compiler that you can use with your PeopleSoft Cloud instances. If this is the case, the Cobol License section of the Cloud Manger Settings detail is the place this information needs to be entered. To complete this, you will need to enter your Micro Focus COBOL compiler serial number and license key into the Cobol License section (Figure 4-15).

Cobol License	
Serial Number	
License Key	•••⊕

Figure 4-15. *Cobol License detail*

Operating System Image Input

For PeopleSoft Cloud Manager to create PeopleSoft images in the Oracle Cloud infrastructure, you will need to provide both a Linux and Windows image for the application to use. Specifically, PeopleSoft Cloud Manager is looking for an Oracle Linux 6.6 image and a Microsoft Windows Server 2012 image. These images should be available in your Compute Classic Images tab, and you can find the appropriate OS Image path by hovering over the image name. Figure 4-16 indicates how the OS Image path is located.

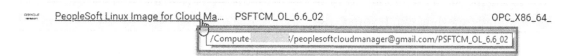

Figure 4-16. *Oracle Linux Image path*

Once you have collected both the Oracle Linux 6.6 and Microsoft Windows Server 2012 image paths, you need to provide the paths in the Operating System Image section of the Cloud Manager Settings page.

In addition to the image path, you will also need to set the Bootable Volume Size for each of these images. The size you indicate in this field needs to be at least 5% bigger than the size of image that you are listing for that OS. In my case, given that the uncompressed size of the Oracle Linux Image is 10.5 GB, I could provide a bootable size for this image as small as 12 GB (10.5 + 5% = 11.025 GB). The Windows Server 2012 image uncompressed size is 25 GB, so therefore I could provide a Bootable Volume Size of 27 GB (25 GB + 5% = 26.25 GB). For simplicity I will provide each image with a 30 GB Bootable Volume Size which is more than adequate for both images we are using. Figure 4-17 shows the information needed for the Operating System Image information in PeopleSoft Cloud Manager.

Operating System Image

The bootable volume size must be at least 5% higher than the uncompressed size of the OS image.

2 rows

Description ◇	OS Version ◇	OS Image ◇	Bootable Volume Size (GB) ◇	OS Default ◇
Oracle Linux	6.6	/Compute-..../peoplesoftcloudmanager@gmail.com/PSFTCM_OL_6.6_02	30	YES
Microsoft Windows Server	2012	/Compute-..../peoplesoftcloudmanager@gmail.com/pcmbook_win_snapshot	30	YES

Figure 4-17.   Operating System Image detail

File Server Details

The File Server Details section of the Cloud Manager Settings at this point in the configuration and setup process should be blank. Additionally, this filed in not editable and cannot be changed from this dialogue. The File Server Host value will populate once you have created a file server within PeopleSoft Cloud Manager. Instructions and detail on creating the file server are in the next section of this book. The location for the File Server Details are shown in Figure 4-18.

File Server Details

File Server Host

Figure 4-18.   PeopleSoft Cloud Manager File Server Details

Add Your Own Public Key

One additional PeopleSoft Cloud Manager Setting that can be entered by each end user is the users public SSH key. This will allow PeopleSoft Cloud Manager the ability to inject that public key into any Linux VM in a PeopleSoft environment that is provisioned by the user.

To complete this task, navigate to the Cloud Manager Home page and click the My Settings tile. Figure 4-19 highlights the My Settings tile on the PeopleSoft Cloud Manager home page.

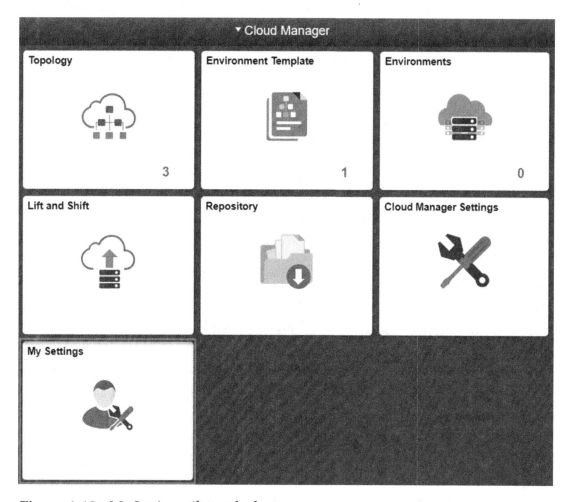

Figure 4-19. *My Settings tile on the home page*

Once on the My Settings page, paste your public SSH key in the My SSH Public Key text window and click save (Figure 4-20).

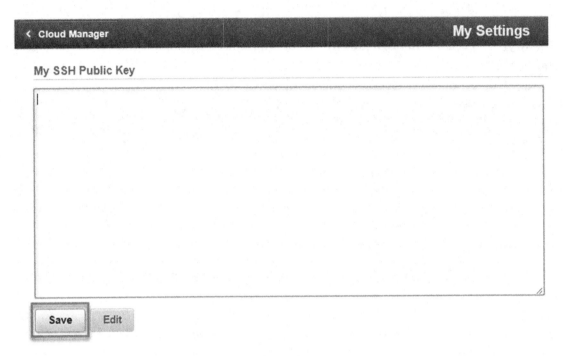

Figure 4-20. *My SSH Public Key*

Creating a File Server for Cloud Manager

A file server is needed be PeopleSoft Cloud Manager to provide space and storage for the various PeopleSoft Images, PeopleTools updates, and Lift & Shift environments you will eventually have stored in Cloud Manager. There are two options available to you when setting up a file server to be used by Cloud Manager. First, you can create a brand-new file server from within the Cloud Manager Settings File Server menu. Second, using the Advanced menu with in the File Server page, you can allow PeopleSoft Cloud Manager to utilize an existing file server volume that is already available in your existing Compute Cloud infrastructure.

Creating a New File Server

Given that you have most of the PeopleSoft Cloud Manager configured, the steps to create a new file server for use by PeopleSoft Cloud Manager are fairly straightforward:

1. Make sure you are properly signed in to PeopleSoft Cloud Manager with your administrator user.

2. From the PeopleSoft Cloud Manager home page, click the Cloud Manager Settings tile as we did earlier to access the Cloud Manager Setting detail.

3. On the left-hand navigation, select File Server from the menu options (Figure 4-21).

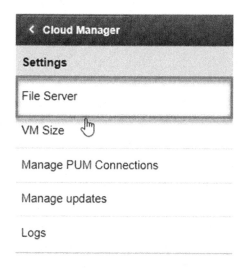

Figure 4-21. *File Server menu option*

4. This will open the File Server Configuration Page. You will need to enter the following information into the various fields on this page:

   - **File Server Name:** You can use any name you like, for this purpose we will be naming this file server pcmBookFileServer.

   - **VM Size:** Small

- **Boot Volume Size:** This should be prefilled based on the information you provided when setting up the Linux image. In our case this is 30GB.

- **Data Volume Size:** You will need to determine the appropriate size necessary for your file server. This will need to be large enough to accommodate the various images, patches, and updates you are planning on storing in PeopleSoft Cloud Manager. I will be using 300 GB as a place to start.

- **Oracle Linux Image:** This value will be prefilled and un-editable based on the information you entered in the File Server Details section (Figure 4-22).

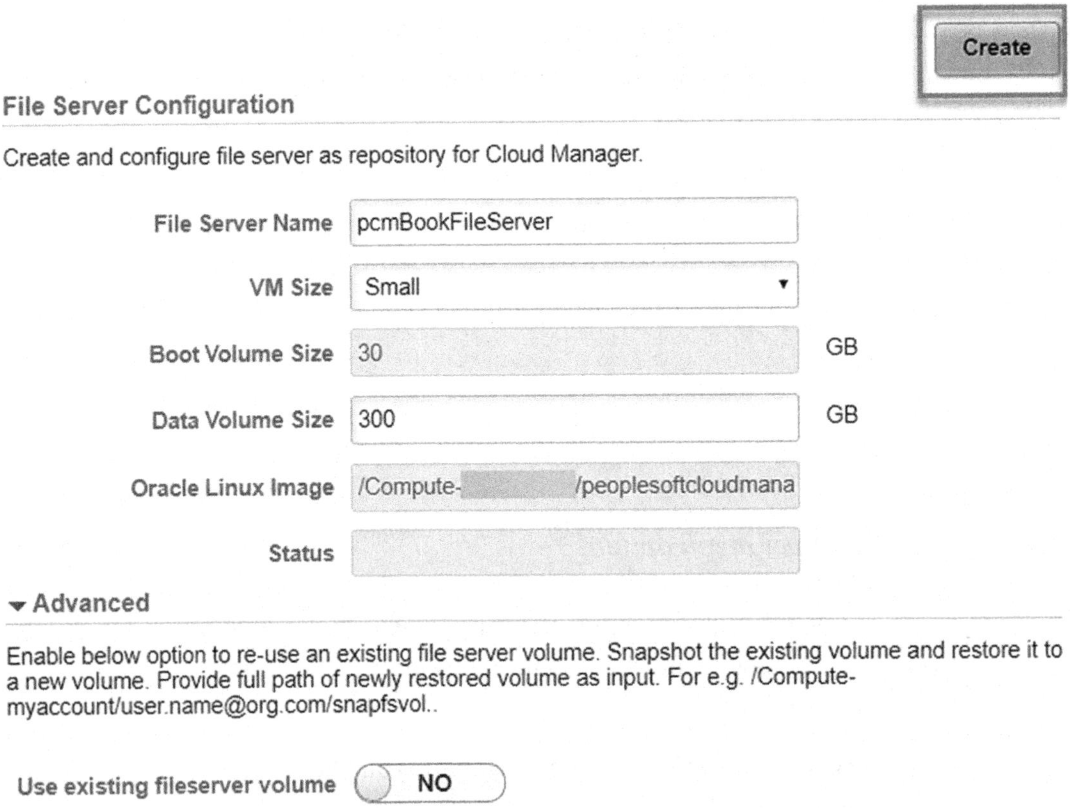

Create

File Server Configuration

Create and configure file server as repository for Cloud Manager.

File Server Name	pcmBookFileServer
VM Size	Small ▾
Boot Volume Size	30 GB
Data Volume Size	300 GB
Oracle Linux Image	/Compute- /peoplesoftcloudmana
Status	

▾ Advanced

Enable below option to re-use an existing file server volume. Snapshot the existing volume and restore it to a new volume. Provide full path of newly restored volume as input. For e.g. /Compute-myaccount/user.name@org.com/snapfsvol..

Use existing fileserver volume ◯ NO

Figure 4-22. *File Server Configuration*

5.   Once all the fields are complete, click Create in the upper right corner of the page.

6.   Click Yes to continue.

7.   The Status field will update as you refresh the page to show In Progress, Configured, or Failed based on how file server instantiation progressed (Figure 4-23).

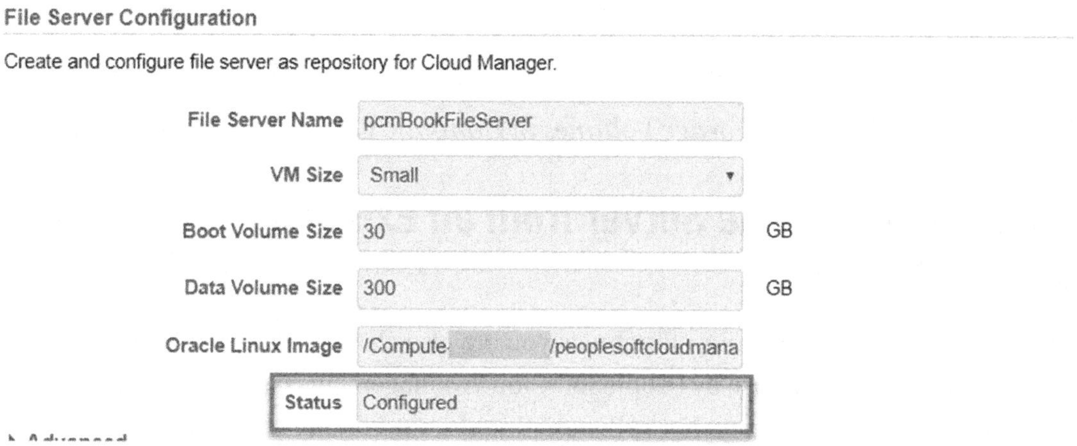

File Server Configuration

Create and configure file server as repository for Cloud Manager.

File Server Name	pcmBookFileServer
VM Size	Small
Boot Volume Size	30 GB
Data Volume Size	300 GB
Oracle Linux Image	/Compute. /peoplesoftcloudmana
Status	Configured

▶ Advanced

Figure 4-23. *File Server Configuration Complete*

You can also see the newly created file server and storage volumes in the Compute Classic instances and Storage tabs. This will also inform you of the current status of the instance and clearly show the size of the storage volume you just created. Figures 4-24 and 4-25 highlight the file server and storage volumes in Compute Classic, respectively.

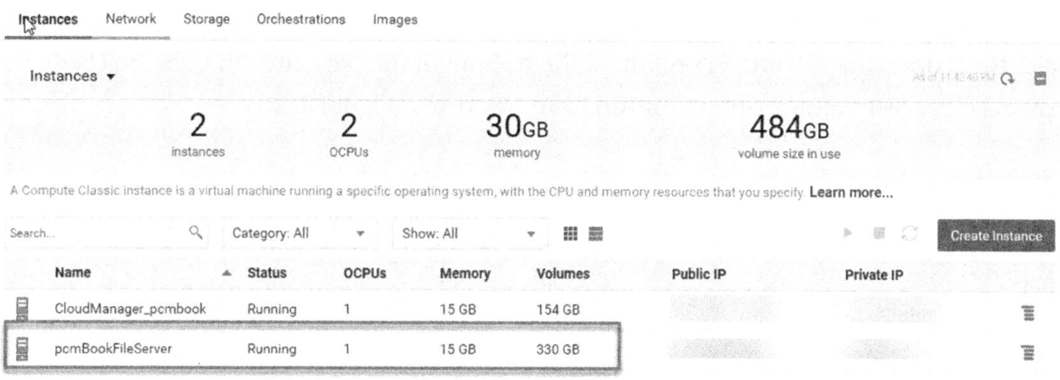

Instances   Network   Storage   Orchestrations   Images

Instances ▾

	2	2	30GB	484GB	
	instances	OCPUs	memory	volume size in use	

A Compute Classic instance is a virtual machine running a specific operating system, with the CPU and memory resources that you specify. Learn more...

Search...   Category: All   Show: All   Create Instance

	Name	Status	OCPUs	Memory	Volumes	Public IP	Private IP	
	CloudManager_pcmbook	Running	1	15 GB	154 GB			≡
	pcmBookFileServer	Running	1	15 GB	330 GB			≡

Figure 4-24. *File Server in Compute Classic Instances tab*

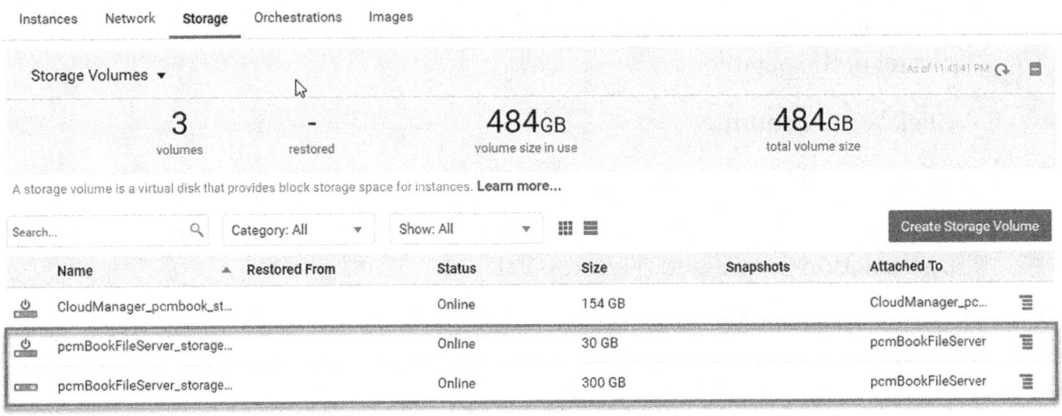

Instances	Network	**Storage**	Orchestrations	Images

Storage Volumes ▾

3 volumes	**-** restored	**484**GB volume size in use	**484**GB total volume size

As of 11:43:41 PM

A storage volume is a virtual disk that provides block storage space for instances. **Learn more...**

Search...	Category: All ▾	Show: All ▾			Create Storage Volume

Name ▲	Restored From	Status	Size	Snapshots	Attached To
CloudManager_pcmbook_st...		Online	154 GB		CloudManager_pc...
pcmBookFileServer_storage...		Online	30 GB		pcmBookFileServer
pcmBookFileServer_storage...		Online	300 GB		pcmBookFileServer

Figure 4-25. *File Server Storage Volumes in Compute Classic Storage tab*

Implementing a File Server from an Existing File Server Storage Volume

Along with creating a brand-new file server, you are also able to reuse an existing file server storage volume for use by PeopleSoft Cloud Manager. This can be accomplished by creating a new storage snapshot of the existing storage volume and then restoring that snapshot. Once the restore of the snapshot you created is complete, take note of the fully qualified name as you will need it once you move to set up the file server PeopleSoft Cloud Manager.

Once you have completed the steps to create your snapshot, restored your snapshot, and retrieved the fully qualified instance name, log back in to PeopleSoft Cloud Manager and click the Cloud Manager Settings tile from the home page. Click File Server in the left-hand navigation.

You will first need to provide a name for your new file server in the File Server Name field. Next, open the Advanced section at the bottom of the page and change the Use existing fileserver volume option button from No to Yes (Figure 4-26).

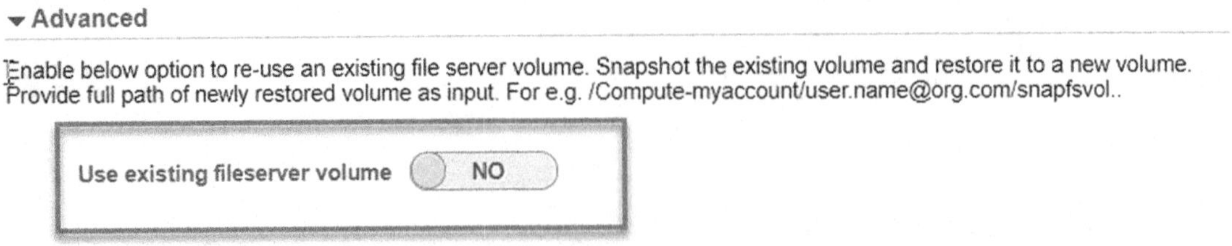

▾ Advanced

Enable below option to re-use an existing file server volume. Snapshot the existing volume and restore it to a new volume. Provide full path of newly restored volume as input. For e.g. /Compute-myaccount/user.name@org.com/snapfsvol..

Use existing fileserver volume   (NO)

Figure 4-26. *Advanced File Server option*

You will now have access to provide the name of the Existing Data Volume. Once this is complete, click Create in the upper right corner of the window, and wait for rh file server to be instantiated.

Additional Cloud Manager Settings

VM Size

Along with Settings and File Server options, you are also able to see and define a virtual machine size (small, medium, large, etc.). You can see how those VM sizes relate to the shape of they are based on. This insight can allow you to more easily select a correctly sized VM when creating instances in the Oracle Cloud. PeopleSoft Cloud Manager comes delivered with three VM sizes: small, medium, and large as shown in Figure 4-27.

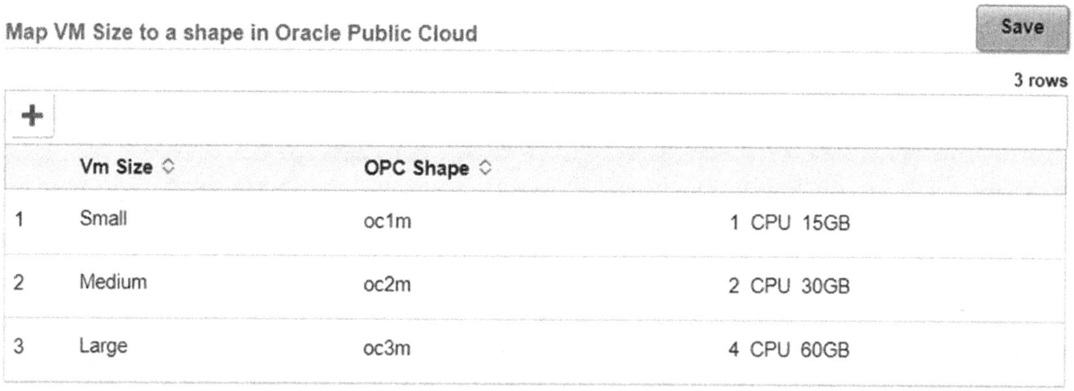

Map VM Size to a shape in Oracle Public Cloud   Save

3 rows

	Vm Size ◇	OPC Shape ◇	
1	Small	oc1m	1 CPU 15GB
2	Medium	oc2m	2 CPU 30GB
3	Large	oc3m	4 CPU 60GB

Figure 4-27. *VM size detail*

Along with being able to see the VM sizes that are currently available, you are also able to add new custom VM sizes to this list. For example, if you had the need to allow for an extra large VM size, you could create it by completing the following steps:

1. Click the plus in the upper right corner of the VM Size list (Figure 4-28).

Figure 4-28. *Add a new VM size*

2. This will add a new row for you to enter a VM size name and
    select the appropriate OPC Shape for the VM size you are adding
    (Figure 4-29).

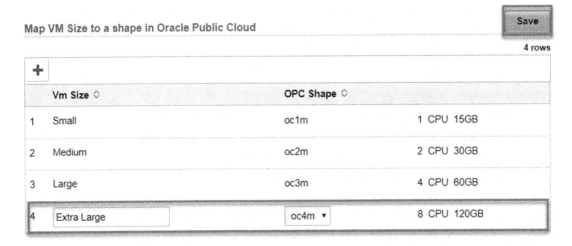

Figure 4-29. *New row for a new VM size*

3. Once you've entered the VM size you need, click Save in the upper
    right corner of the window. Figure 4-30 shows the updated VM
    sizes.

	Vm Size ◇	OPC Shape ◇	
1	Extra Large	oc4m	8 CPU 120GB
2	Small	oc1m	1 CPU 15GB
3	Medium	oc2m	2 CPU 30GB
4	Large	oc3m	4 CPU 60GB

Figure 4-30. *Updated VM sizes*

Logs

From the Cloud Manager Settings left navigation, you have access to all the logs created within your PeopleSoft Cloud Manager instance. The Logs window consists of three major user inputs, selection of the log file you are looking to explore, the number of lines of the log you would like to see at one time (defaults to ten rows), and the search criteria. One additional aspect of the Logs window is the ability to search the selected log files via regular expression. Figure 4-31 shows the detail on the fetch log data dialogue in PeopleSoft Cloud Manager.

File server logs

*Log file	out.log ▾
No of lines	10
Search	

Default Value: 10

Regex search   D

Fetch Logs

Log data

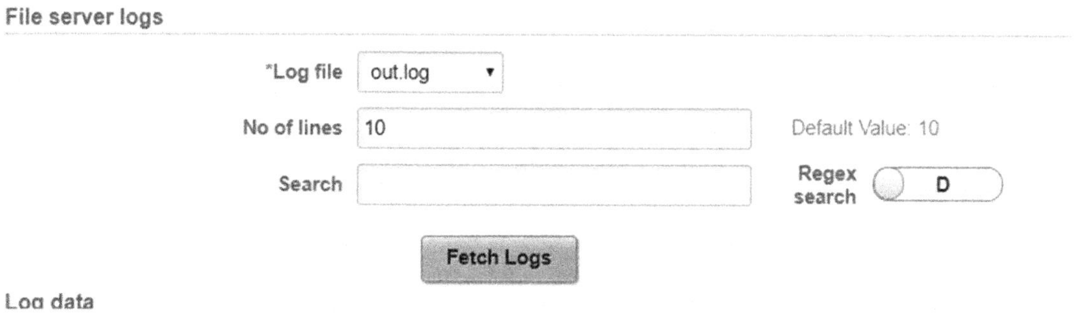

Figure 4-31. *Fetch Log data dialogue*

CHAPTER 5

The Cloud Repository

The previous four chapters have focused exclusively on the steps and processes necessary to get PeopleSoft Cloud Manager up and running in the Oracle Cloud. From this point forward, we will be focused on the process of provisioning PeopleSoft environments in the Oracle Cloud and understanding and utilizing all the features and tools that PeopleSoft Cloud Manager offers. There are four key components that need to be understood in order to properly provision and manage PeopleSoft instance in Cloud Manager: the repository, the topology, the template, and finally the PeopleSoft environment. These four components work together to automate and streamline the environment provisioning process within Cloud Manager.

The first step in provisioning a PeopleSoft environment in Cloud Manager requires downloading and accessing a PeopleSoft image to the repository. The repository within PeopleSoft Cloud Manager provides you with an easy way to both download and manage PeopleSoft images, patch sets, tools updates, and custom PeopleSoft images. The file server we created in Chapter 4 provides Cloud Manager a Network File System (NFS) repository where these images and downloads are stored. The subscription channels found within the repository allow administrators the ability to pick and choose which applications and maintenance content they want to download to the repository. From here, the download manager helps to automate the process of downloading and saving these images from Oracle Support.

Accessing the Repository

To get started building your repository and automating your image download process, you need to start by logging in to the PeopleSoft Cloud Manager as an administrative user. Once you have logged in to the application, gaining access to your repository is a simple task of clicking the Repository tile on your Cloud Manager home page. Figure 5-1 indicates the location of the Repository tile.

© Aaron Engelsrud 2019
A. Engelsrud, *Managing PeopleSoft on the Oracle Cloud*, https://doi.org/10.1007/978-1-4842-4546-0_5

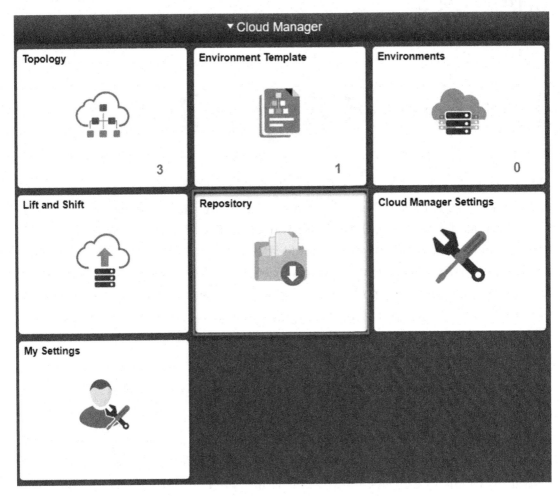

Figure 5-1. *Repository tile*

Once you are in the repository, you will see you have four main menu options on the left-hand navigation of the page: My Downloads, Download Subscriptions, Download History, and Logs. Each of these menu options will be covered in the following sections of this chapter. Figure 5-2 displays the menu options on the left-hand navigation of the repository page.

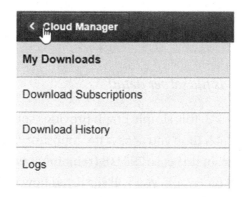

Figure 5-2. *Repository menu options*

My Downloads

The first page that opens after accessing the Repository tile is the My Downloads page. If you are just getting started with PeopleSoft Cloud Manager, this page will largely be empty aside from the size of file server you created in the last chapter and the available space this file server provides. Once you have subscribed to some channels and have downloaded either some PeopleSoft images or PeopleSoft Release Patchsets, you will see the artifacts of those downloads listed here.

There are two main sections to the My Downloads page. First, the top of the page includes basic detail about the file server you have associated with PeopleSoft Cloud Manager. Second, the bottom half of the page details the artifacts that have been downloaded to your file server. Together, these two pieces of data provide you with a basic understanding of how much space you have available, how much you are using, and what has been downloaded.

File Server Information

The top half of the My Downloads page provides you with the basic detail you need to understand how much file server space you are currently using, how much you have allocated, and how much space you have left. This is important information as your cloud repository grows as more patchsets and images are downloaded to your file server; you will need to manage this space accordingly. Figure 5-3 shows the storage space detail.

Figure 5-3. *My Downloads file server detail*

As you can see in image 5-3, this simple graph provides some very important and simple information to you each time you access the repository. On the top left, you will see listed the File Server Size, in this case 295 GB (remember we created a 300 GB file server). In the middle of the bar graph, you will see listed how much of the file server space is currently available, in this case 263 GB. Quite easily, we can determine that we are currently using 32 GB of file space on the server (295GB – 263GB = 32GB). At a glance, we are provided with all the information we need to know if we need to add more space or if we have enough space to continue to download artifacts to the file server.

File Server SSH Access

Accessing your file server via SSH, which you will need to do to expand your file server, is a two-step process. First you will access your Cloud Manager virtual machine using the SSH command coupled with your public and private key pair. Once you have done this, you will then create an additional SSH session to your file server virtual machine using the Cloud Manager private SSH key.

To access your file sever via SSH, complete the following steps:

1. Open a PuTTY or other terminal application and start a ssh session using the opc user to your Cloud Manager virtual machine. If you look back in your notes from your installation, you should have the command you need. For reference, the command looks like this: `ssh -i <path_to_private_key_file>/<private_key_name> -o ServerAliveInterval=5 -o ServerAliveCountMax=1 opc@<public_ip_address_of_instance>`

2. Once you have successfully logged in as the opc user, sudo to the psadm2 user on that VM. Sudo is a Unix command that allows you to elevate your privileges on the server to that of the user you are sudoing as, in this case psadm. The command looks like this: `sudo su - psadm2`

3. You'll note the use on your command prompt has now changed to psadm2 rather than opc.

4. Change your present working directory (pwd) to /home/psadm2/
    psft/data/cloud/opchrome/<identity_domain_name>/<opc_
    user_id>/.ssh. In my case I will use this command to move to
    the correct directory: `cd /home/psadm2/psft/data/cloud/`
    `opchome/6xxxxxxx3/peoplesoftcloudmanager\@gmail.com/.ssh`

5. In this directory, you will find the id_key_rsa.pub file. You can view
    the directory contents by entering the `ls` command at the prompt.

6. Now you can enter a new SSH session using the id_key_rsa file
    located here. To do this, enter the following command at the
    Linux prompt: `ssh -i id_key_rsa opc@<file_server_name>`.
    In my case this command equates to `ssh -i id_key_rsa opc@`
    `pcmBookFileServer`.

7. You will be prompted if you want to continue connecting; select
    yes and add the file server to your list of known hosts on the Cloud
    Manager VM.

8. Once again, you will see your user and server name change at
    your command prompt, this time to opc@pcmbookfileserver. You
    are now connected to the file server virtual machine.

Expanding Your File Server

You can increase your file server space if you created your file server in Oracle Storage
Classic. To expand your file server, complete the following steps:

1. Start by starting a new SSH session and connecting to your Cloud
    Manager virtual machine. This was covered in step 1 of the
    previous section.

2. Determine the name of the device mounted on /cm_psft_dpks –
    you can find this device by using the `df` command from the Linux
    command prompt. Note this device name as you will need it later
    the process.

3. Issue this command: `unmount /cm_psft_dpks` in the Cloud
    Manager virtual machine as the opc user.

4. Once this is complete, SSH to the File Manager virtual machine as described in the following section. Here you will need to stop both the NFS service and the smb service. Issue the following commands at the file server virtual machine dcommand prompt:

   ```
   /sbin/service nfs stop
   /sbin/service smb stop
   ```

5. Next unmount the storage disk: `unmount /u01/app/oracle/ product`

6. Next, you need to switch over to the Oracle Compute Cloud Service Console window. To do this, log in to `http://oracle. cloud.com` and navigate to the Compute Cloud Service Console from your Cloud Dashboard.

7. In the Service Console in the instance tab, click the file server instance to view the server details; in my case the file server is named pcmBookFileServer, and copy down the name of the storage disk attached to the file server. In my case, this storage is named pcmBookFileServer_storage_2.

8. Navigate back to your main Compute Classic Service Console page and click the storage tab.

9. Find the disk associated with the file server as highlighted in Figure 5-4.

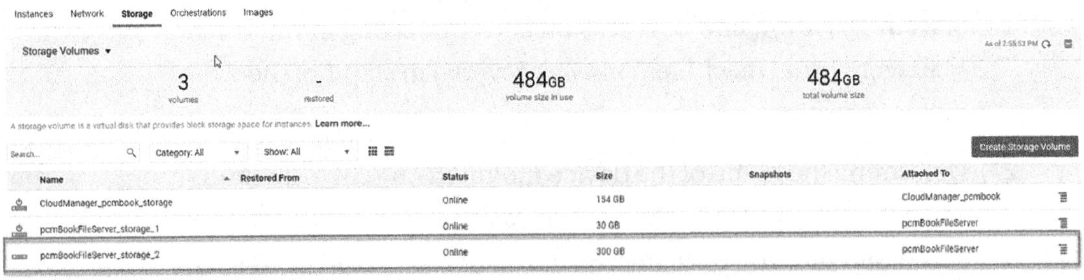

Figure 5-4. Storage tab, file server volume

10. Click the menu icon on the right of the storage volume and select Update (Figure 5-5).

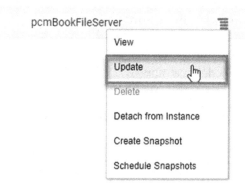

Figure 5-5. *Update file server volume*

11. Input the size required on the Size field (Figure 5-6).

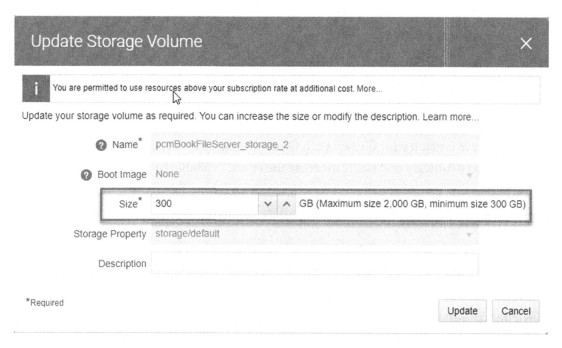

Figure 5-6. *Update Storage Volume*

12. Click Update to increase the size as desired.

13.   Back on the file server virtual machine (where you should still
      have a valid SSH connection), you need to run two different
      commands to expand the file system in the attached disk. From
      the Linux command prompt, run

```
e2fsck -f /dev/<device name>
resize2fs /dev/<device name>
```

In both cases, use the device name you determined in step 2 of
this process.

14.   Again, on the file server virtual machine, issue the following
      commands to mount the newly expanded disk, verify the new file
      server volume, and start both the NFS and SMB services:

```
mount -a
df -h /u01/app/oracle/product
/sbin/service nfs start
/sbin/service smb start
```

15.   Exit out of your file server SSH connection.

16.   Back in the Cloud Manager virtual machine, remount the file
      server share: `mount -a`

IF you have created your file server in Oracle Storage Classic, following these steps
will allow you to quickly and easily increase the space available to you on your file server.

Download Detail

Along with the File Server Size detail, the My Downloads page also provides a detailed
list of the artifacts that have been downloaded to your server. Each artifact downloaded
is listed and, at a glance, provides detail as to the name of the artifact, the type of artifact
downloaded, what product line the artifact belongs, to which release it is associated
with, the version number, the native platform, and the size of the artifact. Figure 5-7
shows the repository download detail.

Name ◇	Type ◇	Product ◇	Release ◇	Version ◇	Platform ◇	Size ◇	
PEOPLESOFT CS UPGRADE SOURCE IMAGE 9.2.002 - NATIVE OS	MOS - Application Upgrade Source Image	CS	9.2	2	Linux	15.73 GB	>
BRON NEEDS EXTRA SERVICE OPERATION FOR PRIOR EDUCATION DUE TO REGULATORY REQ	MOS - PRP	CS	9.2	11	Generic	2.19 MB	>
POTENTIAL SECURITY VULNERABILITY	MOS - PRP	CS	9.2	11	Generic	494.77 KB	>
ACAD PROG TABLE ISSUE AND SFP INTEGRATION PHASE 2	MOS - PRP	CS	9.2	11	Generic	494.31 KB	>
2019 - 2020 AID YEAR UPDATES FOR NSLDS	MOS - PRP	CS	9.2	11	Generic	983.85 KB	>
PEOPLESOFT CS UPDATE IMAGE 9.2.011 - NATIVE OS	MOS - Application Update Image	CS	9.2	11	Linux	15.99 GB	>
HESA - DATA FUTURES - PHASE 2	MOS - PRP	CS	9.2	11	Generic	3.2 MB	>
CS9.2 PUM11 THE PS_MAINTENANCE_LOG IS EMPTY	MOS - PRP	CS	9.2	11	Generic	1.11 MB	>
POTENTIAL SECURITY VULNERABILITY	MOS - PRP	CS	9.2	11	Generic	541.03 KB	>
CHANGE PACKAGE FROM MULTI LANGUAGE CAMPUS SOLUTIONS 9.2 PUM 11 FAILS	MOS - PRP	CS	9.2	11	Generic	500.2 KB	>

Figure 5-7. *Download detail*

Using the filter at the top of the page allows you to quickly and easily limit the
number of artifacts listed. If you click the filter icon in the upper left corner of the list,
you will get the filter pop-up window. This Filter dialogue allows you to search by name,
patch type, product, version, or platform. To use it, simply select your preferred search
term and click Done in the upper right corner. Your list will return filtered appropriately.
When you are done with your filtered list, click the filter icon, and then click the Clear
Filter button in the middle of the Filter dialogue window. Figure 5-8 shows the download
filter detail, and Figure 5-9 provides a view of the filtered list.

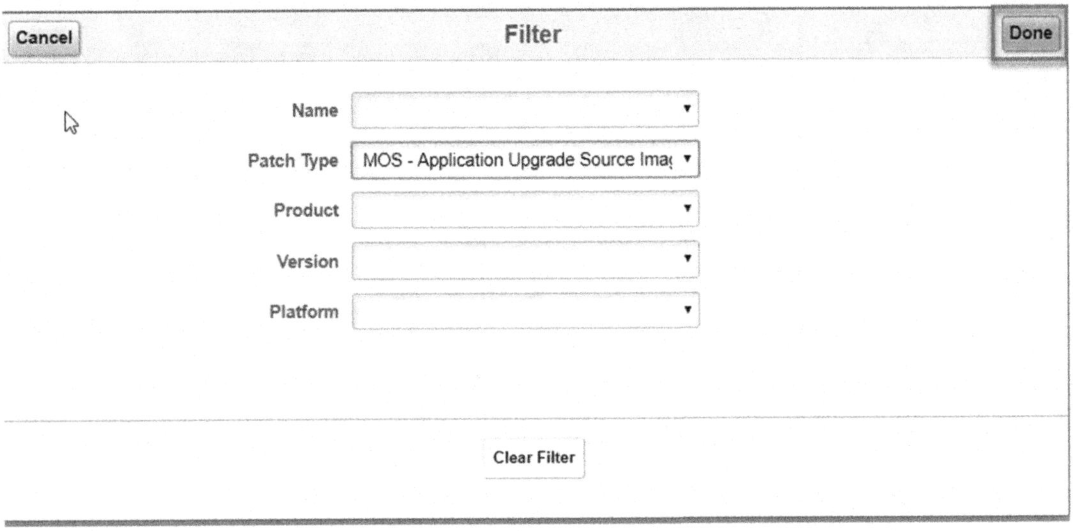

Figure 5-8. *Download filter*

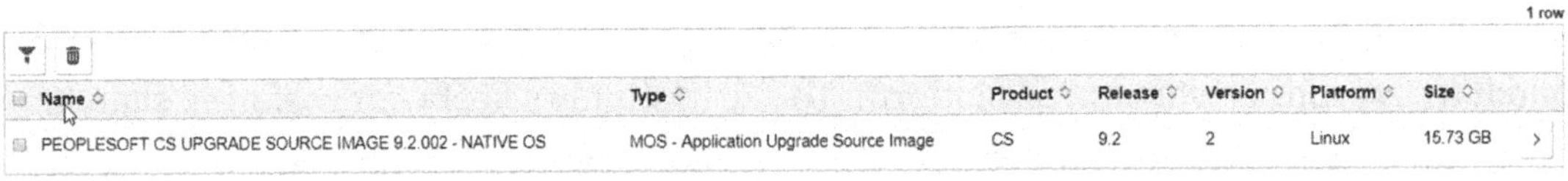

Figure 5-9. *Filtered list*

Along with the row level detail, the My Downloads page also provides more granular detail on each artifact downloaded to the repository. By clicking either the name of the artifact or the arrow button located on the far-right side of the row, you can access more detail on the artifact. This includes a list of basic information about the patchset or image including the bug number (which can be referenced in Oracle Support), a description of the patchset, the release language, the classification of the artifact, and the date it was updated and released, along with the location of the artifact on the file server. Additionally, the detail contains what bugs were fixed with the patchset and what files were downloaded as part of the release. Figure 5-10 captures a view of the artifact detail.

CS   ×

Bug Number 28068969

Description BRON NEEDS EXTRA SERVICE OPERATION FOR PRIOR EDUCATION DUE TO REGULATORY RE

Language American English

Translations Available No

Classification Legislative

Updated Date 12/21/2018 11:12:22

Released Date 12/21/2018 11:12:22

Patch Location /cm_psft_dpks/prp/generic/CS/11/updPRJ28068969.zip

Fixed Bugs   7 rows

Bug Number ⌄	More Information ⌄
29016800	BRON NEEDS EXTRA SERVICE OPERATION FOR PRIOR EDUCATION DUE TO REGULATORY REQ(CC OBJECTS - POPSELECT)
28994552	DO BRON VAVO - NEW INTERFACE NEEDED FOR EXCHANGE OF DATA WITH DUO - (ADS OBJECTS)
28511610	CAF ATTRIBUTES RELATED OBJECTS FOR BRON-VAVO LEGISLATIVE CHANGE
28473892	BRON-BO: NEED NEW EXEMPTION CODE OF KZDL FOR BRON BO SETUP
28142340	SYSTEM DATA CAF ATTRIBUTES FOR BRON-VAVO LEGISLATIVE CHANGE
28068969	BRON NEEDS EXTRA SERVICE OPERATION FOR PRIOR EDUCATION DUE TO REGULATORY REQ
27506607	DO BRON VAVO - NEW INTERFACE NEEDED FOR EXCHANGE OF DATA WITH DUO

Patch Files   1 row

File Name ⌄	Size ⌄
updPRJ28068969.zip	2.19 MB

Figure 5-10. *Artifact detail*

Download Subscriptions

The next menu item in the repository is Download Subscriptions. This page allows you
to see what channels you are subscribed to and what channels are available for you
to subscribe to, to create new subscription channels, and to initiate downloads to the
Cloud Manager repository. To help you quickly get started, PeopleSoft Cloud Manager
comes ready to go with a set of default channels, one for each PeopleSoft application
and one for each major PeopleTools release. Figure 5-11 shows the high-level repository
subscription.

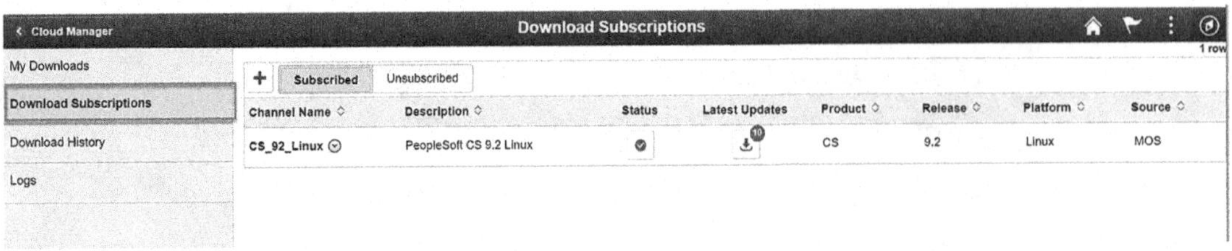

Figure 5-11. *Download Subscription page detail*

Subscribing to Channels

The concept of subscribing to channels is a new concept to PeopleSoft users. Within PeopleSoft Cloud Manager, channels consist of automated access to downloads for the current PeopleSoft image for a specific PeopleSoft application or PeopleSoft PeopleTools only releases for the major PeopleTools releases starting with 8.55. PeopleSoft Cloud Manager comes with several channels already predefined, one for each major application on the Linux platform and one for each major PeopleTools release on the Linux platform. Any additional channels you may want to subscribe to can be created through the Download Subscription page. Figure 5-12 provides a view of what predefined subscription channels are included.

Channel Name ◇	Description ◇
CRM_92_Linux ⊙	PeopleSoft CRM 9.2 Linux
ELM_92_Linux ⊙	PeopleSoft ELM 9.2 Linux
FSCM_92_Linux ⊙	PeopleSoft FSCM 9.2 Linux
HCM_92_Linux ⊙	PeopleSoft HCM 9.2 Linux
IH_91_Linux ⊙	PeopleSoft IH 9.1 Linux
PCM_91_Linux ⊙	PeopleSoft Cloud Manager 9.1 Linux
Tools_855_Linux ⊙	PeopleSoft PeopleTools 8.55 Linux
Tools_856_Linux ⊙	PeopleSoft PeopleTools 8.56 Linux
Tools_857_Linux ⊙	PeopleSoft PeopleTools 8.57 Linux

Figure 5-12. *Cloud Manager predefined subscription channels*

Subscribing from the Unsubscribed Page

The main section of the Download Subscription page consists of two main tabs, subscribed and unsubscribed. Any channels that you are already subscribed to and downloading content from will show up in the subscribed tab; if you have not yet subscribed to any channels, this page will be blank. Conversely, when you switch over to the Unsubscribed tab of the Download Subscriptions page, you will have access to any of the predefined channels you are not yet subscribed to.

To subscribe to one of the predefined channels and begin downloading content for that channel, do the following:

1. Log in to PeopleSoft Cloud Manager.

2. Click the Repository tile from the Cloud Manager home page (Figure 5-13).

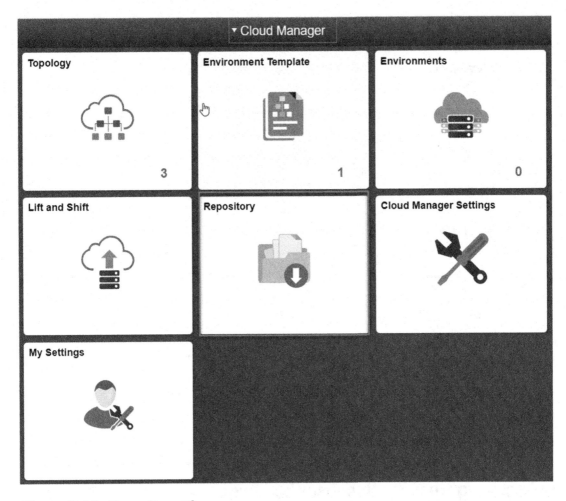

Figure 5-13. *Repository tile*

3. From the left-hand menu, select Download Subscriptions
    (Figure 5-14).

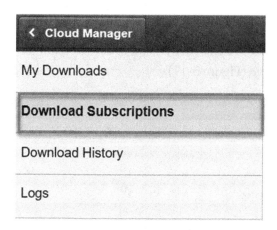

Figure 5-14. *Download Subscriptions menu option*

4.   Select the Unsubscribed button at the top of the page (Figure 5-15).

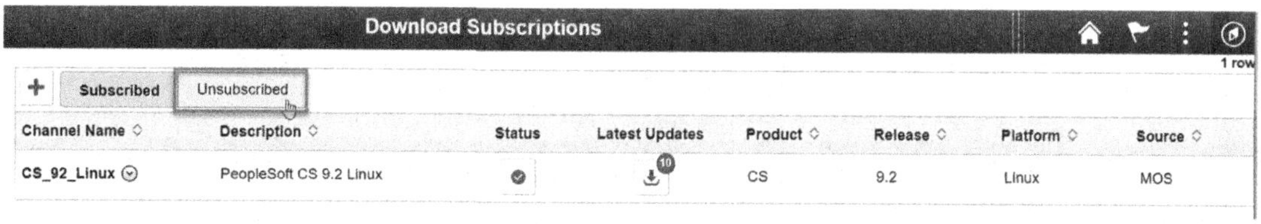

Channel Name ◇	Description ◇	Status	Latest Updates	Product ◇	Release ◇	Platform ◇	Source ◇
CS_92_Linux ⊙	PeopleSoft CS 9.2 Linux	✓	⬇30	CS	9.2	Linux	MOS

Figure 5-15. *Unsubscribed button*

5.   Find the channel you'd like to subscribe to from the list of unsubscribed channels. For this example we will be using the ELM_92_Linux channel.

6.   Click the related actions drop-down button to the right of the channel name and select Subscribe from the pop-up menu (Figure 5-16).

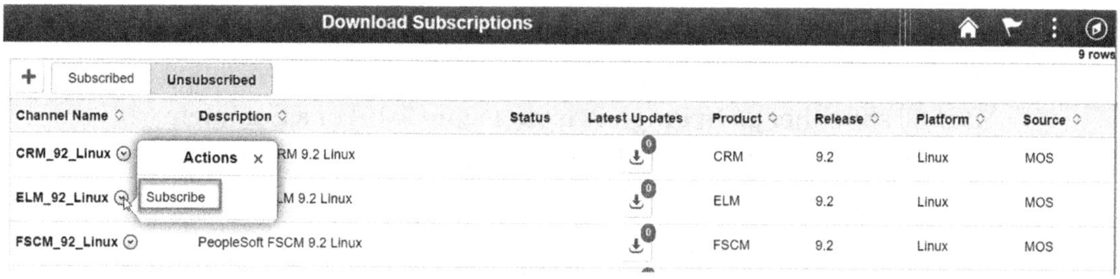

Channel Name ◇	Description ◇	Status	Latest Updates	Product ◇	Release ◇	Platform ◇	Source ◇
CRM_92_Linux ⊙	**Actions** × RM 9.2 Linux		⬇0	CRM	9.2	Linux	MOS
ELM_92_Linux ⊙	Subscribe LM 9.2 Linux		⬇0	ELM	9.2	Linux	MOS
FSCM_92_Linux ⊙	PeopleSoft FSCM 9.2 Linux		⬇0	FSCM	9.2	Linux	MOS

Figure 5-16. *Channel Subscribe pop-up*

157

7. Click the Subscribed button at the top of the page.

8. You will now see the channel you just subscribed to listed on the
    Subscribed page (Figure 5-17).

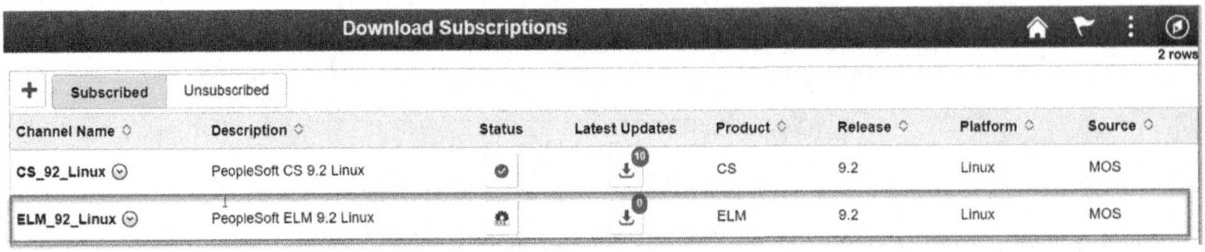

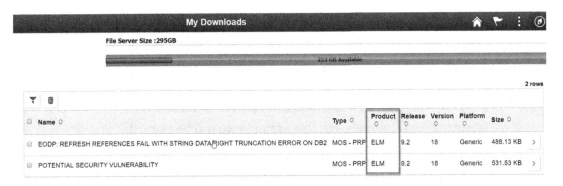

Figure 5-17. *Newly subscribed channel*

9. If you switch back to the My Downloads page within the
    repository, you will begin to see that artifacts from your channel
    subscription start to appear in the list of artifacts. In our example,
    ELM artifacts are now displayed in My Downloads (Figure 5-18).

Figure 5-18. *New artifacts in My Downloads*

10. Downloading a channel will take some time. You can check on the
    status of your channel, by going to the Download Subscriptions page
    and looking at the Status column for the channel you are watching.
    You will see either an In Progress Icon (Figure 5-19) or a Complete
    Icon (Figure 5-20) indicating the progress of the download.

| ELM_92_Linux ⊙ | PeopleSoft ELM 9.2 Linux | 🏛 | ⬇ | ELM | 9.2 | Linux | MOS |

Figure 5-19. *Channel In Progress*

| CS_92_Linux ⊙ | PeopleSoft CS 9.2 Linux | ✓ | ⬇⑩ | CS | 9.2 | Linux | MOS |

Figure 5-20. *Channel Complete*

Creating a New Channel

There may be cases where the pre-delivered channels do not meet your needs. You may have a need to create a subscription to a CRM 9.2 Windows platform in order to meet the needs of your organization. To complete this, Cloud Manager allows you the ability to create your own custom channels. To create a new channel, complete the following steps.

1. Assuming you are already logged into the Cloud Manager application and on the Download Subscription page, click the plus (+) sign at the top of the page (Figure 5-21).

Download Subscriptions							⌂ 🏴 ⋮ ◉
+ **Subscribed** Unsubscribed							2 rows
Channel Name ◇	Description ◇	Status	Latest Updates	Product ◇	Release ◇	Platform ◇	Source ◇
CS_92_Linux ⊙	PeopleSoft CS 9.2 Linux	✓	⬇⑩	CS	9.2	Linux	MOS
ELM_92_Linux ⊙	PeopleSoft ELM 9.2 Linux	⚙	⬇①	ELM	9.2	Linux	MOS

Figure 5-21. *Create a new channel*

2. This will open the Create Channel dialogue window. This dialogue allows you to enter the following information:

- **Channel Name:** This can be a name of your choice. For this example, we will follow the naming convention used by the delivered channels and name this new channel CRM_92_Windows.

- **Description:** A brief description of what the channel contains. In this vcase CRM 9.2 Windows will be used.

- **Product Name:** Select the appropriate product from the drop-down list.

- **Release Name:** Select the appropriate release from the drop-down list.

- **Platform:** Select the platform you want from the drop-down list. In this case, we will be selecting Windows.

- **Source:** Select the download source from the drop-down list.

Figure 5-22 provides a view of this dialogue detail.

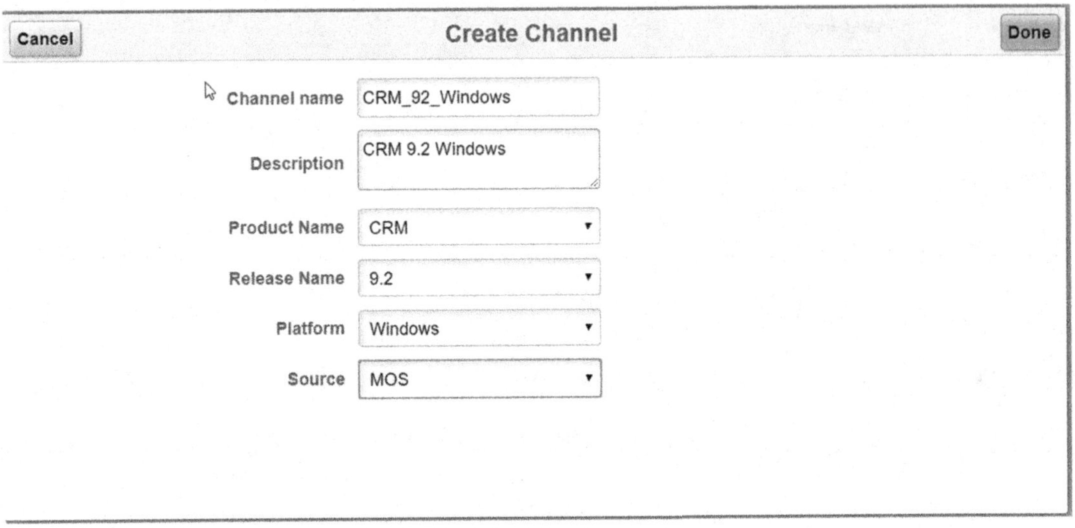

Figure 5-22. *Create Channel dialogue*

3. Once this detail is entered, click Done in the upper right corner of
    the window.

4. Your new channel should now show up in the Subscribed list of
    Channels.

Download History

Once you have subscribed to content within PeopleSoft Cloud Manager, it may be
necessary to see the history of what has been downloaded to your repository and when
it was downloaded. This detail can be found in the Download History page within
the repository. To get to the Download History page, click the Repository tile on the
home page of PeopleSoft Cloud Manager, and then select Download History from the
navigation on the left-hand side of the page (Figure 5-23).

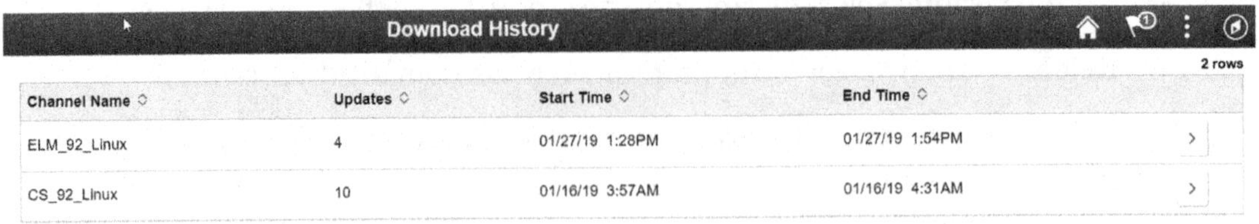

Figure 5-23. *Download History detail*

This detail provides the channel name, the number of updates downloaded, and the start and end times for downloads within the channel. You can get more information on each of the subscription channels by either clicking directly on the channel name or by clicking the arrow to the right of the channel history row. This will provide you with detail of the sync and the status for the channel as well as the status of each patch file included in the download (Figure 5-24).

ELM_92_Linux - Patch List					✕
Sync finished for the channel					
Patch Download Status					
Patch Location ◇	Status ◇	Download Time ◇	Size ◇	Name ◇	
/cm_psft_dpks/dpk/linux/ELM/18/ELM-920-UPD-018-LNX_8of11.zip	Download complete	00:11:34	3.2 GB	PEOPLESOFT ELM UPDATE IMAGE 9.2.018 - NATIVE OS	
/cm_psft_dpks/dpk/linux/ELM/18/ELM-920-UPD-018-LNX_1of11.zip	Download complete	00:00:23	180.6 MB	PEOPLESOFT ELM UPDATE IMAGE 9.2.018 - NATIVE OS	
/cm_psft_dpks/dpk/linux/ELM/03/ELM-920-UPG-003-LNX_2of11.zip	Download complete	00:08:25	1.76 GB	PEOPLESOFT ELM UPGRADE SOURCE IMAGE 9.2.003 -	
/cm_psft_dpks/dpk/linux/ELM/18/ELM-920-UPD-018-LNX_10of11.zip	Download complete	00:01:03	539.93 MB	PEOPLESOFT ELM UPDATE IMAGE 9.2.018 - NATIVE OS	
/cm_psft_dpks/dpk/linux/ELM/18/ELM-920-UPD-018-LNX_6of11.zip	Download complete	00:02:17	1.25 GB	PEOPLESOFT ELM UPDATE IMAGE 9.2.018 - NATIVE OS	
/cm_psft_dpks/dpk/linux/ELM/18/ELM-920-UPD-018-LNX_11of11.zip	Download complete	00:01:03	524.95 MB	PEOPLESOFT ELM UPDATE IMAGE 9.2.018 - NATIVE OS	
/cm_psft_dpks/dpk/linux/ELM/03/ELM-920-UPG-003-LNX_3of11.zip	Download complete	00:06:44	2.5 GB	PEOPLESOFT ELM UPGRADE SOURCE IMAGE 9.2.003 -	
/cm_psft_dpks/dpk/linux/ELM/18/ELM-920-UPD-018-LNX_5of11.zip	Download complete	00:02:49	1.5 GB	PEOPLESOFT ELM UPDATE IMAGE 9.2.018 - NATIVE OS	
/cm_psft_dpks/dpk/linux/ELM/03/ELM-920-UPG-003-LNX_8of11.zip	Download complete	00:14:01	3.06 GB	PEOPLESOFT ELM UPGRADE SOURCE IMAGE 9.2.003 -	

Figure 5-24. *Download History patch detail*

Repository Logs

You can easily view the content within the Downloads Logs through the Logs page. You can get to the Logs page by clicking the Repository tile on the home page and selecting Logs from the left-hand menu. This page provides you the opportunity to view the log output for any of the channels you are subscribed to as well as the output for each specific patch file within a channel.

The page provides you with several search options to help limit the results you return. You will want to select from the following options to limit your search and include only the log files you are expecting:

- **Channel Name:** Select the channel name from where you would like to search the log files. In our case, we will search ELM_92_Linux channel.

161

- **Log File:** Allows you to select from a drop-down list the log file you would like to look at. Here we will be searching the ELM_92_Linux261.log file for details about the download process.

- **Number of Lines to Display:** Limit the number of lines returned to something manageable. This defaults to ten lines.

- **Search String:** Enter the search string you are looking for in the log file. In our case we will look for the string "29057111" to find log detail about that particular bug number (Figure 5-25).

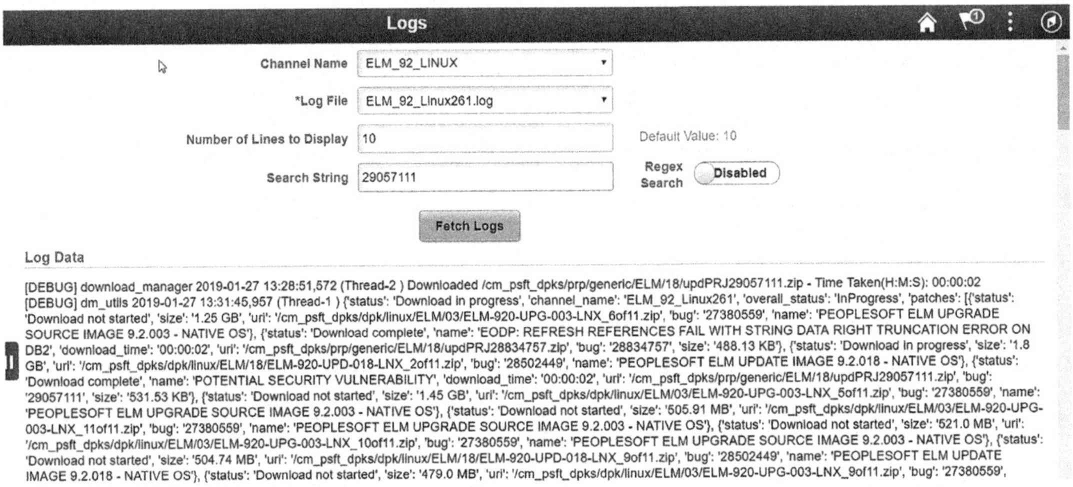

Figure 5-25. *Repository download logs*

CHAPTER 6

Creating and Managing Topologies

The previous chapter focused on the repository and the functionality available from PeopleSoft Cloud Manager to simplify and automate the process of downloading and managing application packages. This chapter will focus on how you can design and manage the infrastructure on which those application packages will run. Cloud Manager uses the concept of topology to help define the various components within your PeopleSoft environment.

During the process of creating a new topology, you will determine how many nodes your PeopleSoft environment will run on, what operating system those nodes will run, the computing power of each node including CPU (virtual CPU) and RAM, and what PeopleSoft components are installed on each of the nodes. Your business requirements may dictate that your PeopleSoft environments include a Linux node for mid-tier components, one Windows node for PeopleSoft client tools which are used for development and updating your system, and a separate Linux node for the database. Within the Cloud Manager Topology, you can define and control these deployment features and provision the environment the way you need. Along with creating custom topologies to meet your needs, PeopleSoft Cloud Manager also comes with three topologies predefined for your use: Lift and Shift, PUM Fulltier, and Lift and Shift – DbaaS.

Accessing the Topology Home Page

To access the Topology home page, start by logging in to PeopleSoft Cloud Manager application with your administrative user. Once you are logged in, from the PeopleSoft Cloud Manager home page, click the Topology tile. This will open the Topology home page. Figure 6-1 highlights the Topology tile on the PeopleSoft Cloud Manager home page.

© Aaron Engelsrud 2019
A. Engelsrud, *Managing PeopleSoft on the Oracle Cloud*, https://doi.org/10.1007/978-1-4842-4546-0_6

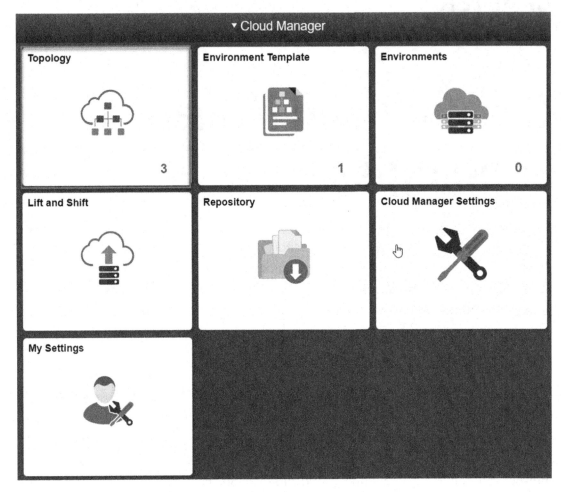

Figure 6-1. *Topology tile on the Cloud Manager home page*

On the topology page, you will see that you have access to the three delivered topologies, you can clone existing topologies, and you can also create new topologies. Each of these functions will be covered in detail in the following sections and is shown in Figure 6-2.

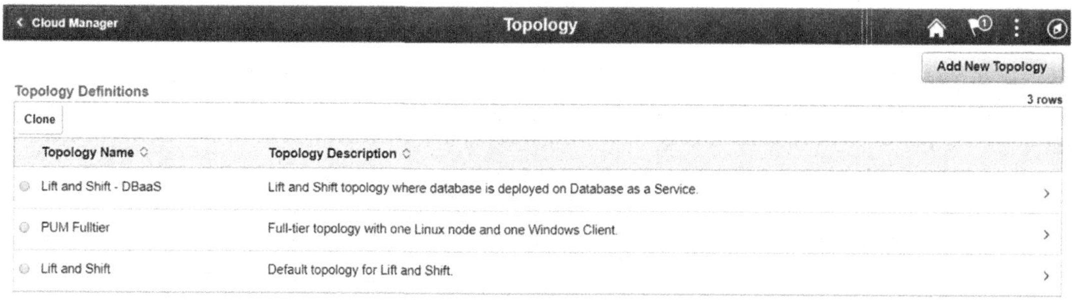

< Cloud Manager
Topology
Add New Topology
Topology Definitions
3 rows
Clone
Topology Name
Topology Description
Lift and Shift - DBaaS
Lift and Shift topology where database is deployed on Database as a Service.
PUM Fulltier
Full-tier topology with one Linux node and one Windows Client.
Lift and Shift
Default topology for Lift and Shift.

Figure 6-2. *Three delivered PeopleSoft Cloud Manager Topologies*

What Is a Topology?

A PeopleSoft Cloud Manager Topology does the following:

- Defines the infrastructure layout of the PeopleSoft environment that will be created in the Oracle Cloud
- Allows the administrator to choose what operating system the node will run on
- Determines how much virtual CPU and memory are allocated to each node within the topology
- Indicates which PeopleSoft components are installed on each node within the topology

Topologies are used within PeopleSoft Cloud Manager to help administrators create environments that meet the needs of the users of that environment. Administrators may create a development topology that is small and consists of only one node, a test topology that can be used when test environments are needed, and a production topology that consists of multiple nodes that are bigger and more powerful than the developer topology allows for. This provides added functionality, consistency, and reusability to PeopleSoft Cloud administrators and makes provisioning environments across the enterprise more straightforward.

Delivered Topologies

PeopleSoft Cloud Manager comes delivered with three unique topologies that can be used in the process of instantiating new PeopleSoft environments in the Oracle Cloud. These three topologies are Lift and Shift, PUM Fulltier, and Lift and Shift – DbaaS. Each of these topologies has a distinct use case and specific purpose. Additionally, these provided topologies can typically be used as a good starting point in creating a new custom topology that better meets the needs of your organization. Let's explore each of these delivered topologies in more detail.

To access the node specific detail within each of the delivered topologies, you can get there by clicking directly on the row containing the name description of the topology you would like to see in more detail. This will bring you to the Topology Definition page. This page provides detail as to how many nodes are defined within topology, the environment type of the node, the size of each node, the operating system of each node, and the disk space of each node.

Lift and Shift

The Lift and Shift topology is delivered with three nodes predefined. A Middle Tier, a Database Tier, and a node for the Peoplesoft client. Unlike topologies that employ a single full-tier node, the Lift and Shift node breaks out the Middle Tier and the database on to separate nodes within the topology. Each of these nodes serves a distinct purpose in the environments created using this topology. You will notice that while you are able to delete our custom created topologies, you cannot delete the Lift and Shift topologies that are used for the lift and shift process, and the Delete button at the top of the page is grayed out and not accessible. Figure 6-3 shows the Lift and Shift topology definition and corresponding environment types.

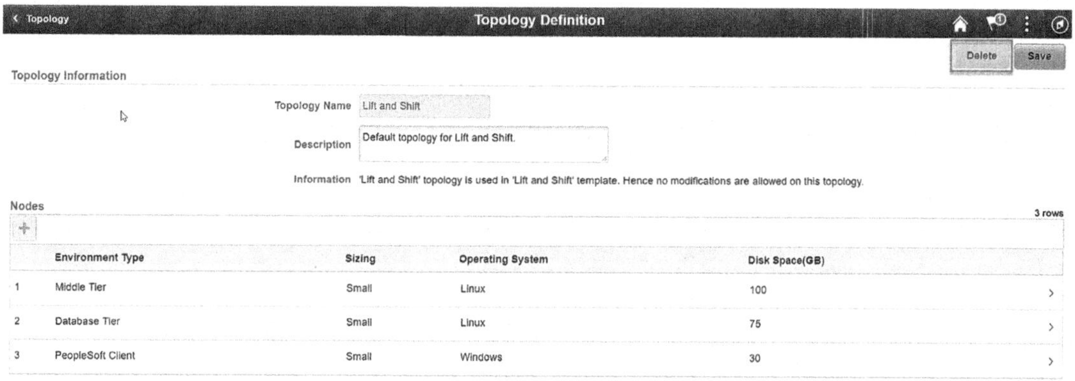

Figure 6-3. *Lift and Shift topology*

Middle Tier Node

If you click the node name, Environment Type in the Topology Definition page, you can see the specific detail about that node. In this case the Middle Tier consists of a Linux host operating system providing the middle tier PeopleSoft components including an appserver, webserver, and process scheduler. These components are built on a size small host (1 OCPU and 15GB RAM) and 100GB of disk space. Currently, it is not possible to remove individual components, such as the appserver or webserver, from the middle tier environment type. Figure 6-4 provides the detail included in the edit node dialogue.

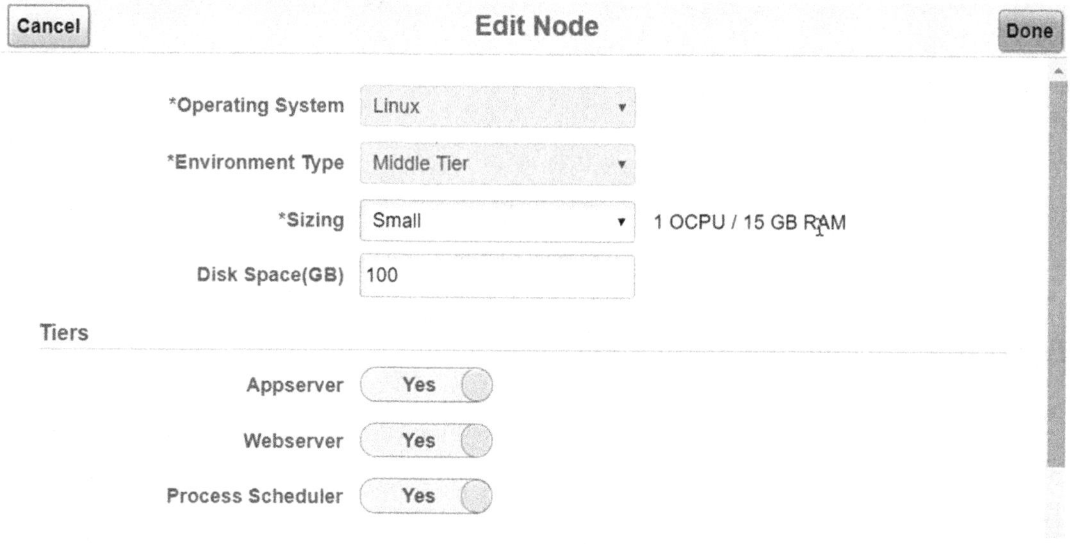

Figure 6-4. *Lift and Shift – Middle Tier*

Database Tier Node

The Lift and Shift Database node consists of a Database environment type build on a Linux host. This host is sized small with 75GB of disk space (Figure 6-5).

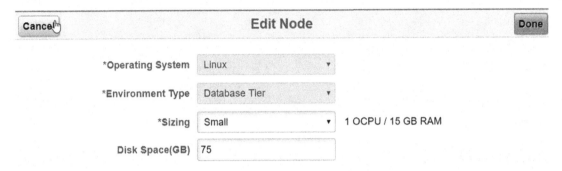

Figure 6-5. *Lift and Shift – Database Tier node*

PeopleSoft Client Node

The third node in this topology is the PeopleSoft Client node. This node consists of a node running the Windows operating system and the PeopleSoft Client tools environment type. The size of this host is small and allows for 30 GB of disk space (Figure 6-6).

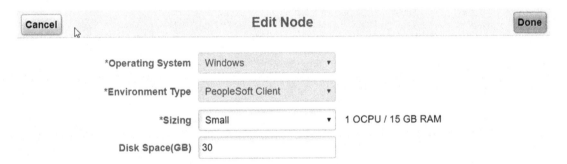

Figure 6-6. *Lift and Shift – PeopleSoft Client node*

PUM Full Tier

The PeopleSoft Update Manager (PUM) Fulltier topology is a delivered topology that consists of one Linux full-tier node and one Window PeopleSoft Client node. This topology is well suited to provisioning PeopleSoft Images for PeopleSoft Update Manager applications. It is a simple and straightforward topology that provides the necessary components to quickly and easily spin up a PeopleSoft environment from a downloaded PeopleSoft Image. Figure 6-7 shows the PUM Fulltier Topology Definition.

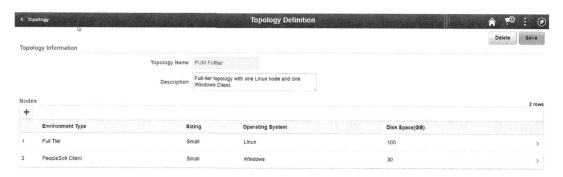

Figure 6-7. *PUM Fulltier*

Full Tier

The full-tier node of the PUM Fulltier topology consists of a Linux host running the Full Tier environment type. This means that an appsever, webserver, process scheduler, and database will all be deployed on this one virtual machine. The size of this node is small, and the host is allocated 100GB of file space (Figure 6-8).

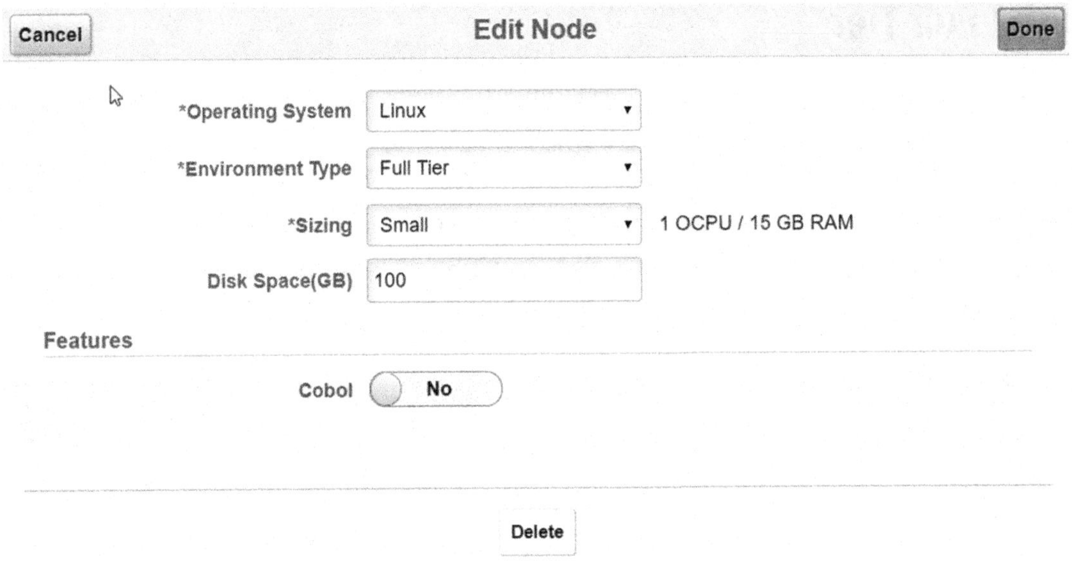

Figure 6-8. *PUM Fulltier – Full Tier*

PeopleSoft Client Node

The second node in the PUM Fulltier topology is a PeopleSoft Client node. This node runs the Windows operating system and deploys the PeopleSoft Client environment type. The size of this host is small and is allocated 30GB of file space. Once deployed, this Windows workstation is accessible via Remote Desktop Manager and can be used for development tasks through PeopleSoft Application Designer and Datamover or update tasks with Change Assistant (Figure 6-9).

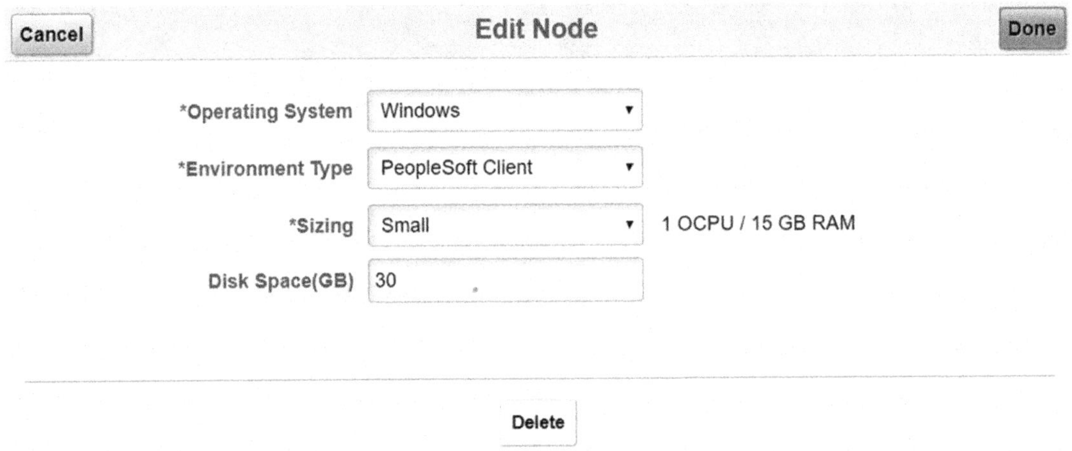

Figure 6-9. *PUM Fulltier – PeopleSoft Client*

Lift and Shift – DBaaS

The third topology delivered by PeopleSoft Cloud Manager is the Lift and Shift – DbaaS topology. This topology is designed specifically for Lift and Shift applications that are going to use Oracle Database as a Service for the database layer of the PeopleSoft application stack. Like the regular Lift and Shift topology, the Lift and Shift – Dbaas topology consists of three separate nodes: a middle tier node, a Database as a Service node, and a PeopleSoft Client node. Figure 6-10 shows the Topology Definition for the Lift and Shift – DBaaS delivered topology.

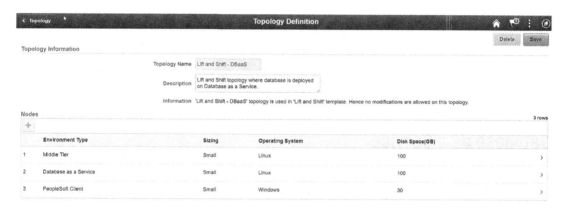

Figure 6-10. *Lift and Shift – DbaaS*

Middle Tier

The Lift and Shift – DbaaS topology Middle Tier consists of a node running the Linux operating system. This is a small-sized node with 1 OCPU and 15 GB of RAM; the node has also been allocated 100 GB of disk space (Figure 6-11).

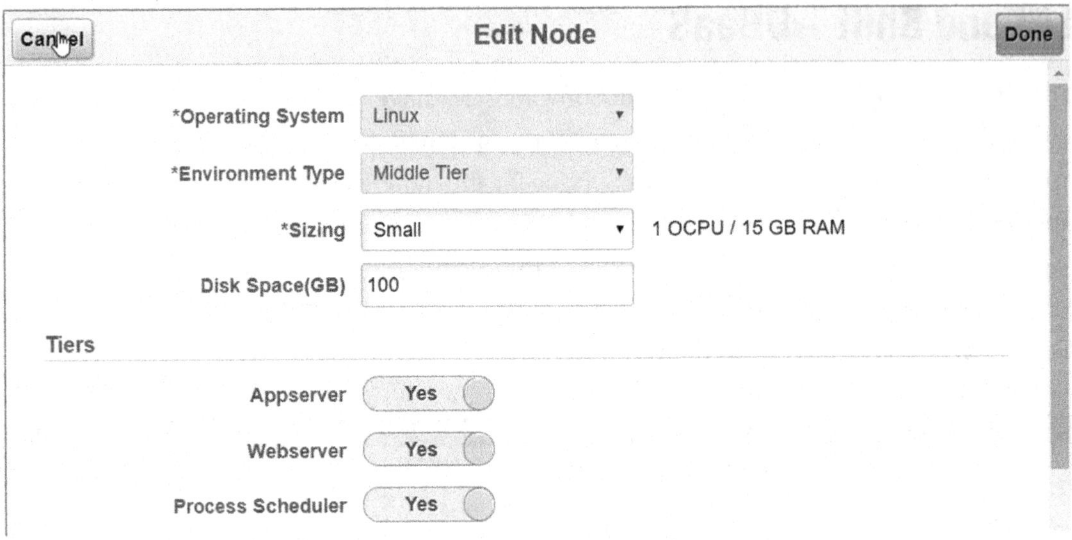

Figure 6-11. *Lift and Shift – DbaaS – Middle Tier*

Database as a Service

The second node in this topology is the Database as a Service node. Like the middle tier node, this node also runs the Linux operating system. This node is sized small, with 1 OPCU and 15 GB of RAM along with 100 GB of disk space (Figure 6-12).

Figure 6-12. *Lift and Shift – DBaaS – Database as a Service*

PeopleSoft Client

Like the other topologies that come delivered with PeopleSoft Cloud Manager, the Lift and Shift – DbaaS topology comes delivered with a Windows-based node to allow for PeopleSoft Client tool access. This is a small-sized host, with 1 OPCU and 15 GB of RAM and 30 GB of disk space (Figure 6-13).

Figure 6-13. *Lift and Shift – DbaaS – PeopleSoft Client*

Creating a New Topology

You will find cases where the delivered topologies do not meet your needs. For example, none of the three delivered topologies would accurately define what you may need for a production, development, or test environment. To address this issue, you will need to create a new topology. To get started defining the components within your custom topology, you will need to log in to PeopleSoft Cloud Manager, and click the Topology tile on the home page. From the main topology page, click the **Add New Topology** button at the top of the page to get started (Figure 6-14).

Figure 6-14. *Add New Topology*

Once you are on the Topology Definition page, you will need to provide the following two pieces of information:

- **Topology Name:** This can be anything you like. It should clearly define what the topology provides in terms of infrastructure to the eventual instance. In our case we are calling this new topology "development (small)."

- **Description:** Again, this can be anything you like; however, the more clearly you define the topology, the less opportunity there will be for accidental misuse. In this example, we are using "This is a small development instance with one middle tier node and one database node" as the description (Figure 6-15).

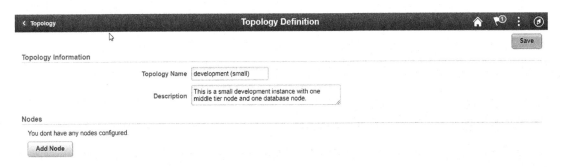

Figure 6-15. *Topology Definition*

Now that you have your topology defined, you will next need to the appropriate nodes to your topology.

Adding a Node

To add a node, start by clicking the Add Node button at the bottom of the Topology Definition page. This will open the Add Node dialogue window. To complete this step and successfully add a new node to your topology, you will need to supply the following input:

- **Operating System:** This is a drop-down box from which you can select either Linux or Windows. For this example, we are going to select Linux.

- **Environment Type:** Here you need to select what type of node this will be. If your operating system is Linux, you will choose from one of the following choices: Database Tier, Database as a Service, Elastic Search Server, Full Tier, or Middle Tier. If you are creating a Windows node, you can only select PeopleSoft Client. For this example, we will select Middle Tier.

- **Sizing:** Here you can choose from the VM sizes you have defined on the VM Size page in Cloud Manager Settings. PeopleSoft Cloud Manager comes delivered with small, medium, and large sizes defined. For this example, we will choose a small size VM.

- **Disk Space:** You will need to provide how much disk space in gigabytes you want allocated to this node. Here, we will follow the standards set in the delivered topologies and allocate 100 GB.

- **Tiers:** The tiers deployed in this instance are appserver, webserver, and process scheduler. You cannot, at this time, modify this setting.

- **Features:** Is Cobol installed on this node or no? For this example, we will leave this set to No.

Figure 6-16 provides a view of the Add Node detail.

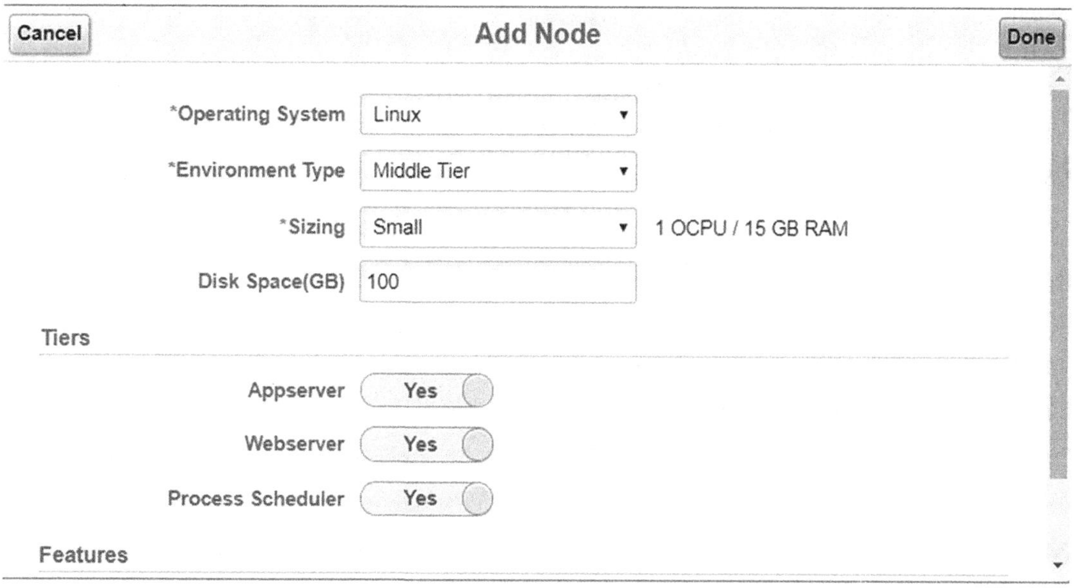

Figure 6-16. *Add Node detail*

Once all the node settings are complete, click Done at the top of the window. You will now see this node added to the Topology Definition (Figure 6-17).

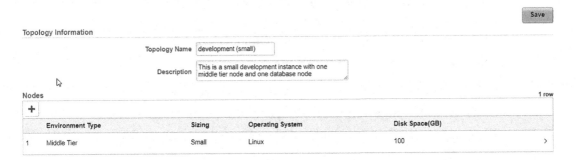

Figure 6-17. *Node successfully added*

Finally, add any other nodes needed for this topology in the same manner, and then click Save in the top left corner of the Topology Definition page (Figure 6-18).

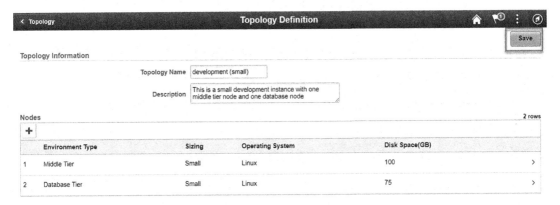

Figure 6-18. *Save the new topology*

You should now see the newly created topology in the list of available topologies on the main Topology page (Figure 6-19).

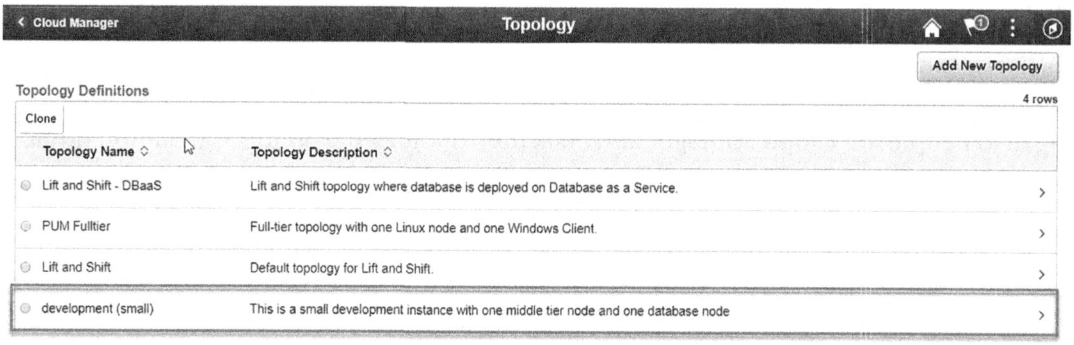

Figure 6-19. *Newly created node, available for use*

Topology Rules

For a topology to have all the components necessary to properly set up and configure a PeopleSoft environment, there are rules for the types of nodes that can or must be included within each topology. These rules are important as you start to define your custom topologies for use in your environment.

If you choose to have a node that is defined as full-tier node, PeopleSoft Cloud Manager will not allow you to have another full-tier node, nor can you have a mid-tier, database, or Database as a Service node included in the topology. You are free to add either a Window Client node or an Elasticsearch Server node if you like.

If you choose to have a node defined as a mid-tier node, given that the mid-tier node splits up some components found in the full-tier node, PeopleSoft Cloud Manager will not allow you to have a full-tier node. Additionally, in order to have a complete topology, you must include either a database or Database as a Service node in the topology. Here too, you can add a Windows Client node or Elasticsearch Server node as needed.

From a Database Tier perspective, if you allocate a database node, you are not able to have either another database node or a Database as a Service node as you are allowed only one database per topology. Additionally, you are not able to create a full-tier node with a database node created. Likewise, if you choose a Database as a Service node, PeopleSoft Cloud Manager will not allow you to allocate a database node nor another Database as a Service node. This is due to the fact that you can only have one database type node per topology. Here too you are unable to add a full-tier node to this configuration.

Editing a Topology

Editing a topology is a straightforward process. To get started editing a topology, first log in to PeopleSoft Cloud Manager and click the Topology tile on the application home page. This will take you to the main Topology page and your list of created topologies. Click the name of the topology you would like to edit to open the Topology Definition page (Figure 6-20).

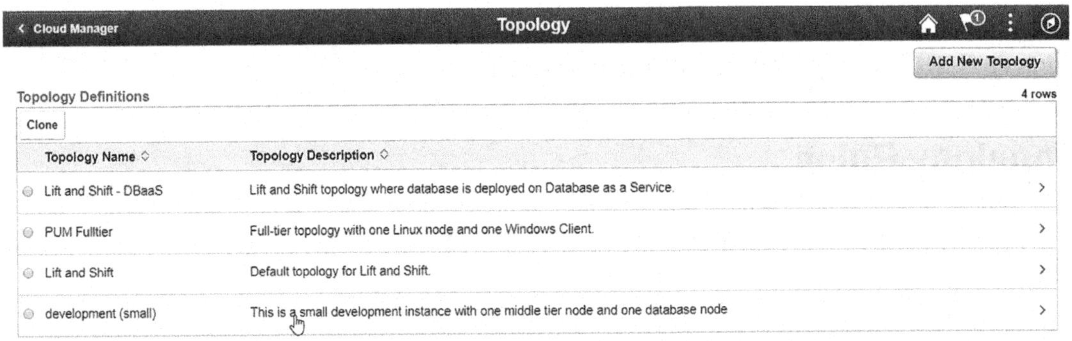

‹ Cloud Manager	Topology		
Topology Definitions			4 rows
Clone			
Topology Name ◇	Topology Description ◇		
○ Lift and Shift - DBaaS	Lift and Shift topology where database is deployed on Database as a Service.		›
○ PUM Fulltier	Full-tier topology with one Linux node and one Windows Client.		›
○ Lift and Shift	Default topology for Lift and Shift.		›
○ development (small)	This is a small development instance with one middle tier node and one database node		›

Figure 6-20. *Click the topology you would like to edit*

From here you can update the description of the topology, click directly on the nodes defined within the topology to modify their definition, or you can add nodes to the existing topology. To edit an existing node, click directly on the environment type to open the Edit Node dialogue window. For this example, we are going to expand the Disk Size of the middle tier node from 100 GB to 125 GB and then save the topology. Figure 6-21 highlights the Edit Node dialogue page.

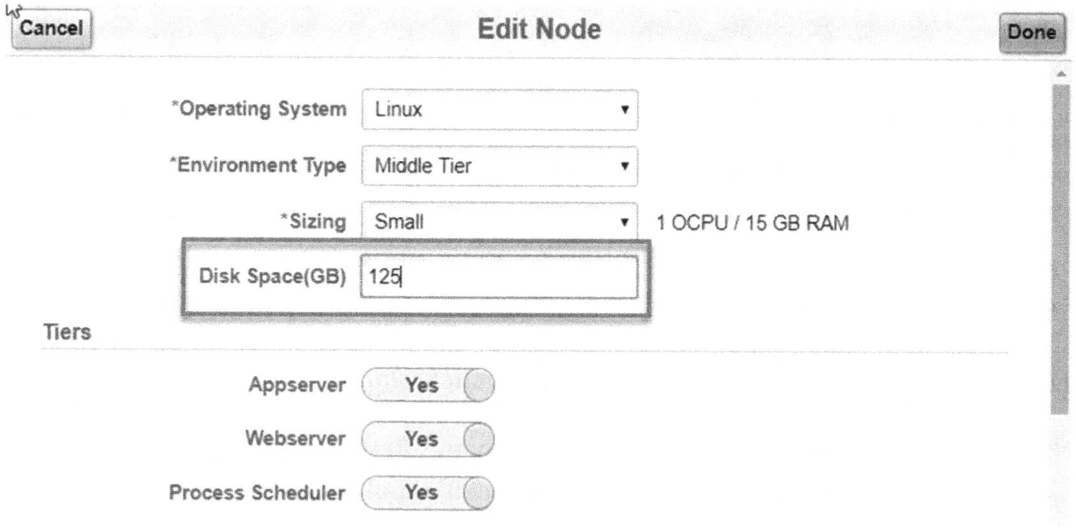

Cancel   **Edit Node**   **Done**

*Operating System   Linux ▾

*Environment Type   Middle Tier ▾

*Sizing   Small ▾   1 OCPU / 15 GB RAM

Disk Space(GB)   125

Tiers

Appserver   (Yes ◯)

Webserver   (Yes ◯)

Process Scheduler   (Yes ◯)

Figure 6-21. *Editing an existing node in a topology*

Once the changes you desire are complete, click Done in the upper right corner of the page to save your edits to the node. You will see any changes you made reflected in the Topology Definition page. Click Save at the top of the page to finish saving your topology edits. You should see a message at the top of the page that your edits were successfully saved.

Cloning a Topology

In some cases, it may be faster for you to create a new topology by starting with an existing topology. This is called cloning. To clone an existing topology, complete the following steps:

1. Go to the the Topology home page, and select the existing topology you would like to clone by selecting the radio button to the left of the topology name.

2. Once the topology is selected, click the Clone button in the top left of the list of topologies (Figure 6-22).

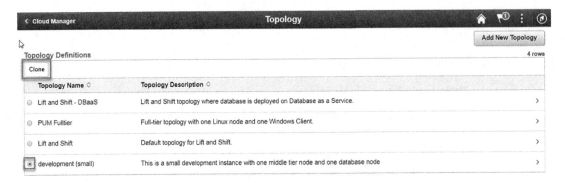

Figure 6-22. Select the topology to clone and click Clone

3. Next, provide the new topology with a name. In this example, we are going to clone the development (small) topology for use as a quality assurance (small) topology (Figure 6-23).

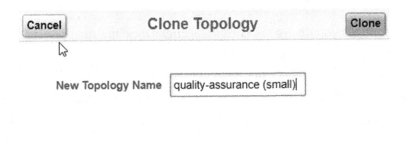

Figure 6-23. Clone Topology

4. Click the Clone button in the top right corner of the window.

5. You will now see your newly cloned topology in your list of available topologies. From here you can edit the topology as needed (Figure 6-24).

Topology Definitions

Clone	

Topology Name ◇	Topology Description ◇
◉ quality-assurance (small)	This is a small development instance with one middle tier node and one database node
◉ Lift and Shift - DBaaS	Lift and Shift topology where database is deployed on Database as a Service.
◉ PUM Fulltier	Full-tier topology with one Linux node and one Windows Client.
◉ Lift and Shift	Default topology for Lift and Shift.
◉ development (small)	This is a small development instance with one middle tier node and one database node

Figure 6-24. *Newly cloned topology*

6. To complete this exercise, we will click the new cloned topology and edit the description to more closely match the name of the topology and save the edits (Figure 6-25).

Topology Definitions

Clone	

Topology Name ◇	Topology Description ◇
◉ quality-assurance (small)	This is a small quality-assurance instance with one middle tier node and one database node
◉ Lift and Shift - DBaaS	Lift and Shift topology where database is deployed on Database as a Service.
◉ PUM Fulltier	Full-tier topology with one Linux node and one Windows Client.
◉ Lift and Shift	Default topology for Lift and Shift.
◉ development (small)	This is a small development instance with one middle tier node and one database node

Figure 6-25. *Cloned and edited topology*

Deleting a Topology

If you have topology that you no longer want available for use, you can permanently delete it from your list of topologies. However, if the topology is in use by any existing environment, you will not be able to delete the topology until the environment is no longer using the topology. To complete this task, click the name of the topology you want to delete, and then, directly from the Topology Definition page, you can completely delete the topology by clicking the Delete button at the top of the page. Once this button is clicked, you will get a confirmation message, and the topology will be removed from your list of topologies (Figure 6-26).

Figure 6-26. *Delete a topology*

CHAPTER 7

Creating a PeopleSoft Cloud Manager Environment Template

Creating a PeopleSoft environment in the Oracle Cloud requires three main components to be created in PeopleSoft Cloud Manager. The first requirement of provisioning an environment is having a database and application available in the repository; this was covered in Chapter 5. The second necessary component required to provision a PeopleSoft instance in the Oracle Cloud is a topology, which was covered in Chapter 6. The third and final piece required to provision a PeopleSoft instance is creating an environment template. The main purpose of the environment template is to tie the application information and the topology together to create a blueprint for how the environment will look once it is provisioned.

Environment Template

The PeopleSoft Cloud Manager Environment Template consists three main components. First the template requires basic information including the name of the environment template and the PeopleSoft Deployment Kit (DPK) that the template will be using to build the environment. Second, one or more topologies are selected for use at environment build time, and the custom attributes for each topology are available to be customized. Finally, security for the template is defined, allowing for administrator access and self-service provisioning to be available base on roles and permissions lists. Once these pieces are combined, you will have a reusable template that can be used to build environments for a variety of purposes.

© Aaron Engelsrud 2019
A. Engelsrud, *Managing PeopleSoft on the Oracle Cloud*, https://doi.org/10.1007/978-1-4842-4546-0_7

Create a New Template

Creating a new template in PeopleSoft Cloud Manager is a four-step, guided process. The four steps in the process follow a guided wizard-like process and includes a progress bar along the top showing the template creation progress as each step in the process is completed. Step 1 includes the input of the basic details of the template, step 2 allows for the selection of available topologies and corresponding attributes, step 3 provides an opportunity in set user security for the template, and step 4 allows an opportunity to review the information input in the previous three steps. In the following sections, each of these steps is explored in detail and the process of creating a new template is shown step by step.

To get started with step 1 in the guided process, you must first log in to PeopleSoft Cloud Manager with your administrator user and click the Environment Template tile on the home page. The Environment Template tile can be seen in Figure 7-1.

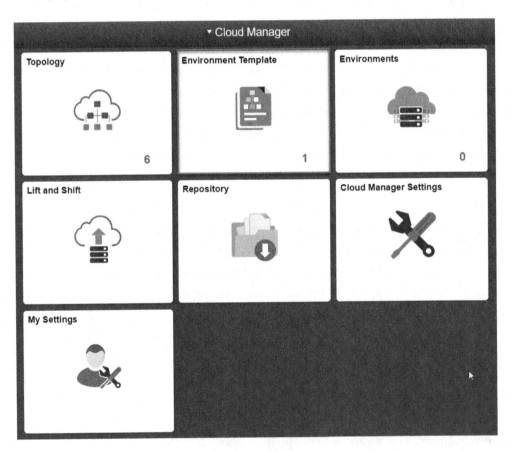

Figure 7-1. Environment Template tile

This tile will take you to the Environment Template homepage. On this page, you should see a listing of any delivered or newly created environment templates. To get started creating a new environment template, click the Add New Template button in the top right-hand corner of the page. This button is highlighted in Figure 7-2.

Figure 7-2. *Add New Template button*

Clicking this button will open the process to create a new environment template, and the four-step process will be shown across the top of the page. These four steps and progress bar are shown in Figure 7-3.

Figure 7-3. *Create Environment Template four-step process*

Step 1 – General Details

The create environment template process starts with a general details section. This step in the process allows you to name, define, and select a database (from your cloud repository) to be used by the environment template when provisioning the environment. For the purpose of this tutorial, we will be creating a new environment template to be used to create new ELM instances for a variety of purposes including development, quality assurance, and test environments. To complete this step, you will need to provide the General Details page with the following information:

- **Name:** ELM Non-Prod
- **Description:** Template to be used to provision non-production ELM instances
- **Database:** PEOPLESOFT ELM UPDATE IMAGE 9.2.018 – NATIVE OS (The database can be selected by clicking the magnify glass icon to the right of the text box and selecting the database from the list provided.)

This detail is shown in Figure 7-4.

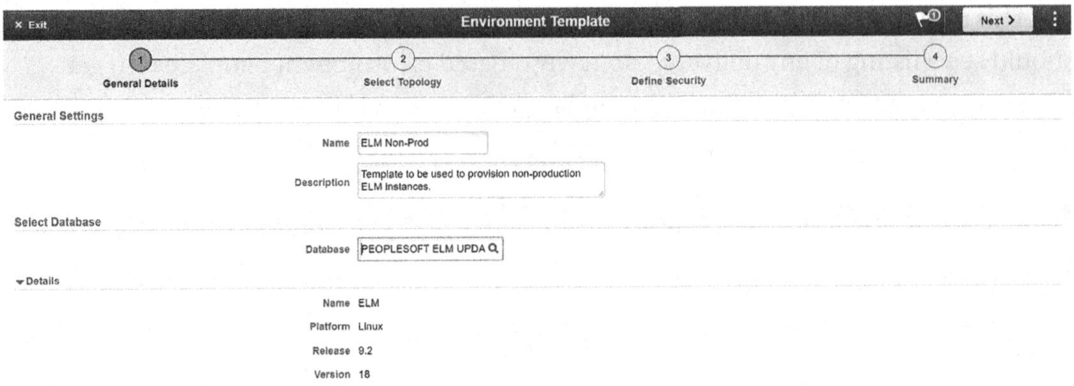

Figure 7-4. *General Details page*

Once the general details page is complete and you have provided the detail necessary, click the next button at the top of the page and move on to step 2, selecting topology.

Step 2 – Select Topology

The Select Topology step allows you to select one or more topologies that can be used to provision environments with this template. Additionally, this page also allows you the opportunity to set a variety of custom attributes that are used by the deployment kit to provision the environment to your requirements. Each of the various tiers has its own set of custom attributes that need to be addressed as the environment template is created. To get started we need to add the topologies that are available for use by this template to the page:

1. Starting from Step 2: Select Topology, add your first topology by clicking the magnifying glass to the left of the topology name filed. This detail can be seen in Figure 7-5.

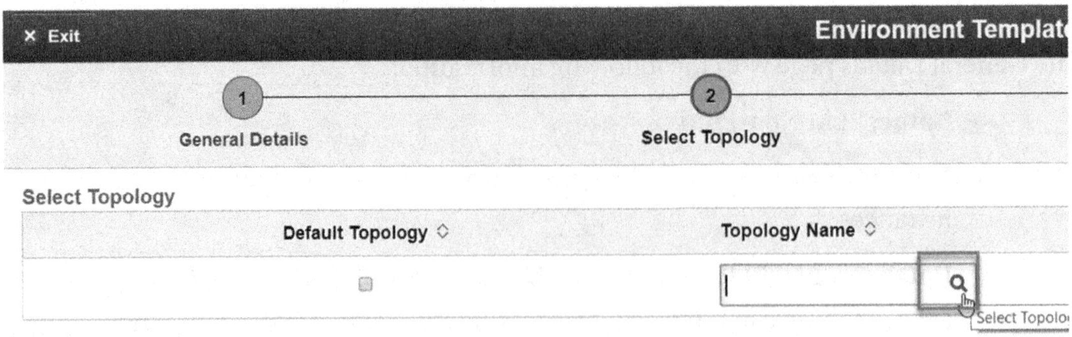

Figure 7-5. *Select a topology*

2. Select the topology you want from the page listing the available topologies. For the purpose of this tutorial, we will select the development (small) topology (Figure 7-6).

Cancel	Lookup		
Search for: Topology Name			
▼ Search Results			
⊞ ☰			6 rows
Topology Name ◇	**Description** ◇		
Lift and Shift	Default topology for Lift and Shift.		
Lift and Shift - DBaaS	Lift and Shift topology where database is deployed on Database as a Service.		
PUM Fulltier	Full-tier topology with one Linux node and one Windows Client.		
development (small)	This is a small development instance with one middle tier node and one database node		
quality-assurance (small)	This is a small quality-assurance instance with one middle tier node and one database node		
test (small)	This is a small test instance with one middle tier node and one database node		

Figure 7-6. *Topology lookup*

3. This topology will automatically be set as the default topology as it is the only option.

4. Based on the eventual use of the environment, a different topology can be selected at environment creation time to allow for different sizing and specifications. Given that we want the ability to use this template for development, quality assurance, and test environments, we are going to add both the quality assurance (small) and test (small) topologies to the template. Do this by clicking the plus (+) to the right of the current topology. The plus (+) sign is highlighted in Figure 7-7.

Figure 7-7. *Add an additional topology to the template*

5. Once you've selected all the topologies you'd like to have available for this environment template, you can move on and start setting the custom attributes for each of the selected topologies (Figure 7-8).

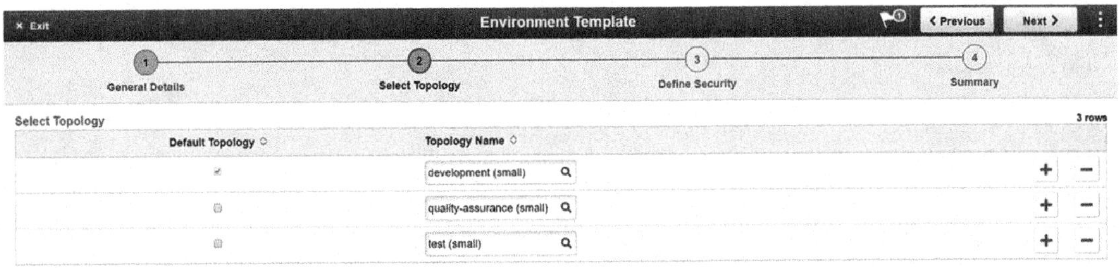

Figure 7-8. *Multiple topologies*

Custom Attributes

To set the custom attributes for each topology, start by expanding the Custom Attributes section at the bottom of the Select Topology step. Here you will find a drop-down to allow you to select the topology you want to edit the attributes of along with an Edit Custom Attributes button. You will note that you can set the custom attribute differently for each of the topologies you select for the environment template. This means you are easily able to allow for different custom attributes based on the topology and the use case of the environment being instantiated.

To get started, let's set the custom attribute for the development (small) topology:

1. Expand the Custom Attributes section at the bottom of the Select Topology page by clicking the word Custom Attributes.

2. From the Topology drop-down, select the development (small) topology and click the Edit Custom Attributes. This button and topology selection can be viewed in Figure 7-9.

Figure 7-9. *Edit Custom Attributes*

3. This will open the tiers that are appropriate to this topology. In this case, you should see Database Tier and Middle Tier as options. If this topology included a PeopleSoft Client tier, you would see that listed as well. The attributes available to you for each tier are listed in the following sections.

Middle Tier

The Middle Tier Custom Attributes consists of three main sections: General Settings, Domain Settings, and Advanced Settings.

General Settings

- **HTTP PIA Port:** The default port for HTTP PIA is 8000. If you are using a different HTTP port per your standards, you can supply that port here.

- **Gateway Administrator Username:** The default username for Gateway access is administrator. If you need to supply a different Gateway Username, you can supply that username in this field.

- **HTTPS PIA Port:** The default HTTPS PIA port is 8443. If your standards require a different HTTPS PORT, update this field with the appropriate port number.

- **Enable EM Agent:** This option allows you to either select NO (Disable)or YES (Enable) for the Enterprise Manager Agent for PeopleSoft. This option will default to NO.

189

- **WLS Port:** This is port for the WebLogic Server which is set to a default of port 7000. Like HTTP and HTTPS, if you require a different WLS port, you can supply that value in this field.

- **WebLogic Administrator Username:** This is the username of the WebLogic Administrator. The default value for this username is system. This is the user that is used to access the WebLogic console.

- **Jolt Port:** This value the port number for the JOLT listener on the appserver. The default value for this port is 9033.

All of these settings can be seen in Figure 7-10.

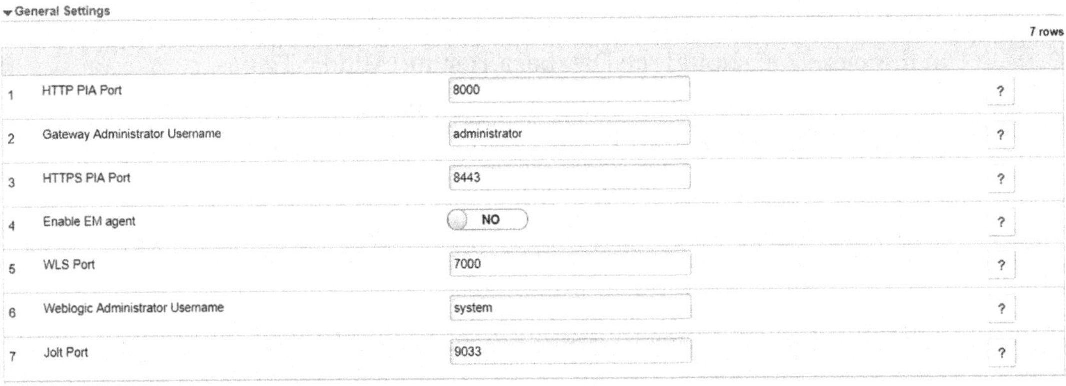

Figure 7-10. *Middle Tier, General Settings*

Domain Settings
Appserver Settings

- **Number of Domains:** This is the number of appserver domains. This value is always set to 1.

- **Number of App Server Instances Per Domain:** This field indicates the number of PSAPPSRV Services that are required. This setting is applied to all appserver domains. The supplied value for this setting is 3.

- **Number of Query Server Instances Per Domain:** Supplied here is the number of PSQRYSRV services required for each domain. Like the PSAPPSRV value, this value is applied to all appserver domains. The default supplied here is 2.

- **Number of SQL Access App Server Per Domain:** This is the number
  of PSSAMSRV instances created per domain. The default value
  supplied is 1.

- **Number of Jolt Listeners Per Domain:** The number of Jolt Listeners
  created per domain. The default in this field is 3 based on the sizing
  of the topology.

These settings can be seen in Figure 7-11.

▾ Appserver Settings

			5 rows
1	Number of Domains	1	?
2	Number of App Server Instance (PSAPPSRV services) Per Domain	3	?
3	Number of Query Server Instances(PSQRYSRV services) Per Domain	2	?
4	Number of SQL Access App Server(PSSAMSRV services) Per Domain	1	?
5	Number of Jolt Listener(Jolt Handler) Per Domain	3	?

Figure 7-11. *Middle Tier, Domain Settings, Appserver Settings*

Process Scheduler Settings

- **Number of Domains:** This value sets the number of Process
  Scheduler Domains created. This value is set to 1.

- **Number of App Engine Server Instances (PSAESRV) Per Domain:**
  This is the number of PSAAESRV Services, application engines,
  that are created. If your standards require a different number of
  application engine servers per domain than what is set, you can
  update this value to your appropriate number.

- **Number of App Engine Server Instances (PSDSTSRV) Per
  Domain:** This value indicates the number of application servers
  required per domain.

These settings can be seen in Figure 7-12.

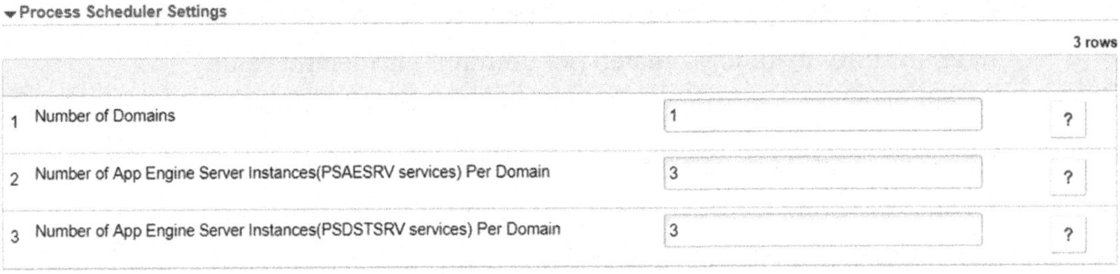

▼ Process Scheduler Settings

			3 rows
1	Number of Domains	1	?
2	Number of App Engine Server Instances(PSAESRV services) Per Domain	3	?
3	Number of App Engine Server Instances(PSDSTSRV services) Per Domain	3	?

Figure 7-12. *Middle Tier, Domain Settings, Process Scheduler Settings*

Process Scheduler Server Definition Parameters

- **Application Engine:** This is the number of process scheduler jobs allowed.

- **XML Publisher:** This value indicates the number of XML Publishers created.

- **COBOL SQL:** Allows you to set the number of COBOL SQL process that can run.

- **Optimization Engine:** Indicates the number of Optimization Engines on the Process Scheduler.

- **SQR Process:** Sets the number of SQR Processes on the process scheduler.

- **SQR Report:** Provides the process scheduler with the number of SQR reports.

- **Max API Aware:** This parameter provides the process scheduler with the max number of API Aware services that can run concurrently on the server. An API Aware task is a process that can update its current status through a specific API.

These settings can be seen in Figure 7-13.

▾ Process Scheduler Server Definition Parameters

			7 rows
1	Application Engine	5	?
2	XML Publisher	3	?
3	COBOL SQL	3	?
4	Optimization Engine	5	?
5	SQR Process	3	?
6	SQR Report	3	?
7	Max Api Aware	5	?

Figure 7-13. *Middle Tier, Domain Settings, Process Scheduler Server Definition Parameters*

Web Server Settings

- **Number of Domains:** This provides the number of PIA web server domains. This value is set to 1.

- **Authentication Domain:** If you have a custom authentication domain, you can enter that value here. The default value is .compute. oracle.com.

These settings can be seen in Figure 7-14.

▾ Web Server Settings

			2 rows
1	Number of Domains	1	?
2	Authentication Domain	.compute.oraclecloud.com	?

Figure 7-14. *Middle Tier, Domain Settings, Web Server Settings*

Advanced Settings

The Advanced Settings in the Custom Attributes section allows you to enter custom YAML data for your appserver or web server configuration. This allows you the ability to create one set of custom configuration data and reuse it for multiple topologies without re-creating the configuration each time. This section contains only one section, Customization YAML, and corresponding text entry box that allows you to paste your YAML data in it (Figure 7-15).

Figure 7-15. *Middle Tier, Advanced Settings*

Database Tier

The Database Tier Custom Attributes allows users to input custom database specific attributes per topology that are then used at environment creation to instantiate the Database Tier in the application stack.

General Settings

- **Enable EM Agent:** This option allows you to either select NO (Disable) or YES (Enable) for the Enterprise Manager Agent for PeopleSoft. This option will default to NO.

- **Database Name:** This allows you to enter a specific naming convention for the database being created in the Database Tier. Given that this is the development (small) topology for an ELM database, we will name the database created in this topology accordingly.

- **Database Operator ID:** Default value is PS. If you require a different Database Operator ID, you can supply that value here.

- **Database Access ID:** The default value is SYSADM.

- **Database Server Port:** This indicates the port that the database server connects on. The default is port 1522.

- **Database Connect ID:** The PeopleSoft Connect ID. Default value is people.

- **PeopleSoft Deployment Path:** This is the path on the host for database deployment. Default path is /u01/app/oracle/product/.

- **Database Type:** This is a drop-down which provides values that allow you to select the database type. In this case DEMO is default, while SYS is another provided database type option.

- **Enable Multi Language:** Turn on (YES) or off (NO) Multi Language Support in the database.

- **Is Database Unicode:** Select YES (Unicode) or NO (non-Unicode) for the database.

These settings can be seen in Figure 7-16.

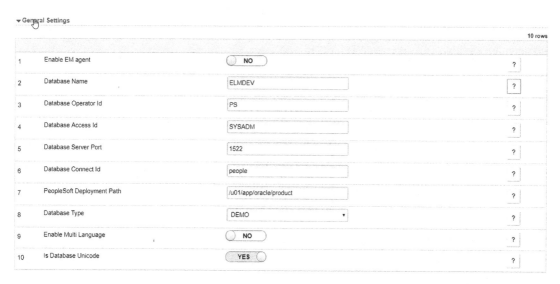

Figure 7-16. *Database Tier, General Settings*

Database as a Service (DBaaS)

While creating an environment template which includes DBaaS components, you have the option to customize various DBaaS attributes. These attributes can be used to allow PeopleSoft Cloud Manager to better create environments that more closely match your needs and business requirements as well as ensure database recovery and backup in case of failures. DBaaS options within PeopleSoft Cloud Manager allow for a truly production-ready and scalable database provisioning in the Oracle Cloud.

General Settings

- **Database Server Port:** This indicates the port that the database server connects on. The default is port 1522.

- **Container Name:** A container is a storage area in the Oracle Cloud Infrastructure that allows users to store and organize data. Here you can provide a container name to be used as the database is provisioned.

- **Character Set:** This setting allows you to set the character set you would like for the database. The default database character set is AL32UTF8.

- **Database Connect ID:** The PeopleSoft Connect ID. Default value is people.

- **Enable EM Agent:** This option allows you to either select NO (Disable) or YES (Enable) for the Enterprise Manager Agent for PeopleSoft. This option will default to NO.

- **Database Name:** This allows you to enter a specific naming convention for the database being created in the Database as a Service tier. For example, if you are setting up a production-ready environment template for ELM, you can choose to name the database being created accordingly.

- **National Character Set:** The default value for this setting is UTF8. If you require a different National Character Set, such as UTFE, you can change that setting here.

- **Database Operator ID:** Default value is PS. If you require a different Database Operator ID, you can supply that value here.

- **Database Access ID:** The default value is SYSADM.

- **Database Type:** This is a drop-down which provides values that allow you to select the database type. In this case DEMO is default while SYS is another provided database type option.

- **Enable Multi Language:** Turn on (YES) or off (NO) Multi Language Support in the database.

These settings can be seen in Figure 7-17.

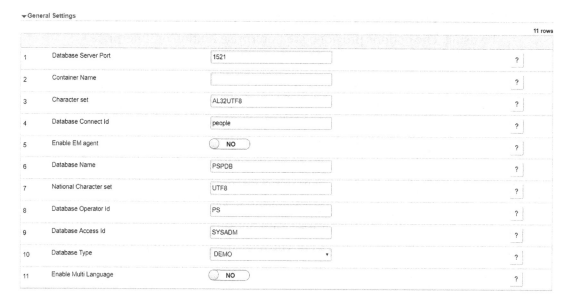

Figure 7-17. *Database as a Service, Custom Attributes, General Settings*

Advanced DBaaS Options

- **Service Level:** This option is not user configurable and defaults to Oracle Database Cloud Service.

- **Metering Frequency:** This field is linked to the billing of your DBaaS service. The two options in the drop-down are Hourly or Monthly. Each option provides you with different a different billing scenario:

    - **Hourly:** This billing option provides you with a price based on the number of hours of the service used.

    - **Monthly:** This billing option provides you with one payment for the month independent of how many hours of service are consumed.

- **Software Release:** Select which release of the Oracle Database you will be using with DBaaS. The options provided here are currently Oracle Database 12c Release 1 and Oracle Database 12c Release 2.

- **Database is RAC:** Allows you to use Oracle Real Application Cluster (RAC) for the database by selecting YES or not by selecting NO.

197

- **Software Edition:** Select the edition of the database software you will be using. The options provided are Enterprise Edition or Enterprise Edition – Extreme Performance. With these options, there are additional licensing constraints that will need to be addressed.

- **Backup Destination:** Provide what type of database backup option will be used. The options provided are Both Cloud and Local Storage or No Backup.

- **Backup Container Name:** If you select the Both Cloud and Local Storage option in the Backup Destination field, you will need to provide a container name for the cloud backup. If you select No Backup, you will not be able to provide a value in this field.

These settings can be seen in Figure 7-18.

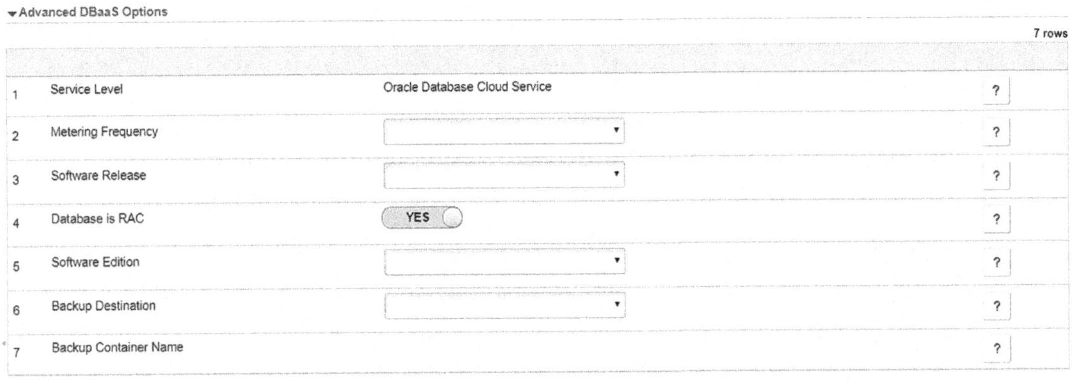

1	Service Level	Oracle Database Cloud Service	?
2	Metering Frequency		?
3	Software Release		?
4	Database is RAC	YES	?
5	Software Edition		?
6	Backup Destination		?
7	Backup Container Name		?

Figure 7-18. Database as a Service, Custom Attributes, Advanced DBaaS Options

Step 3 – Define Security

Step 3 in the Environment Template creation process involves setting not only what type of zone the environment should be created in but also the security roles that should have access to this template. The complete this step in the process first select a zone name from the zone name list. You can get this list of values by clicking the magnifying glass to the right of the Zone Name field (Figure 7-19).

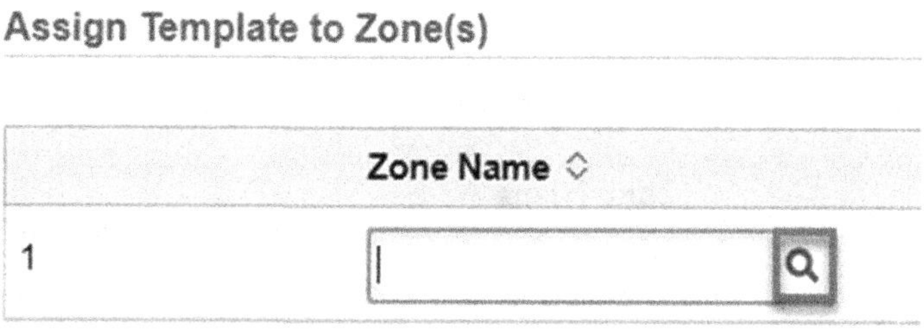

Assign Template to Zone(s)

	Zone Name ◇
1		🔍

Figure 7-19. *Zone Name Selection*

From the list of values provided, select the value that is appropriate for the template you are creating. In this case, Development is the most appropriate considering this is a non-production template. If you have too many different zones and need help finding the correct one, you can use the search functionality at the top of the page as noted in Figure 7-18. PeopleSoft Cloud Manager comes delivered with Development, Production, and Test zones defined. Select the zone you want (in this case Development and Test are most appropriate), and it will populate the Zone Name filed on step 3. Once you add Development, click the Plus icon on the right of the page and add Test in the same manner. The Zone Lookup dialogue can be seen in Figure 7-20, and the Zone Assignment dialogue can be seen in Figure 7-21.

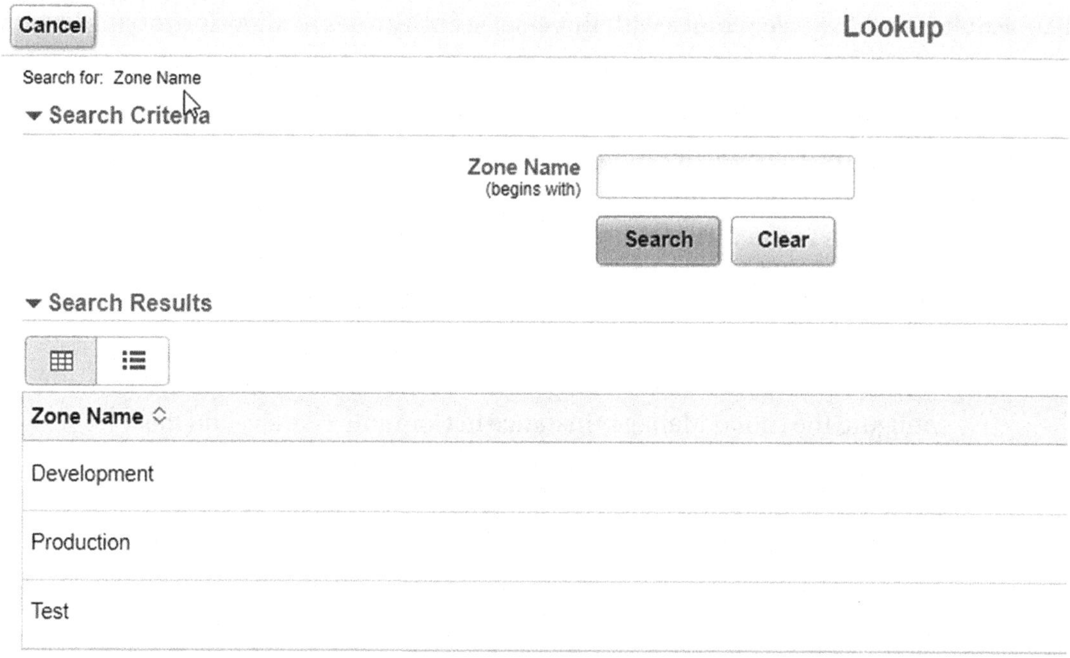

Cancel		Lookup

Search for: Zone Name
▼ **Search Criteria**

Zone Name
(begins with)

Search   Clear

▼ **Search Results**

⊞ ☰

Zone Name ◇
Development
Production
Test

Figure 7-20. *Zone Lookup*

Assign Template to Zone(s)

Zone Name ◇
1   Development ◎
2   Test Q

Figure 7-21. *Zone Assignment*

Now that the zones have been selected, the next step in the process to complete is
to select which roles are going to have access to this template once it is created. There
may be instances where you only want administrators to have access to a template for
provisioning a production environment, but other instances where you want to grant
users the ability spin up an instance without any assistance. The three-key PeopleSoft
Cloud Manager delivered roles and associated permission lists are covered next.

Cloud Manager Delivered Roles and Permission Lists

PeopleSoft Cloud Manager comes with three-set security roles to allow for varying levels
of access to the application. The roles delivered are Cloud Administrator, PeopleSoft
Cloud Administrator, and Self-Service User. Each of these roles provides a specific set
of permissions to the users that allow or disallow access to certain components within
PeopleSoft Cloud Manager. Further, these roles can be used to define who has access or
does not have access to the various Environment Templates as they are created:

- **Cloud Administrator (PACL_CAD):** The Cloud Administrator
  role allows users the ability to download and initiate the Cloud
  Manager Image from the Oracle Cloud Marketplace, can set up and
  configure the Cloud Manager instance in Compute Classic, and has
  full access to set up the repository to auto-download content from
  MOS. Additionally, the Cloud Administrator has full access to every
  tile in Cloud Manager, can add the Cloud PeopleSoft Administrator
  and Self-Service User role to other users, and can manage all

created environments. This is the most powerful role in PeopleSoft Cloud Manager and should be granted only where necessary and appropriate.

This user is granted the PACL_001 (Cloud Administrator) permission list, PACL_002 (PeopleSoft Admin for Cloud) permission list, and the PACL_003 (Cloud Self Service) permission list for appropriate access. This is shown in Figure 7-22.

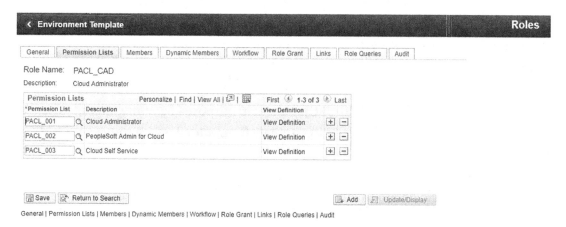

Figure 7-22. *Cloud Administrator Role*

- **Cloud PeopleSoft Administrator (PACL_PAD):** Users assigned the Cloud PeopleSoft Administrator Role can create deployment templates based on downloaded PeopleSoft images or other environments in Compute Classic. This user has access to the Topology, Environment Template, Environments, and My Settings tiles from the PeopleSoft Cloud Manager home page and can also manage all created environments.

  This user is granted only the PACL_002 (PeopleSoft Admin for Cloud) permission list and the PACL_003 (Cloud Self Service) permission list for appropriate access. This is shown in Figure 7-23.

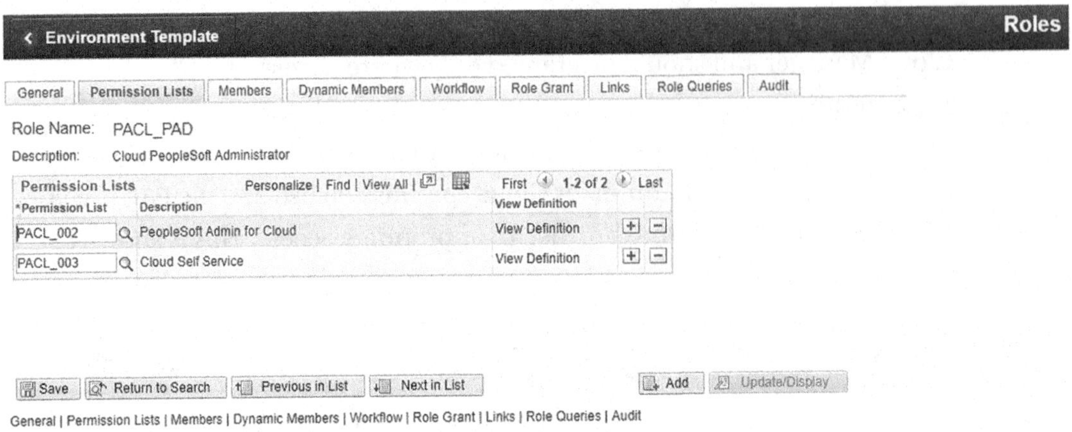

Figure 7-23. *Cloud PeopleSoft Administrator Role*

- **Self-Service User (PACL_SSC):** The main purpose of granting this
  role is to allow users the ability to create Compute Classic instances
  from templates that are available to them. They can also stop, start,
  and delete those instances that they have created. These users will
  only see the Environments and My Settings tiles on the PeopleSoft
  Cloud Manager home page.

  This user is granted only the PACL_003 (Cloud Self Service) permission list for
  appropriate access. This is shown in Figure 7-24.

Figure 7-24. *Self-Service User Role*

Assigning Environment Template Security

Now that you have a better understanding of the three-key delivered PeopleSoft Roles within PeopleSoft Cloud Manager you can finish defining and setting up security within the Environment Template. To finish defining security, you need to assign the proper security roles to the Environment Template you are creating. Given that the template being created is a development or test template, we will grant everyone access to use this template to create environments. To do this, like with zone selection, click the magnifying glass next to the Role Name text box. This will give you a list, a rather long list, of every permission list in PeopleSoft Cloud Manager. To find the roles you are looking for, type PACL in the Role Name search box at this top of the page as shown in Figure 7-25.

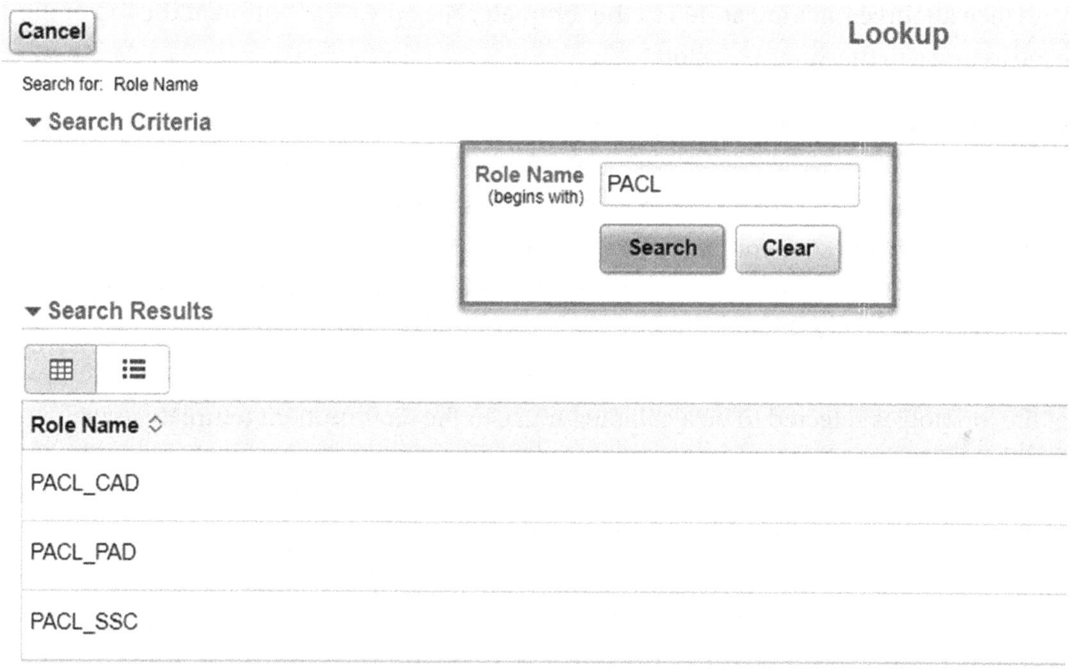

Figure 7-25. *Role search for PACL roles*

Add the three PeopleSoft Cloud Manager Roles, PACL_CAD, PACL_PAD, and PACL_ SSC to the template until your assigned roles are added. The dialogue to assign security to the Template is shown in Figure 7-26.

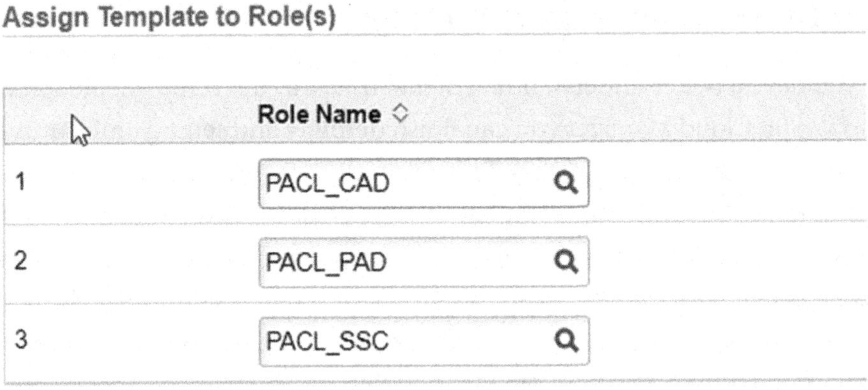

Assign Template to Role(s)

	Role Name ◇	
1	PACL_CAD	🔍
2	PACL_PAD	🔍
3	PACL_SSC	🔍

Figure 7-26. *Assigned Cloud Roles*

Once all three roles are added to the template, click the Next button at the top of the page to move to the Summary step.

Step 4 – Review and Submit Template

The final step in Environment Template creation is to review and, if the details are correct, submit and save your template. This page, as shown in Figure 7-27, has three main sections: General Details, Topology, and Security. The General Details section allows you to review the environment template name, the description you provided, and the database included in the template. The topology section provides you with a review of the topologies selected to be available for use in the environment template as well as what the default topology is. Finally, the security section allows you to review which zones are available to the template, this list of roles that have access to the template, and if passwords will be auto generated by the template. If you are not satisfied with any of these details, use the previous button at the top of the page to change the setting you provided. Once you are satisfied with the summary, click the Submit button at the top of the page, and the environment template will be saved and available for use. Step 4, the Summary step, is shown in Figure 7-27, and the newly created environment template is shown in Figure 7-28.

Figure 7-27. *Summary, Step 4*

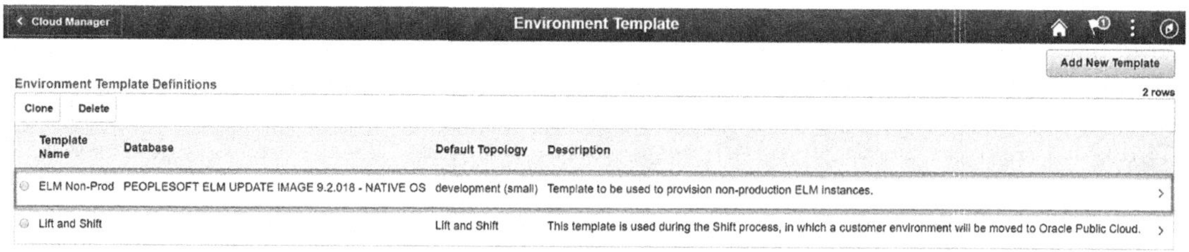

Figure 7-28. *Newly created Environment Template*

Edit an Existing Template

The process to edit an existing environment template starts with selecting and clicking the environment template you would like to edit. For example, to edit the ELM Non-Prod template we previously created, you can start by clicking the template name. This will open the four-step environment template creation process, and all of your options, with the exception of the template name, will be changeable. Edit functionality is shown in Figure 7-29.

Figure 7-29. *Editing an Environment Template*

Using the next button at the top of the page, complete or edit the details on each step, review the summary page, and then click submit to save your changes to the environment template.

Clone an Existing Template

The process to clone (copy) an existing environment template starts with selecting the radio option to the left of the environment template you would like to clone. This radio button is highlighted in Figure 7-30.

Environment Template Definitions

Clone	Delete			
Template Name	Database		Default Topology	Description
⦿ ELM Non-Prod	PEOPLESOFT ELM UPDATE IMAGE 9.2.018 - NATIVE OS		development (small)	Template to be used to provision non-production ELM instances.
○ Lift and Shift			Lift and Shift	This template is used during the Shift process, in which a customer e

Figure 7-30. *Clone radio option button selection*

Once you have the template you would like to clone (copy) selected, click to Clone button at the top of the Environment Template Definitions section. This will open a new Clone Template dialogue box. Provide the field with a new template name; in this case we will use a new name of CS Non-Prod, and click Clone in the upper right corner of the window. You will now see your newly cloned environment in your Environment Template list, shown in Figure 7-31. To update this cloned template with changes, use the steps outlined in the section on editing an existing template.

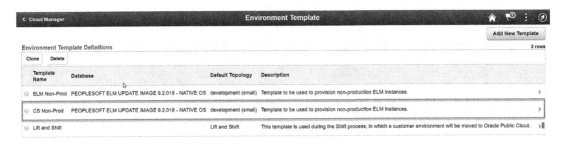

Figure 7-31. *Cloned template*

Delete an Existing Template

To delete an existing template, select the radio option button to the left of the environment template you would like to delete. Once you have seleted the environment template to delete, as seen in Figure 7-32, click the Delete button at the top of the Environment Template Definitions section.

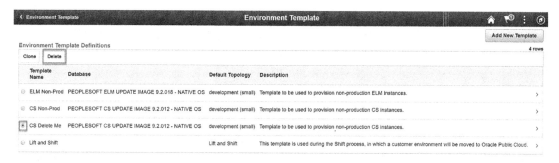

Figure 7-32. *Template to be deleted*

If you wish to continue deleting the template, click the Yes button in the pop-up dialog seen in Figure 7-33. The environment template will be deleted permanently.

Are ẙou sure you want to delete 'CS Delete Me' template?

Figure 7-33. *Delete template confirmation button*

CHAPTER 8

Creating and Managing Environments in PeopleSoft Cloud Manager

PeopleSoft Cloud Manager allows users assigned the necessary roles and permission lists the ability to quickly and easily provision PeopleSoft environments in the Oracle Cloud with just a few clicks. Combining the downloaded database with a topology to create an environment template allows users everything they need to create a working PeopleSoft environment in the cloud. Previous chapters, including Chapters 5, 6, and 7, have focused solely on building the pieces needed to create a new environment.

This chapter will use the foundation built in previous chapters to provide you with the knowledge necessary to not only create new PeopleSoft environments but to also manage cloud environments and troubleshoot as necessary when problems arise. Given this, the chapter is broken up into two main sections. The first section will cover all the details required to create a new environment utilizing the topologies and environment template we created previously. The second section of the chapter will provide insight to all the utilities PeopleSoft Cloud Manager provides to manage existing PeopleSoft environments in the Oracle Cloud. All the functionality detailed in this chapter can be accessed by navigating to the PeopleSoft Cloud Manager home page and clicking the Environments tile, as pictured in Figure 8-1.

© Aaron Engelsrud 2019
A. Engelsrud, *Managing PeopleSoft on the Oracle Cloud*, https://doi.org/10.1007/978-1-4842-4546-0_8

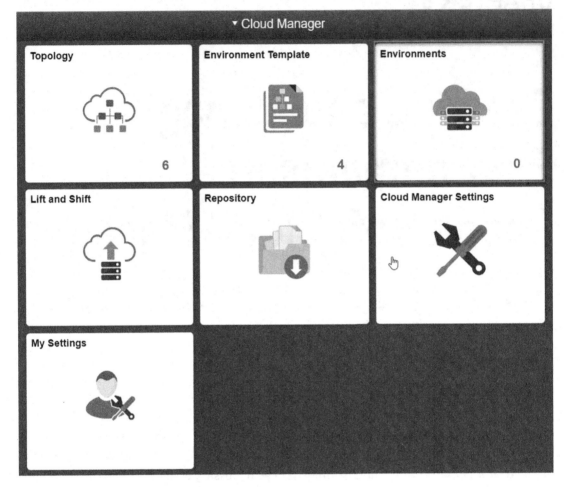

Figure 8-1. *The Environments Tile*

After navigating to the Environments page, you will see a list of any environments that have been previously created. If you have not yet created any PeopleSoft environments in the Oracle Cloud, the Environments home page will be empty.

Creating a New Environment

Where creating a new PeopleSoft environment has traditionally proved to be a time-consuming, highly technical, and labor-intensive process, creating a PeopleSoft environment through PeopleSoft Cloud Manager is simple, quick, and nontechnical. PeopleSoft Cloud Manager removes the complexity of the DPK installation process, provides users with a simple interface to provide the details required to provisioning, and allows administrators the ability to hand off the environment creation process to the very people that need the environments provisioned.

To get started creating a new PeopleSoft environment after clicking the Environments tab or the Cloud Manager home page and navigating to the Environments page, simply click the Create Environment button at the top of the page as shown in Figure 8-2. This will open the Create Environment page and user input dialogue.

Figure 8-2. *Create a new environment*

Provide the following information to start provisioning a new PeopleSoft Environment:

- **Environment Name:** Provide a name for the environment. All users will see this name, so focus on making it something that clearly describes the environment being created. The environment we will be creating here will be named ELMDEV18. ELM is the application, DEV is the type of environment, and 18 is the image that the environment is based on.

- **Description:** Provide a brief description of the environment. This can provide an expanded version of the detail provided in the environment name. A good description for this environment is Development ELM application using ELM PeopleSoft image 18.

- **Template:** Choose the template you want to use to provision the environment. This is a drop-down field and contains a list of all the environment templates you have created in PeopleSoft Cloud Manager. For this environment, we will select the ELM Non-Prod environment template we created in Chapter 7. Once you select the appropriate environment template, more options will build on the page.

- **Zone:** This field will appear once you have selected an environment template. If you have more than one zone available as options in your environment template, you will be able to choose which one you want. For our purposes for this environment, the development zone is the best option to select.

The Create Environment detail can be found in Figure 8-3.

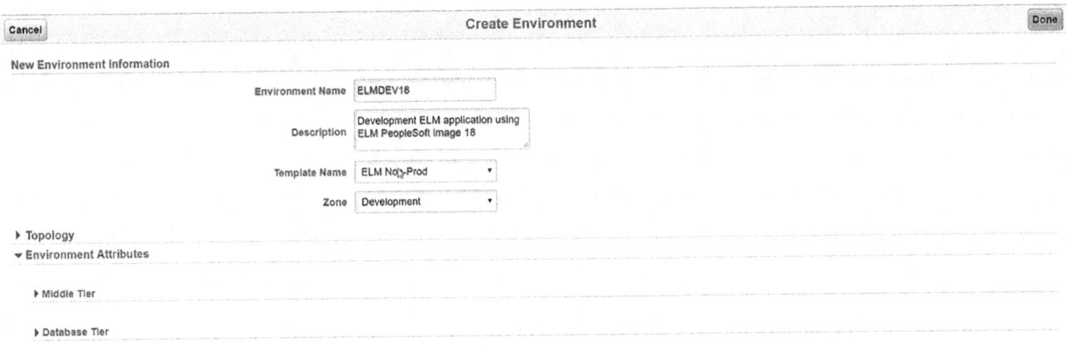

Figure 8-3. *New Environment Information*

Select a Topology

The next step in creating a new environment is to make some decisions about the topology you want to use when the environment is provisioned. To do this, start by expanding the Topology section on the Create Environment page. You can find this section directly below the new environment information you just provided. This section is shown in Figure 8-4. This section allows you to first see which topology is currently selected and second, override the default topology and select a different topology. To override the default topology, change the Override Topology selector to YES, this will allow you to select a different topology from the topology drop-down list. The drop-down will include any of the topologies that are available within the environment template.

- **Override Topology:** This selector switch allows you the option to not override the default topology (NO) or to override the default topology and select a different one (YES).

- **Topology:** If YES is selected it the Override Topology selector switch, this drop-down will provide the topology options available within the environment template. If NO is selected in the Override Topology selector, this drop-down is not editable.

- **Description:** This field is not editable and only provide detail for the topology selected (Figure 8-4).

Figure 8-4. Topology section

Figure 8-5 highlights the section changes and topology options when the Override Topology selector switch is set to Yes.

Figure 8-5. Override Topology and drop-down values

Input Required – Environment Attributes

After selecting the appropriate topology for use in provisioning your new PeopleSoft environment, there is a bit more user input that is required to ensure that all necessary information is provided. Below the Topology section, you will find a section titled Environment Attributes with a series of subsections that closely match what you encountered when setting up the environment template.

Middle Tier – Credentials

Under Environment Attributes you will find a section for your Middle Tier settings. The first sub-section allows you to enter the password values for the WebLogic Administrator, the Gateway Administrator, and the Web Profile Password for the PTWEBSERVER user. Enter these values per your organizational requirements as shown in Figure 8-6.

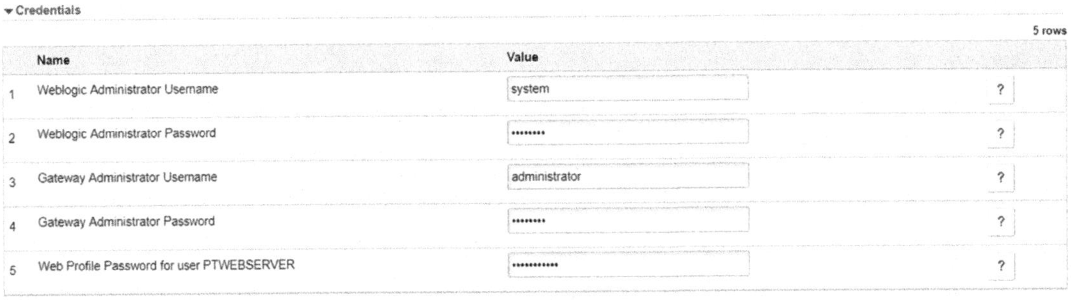

▼ Credentials

5 rows

	Name	Value	
1	Weblogic Administrator Username	system	?
2	Weblogic Administrator Password	••••••••	?
3	Gateway Administrator Username	administrator	?
4	Gateway Administrator Password	••••••••	?
5	Web Profile Password for user PTWEBSERVER	••••••••••	?

Figure 8-6. *Middle Tier – Credentials*

Middle Tier – General Settings

The Middle Tier – General Settings section allows you the ability to change HTTP, HTTPS, WLS, and Jolt Port settings as well as enable the EM agent for the environment you are provisioning. These can be left as they are set in the topology or they can be altered to allow for environment specific settings. This is shown in Figure 8-7.

▾ General Settings

	Name	Value		5 rows
1	HTTP PIA Port	8000		?
2	HTTPS PIA Port	8443		?
3	Enable EM agent	NO		?
4	WLS Port	7000		?
5	Jolt Port	9033		?

Figure 8-7. *Middle Tier – General Settings*

Middle Tier – Domain Settings

The Middle Tier – Domain Settings section of the environment configuration allows you to modify the settings for the appserver, process scheduler, and web server for the environment that you are provisioning.

Appserver Settings

Appserver Settings, shown in Figure 8-8, allows you to modify the following values:

- The number of appserver domains created

- The number of PSAPPSRV services created per domain

- The number of PSQRYSRV services created per domain

- The number of PSSAMSRV created per domain

- The number of Jolt Listeners created per domain

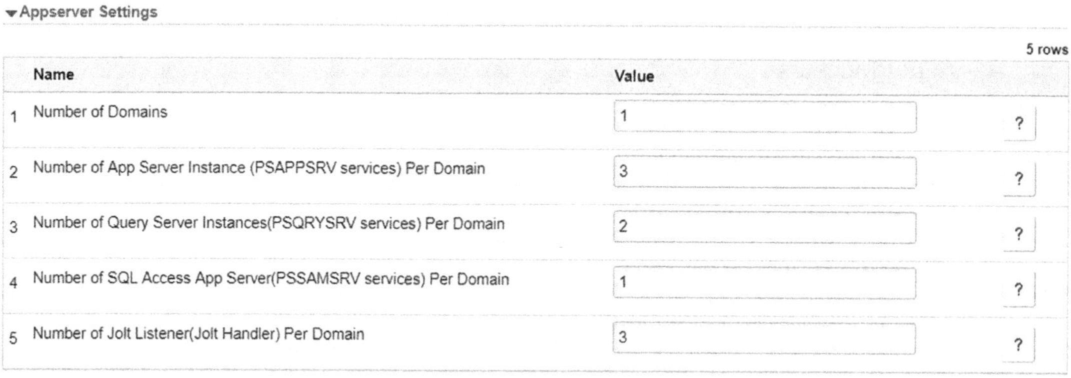

▾ Appserver Settings

	Name	Value		5 rows
1	Number of Domains	1		?
2	Number of App Server Instance (PSAPPSRV services) Per Domain	3		?
3	Number of Query Server Instances(PSQRYSRV services) Per Domain	2		?
4	Number of SQL Access App Server(PSSAMSRV services) Per Domain	1		?
5	Number of Jolt Listener(Jolt Handler) Per Domain	3		?

Figure 8-8. *Middle Tier – Domain Settings – Appserver Settings*

Process Scheduler Settings

The Process Scheduler Settings section, shown in Figure 8-9, allows you to modify the following settings:

- The number of process scheduler domains

- The number of PSAESRV services created per domain

- The number of PSDSTSRV services created per domain

▼ Process Scheduler Settings

3 rows

	Name	Value	
1	Number of Domains	1	?
2	Number of App Engine Server Instances(PSAESRV services) Per Domain	3	?
3	Number of App Engine Server Instances(PSDSTSRV services) Per Domain	3	?

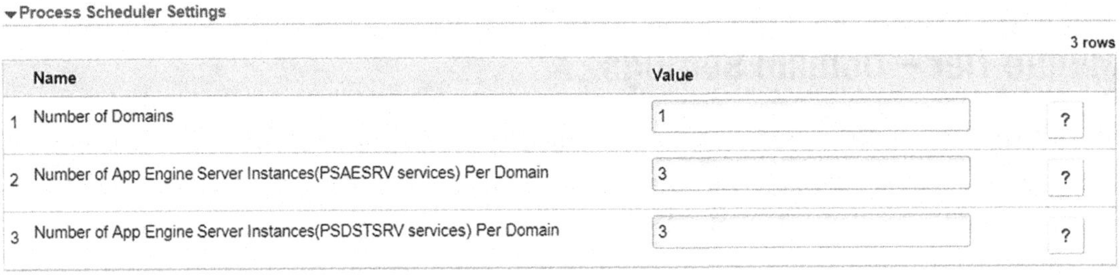

Figure 8-9. *Middle Tier – Domain Settings – Process Scheduler Settings*

Process Scheduler Server Definition Parameters

The Process Scheduler Server Definition Parameter section, shown in Figure 8-10, allows you to modify the following settings before creating your environment:

- Application Engine

- XML Publisher

- COBOL SQL

- Optimization Engine

- SQR Processes

- SQR Reports

- Max API Aware

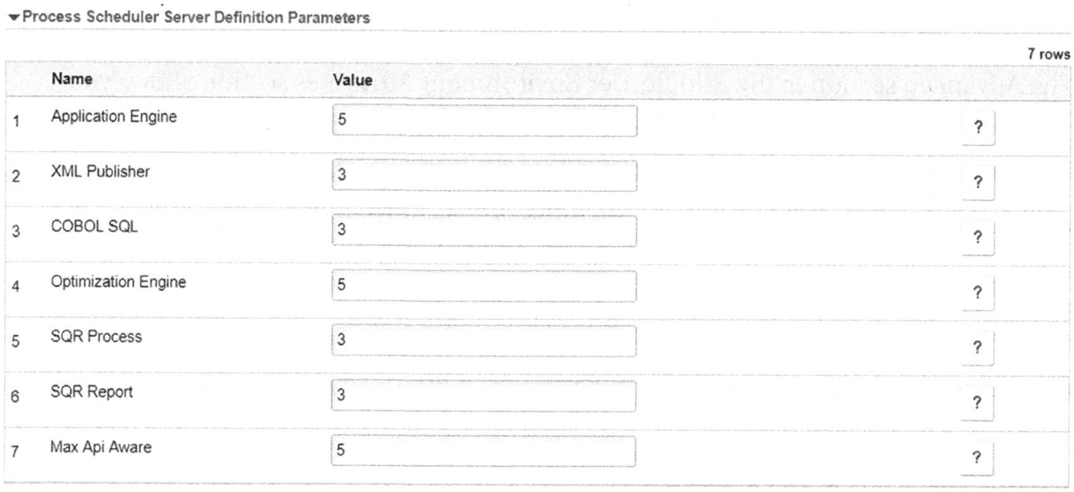

▼ Process Scheduler Server Definition Parameters

7 rows

	Name	Value	
1	Application Engine	5	?
2	XML Publisher	3	?
3	COBOL SQL	3	?
4	Optimization Engine	5	?
5	SQR Process	3	?
6	SQR Report	3	?
7	Max Api Aware	5	?

Figure 8-10. *Middle Tier – Domain Settings – Process Scheduler Server Definition Parameters*

Web Server Settings

Once you have completed the Process Scheduler Server Definitions Parameter section, you will need to pay some attention to the Web Server Settings. The Web Server Settings can be viewed in Figure 8-11. This section allows you to modify the following settings:

- The number of web server domains to create

- Any specific authentication domain you need the environment web server configuration to use

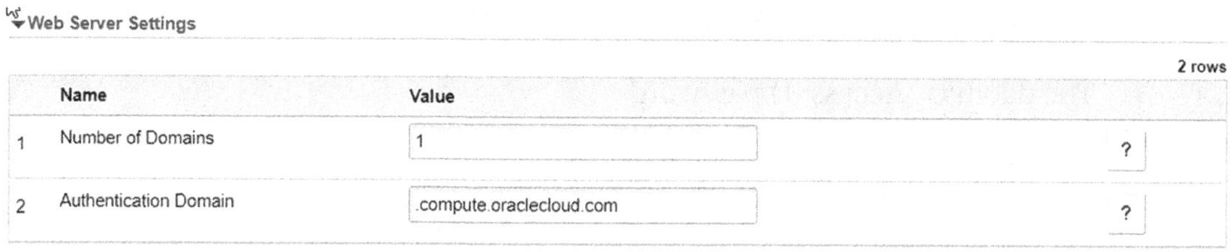

▼ Web Server Settings

2 rows

	Name	Value	
1	Number of Domains	1	?
2	Authentication Domain	.compute.oraclecloud.com	?

Figure 8-11. *Middle Tier – Domain Settings – Web Server Settings*

217

Advanced

The Advanced section in the Middle Tier Environment Attributes section allows you to provide custom YAML data that can be used during provisioning to create the cloud environment. This configuration data needs to be entered as properly formatted YAML data in the provided text box. The YAML input box is shown in Figure 8-12.

Figure 8-12. *Middle Tier – Domain Settings – Advanced (YAML Input)*

Database Tier – Credentials

Now that you have all the Middle Tier specific data entered and configured to your liking, next move on to the specifics of the Database Tier settings. This section covers the settings applicable to a typical Database Tier, not a database being created on Database as a Service. To get started, the first setting to be configured is, similar to the Middle Tier section, the necessary credentials. This section, as shown in Figure 8-13, allows you to input/update the following bits of data:

- The database Operator ID (Defaults to PS)
- The database Operator ID password
- The database Connect ID (Defaults to people)
- The database Connect ID password
- The database Access ID (Defaults to SYSADM)
- The database Access ID password
- The database Administrator Password

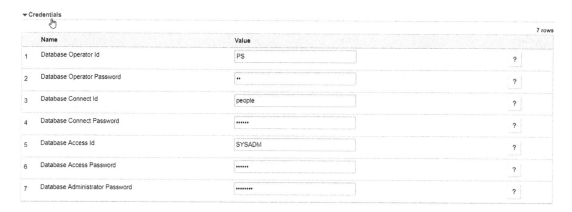

Figure 8-13. *Database Tier – Credentials*

Database Tier – General Settings

The General Settings in the Database Tier Environment Attributes section, shown in Figure 8-14, allows you to select or modify the following settings:

- To enable (YES) or disable (NO) the EM Agent

- The name of the database to be created

- The database server port

- The PeopleSoft deployment path

- The type of database being created (DEMO or SYS)

- Enable (YES) or Disable (NO) multi-language support

- Determine if the database to be created is (YES) or is not (NO) Unicode

▼ General Settings

7 rows

	Name	Value	
1	Enable EM agent	◯ NO	?
2	Database Name	ELMDEV	?
3	Database Server Port	1522	?
4	PeopleSoft Deployment Path	/u01/app/oracle/product	?
5	Database Type	DEMO ▼	?
6	Enable Multi Language	◯ NO	?
7	Is Database Unicode	YES ◯	?

Figure 8-14. *Database Tier – General Settings*

Complete Environment Creation

Once the correct topology is selected and all the Environment Attributes are completed to your satisfaction, you can finish the environment creation process. To finish this, all you need to do is click the Done button in the top right-hand corner of the Create Environment setup page. This button is highlighted in Figure 8-15. This will take you back to the main environment home page, and you will see your new environment listed. It may take some time for the environment to get set up, and during that time, it will be listed in a "provisioning" status.

Figure 8-15. *Finish the environment creation*

Managing Existing Environments

There are multiple pages within the environment detail section that allow to properly manage most all aspects of the environments you have provisioned within PeopleSoft Cloud Manager. These sections include environment detail, manage attributes, health check, manage PUM connections, apply PeopleTools patch, upgrade PeopleTools, provisioning status, and logs. Each of these pages is available for each provisioned environment and will contain the relevant and environment specific detail that is relevant to the environment you are managing.

Environment Detail

The Environment Detail page, the first menu on the left of the Environment page and also shown in Figure 8-16, contains some very basic information about the environment you are managing. This detail includes the name of the environment, the current status of the environment, the zone within which the environment was provisioned, the name of the topology used to provision the environment, and the URL to the PIA for the provisioned environment. This is all the basic information that will be useful to have at a glance while managing PeopleSoft Cloud Manager environments.

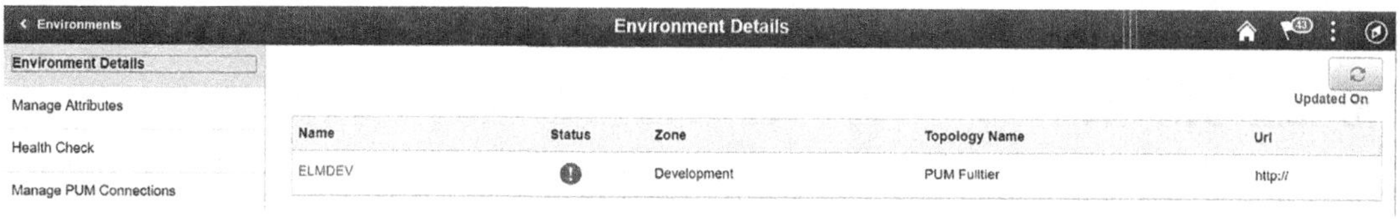

Figure 8-16. *Environment Detail page*

Manage Attributes

The Manage Attributes page allows you to manage all of the Environment Attributes you provided to PeopleSoft Cloud Manager at the time you provisioned the environment. You can change credential information, including passwords for the PTWEBSERVER user (the user used by PeopleSoft to start the PIA), WebLogic, and your Gateway Administrator. Additionally, through this page you are able to manage and update ports used by the application, the database name, and the database type. This level of access allows you the ability to configure and update many of the key attributes within the PeopleSoft application without ever having to access the psadmin console. The information contained in the Manage Attributes page is shown in Figure 8-17.

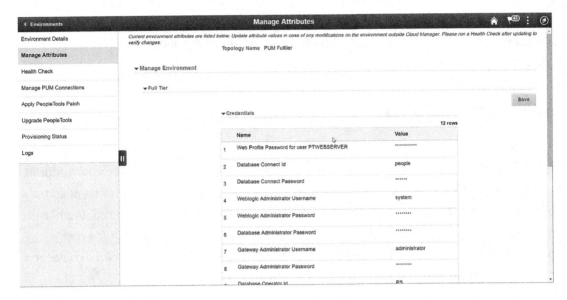

Figure 8-17. *Manage Attributes page*

Health Check

With the simple click of the Retrieve Health Check button at the top of the Health Check page, PeopleSoft Cloud Manager will run an automated process to determine the overall status of your provisioned environment. This can help you uncover unknown issues within your environment or determine where your PeopleSoft environment is improperly configured. This button is shown in Figure 8-18.

Figure 8-18. *Retrieve Health Status*

Manage PUM Connections

The Manage PUM Connections page, shown in Figure 8-19, within the Environment Details section, allows you the ability to not only see the details about the PUM Source environment but also allows you the ability to add target databases from your provisioned environments in PeopleSoft Cloud Manager. This provides you one location where you can manage both your PeopleSoft Update Manager image and the environments that image is able to update within PeopleSoft Cloud Manager.

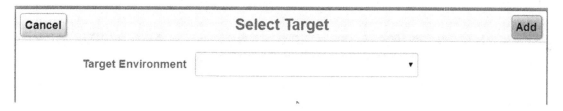

Figure 8-19. *Manage PUM Connections page*

The Select Target dialogue is shown in Figure 8-20.

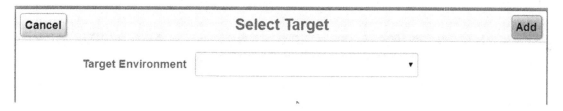

Figure 8-20. *Add target environment for PUM connection dialogue window*

Apply PeopleTools Patch

The Apply PeopleTools Patch page, found in Figure 8-21, allows you the ability to do exactly what you might think it would; the page allows you to select and apply a PeopleTools patch to your PeopleSoft Cloud Manager provisioned environment. Keep in mind, in order to select a particular PeopleTools patch, you must have already subscribed to and downloaded that patch in your repository. The process is simple;

223

select the tools patch you would like applied from the drop-down list of available patches, and then click the Update button. PeopleSoft Cloud Manager takes care of the rest of the work.

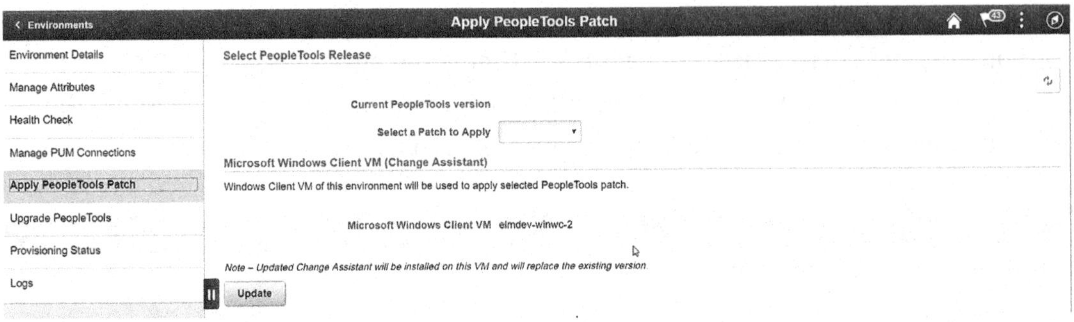

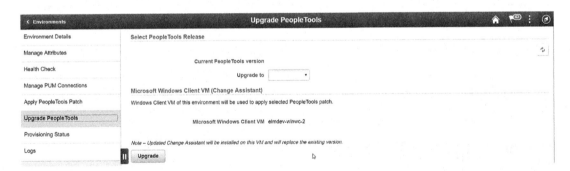

Figure 8-21. *Apply PeopleTools Patch page*

Upgrade PeopleTools

Like applying a PeopleTools patch, PeopleSoft Cloud Manager also allows you the ability to upgrade PeopleTools within PeopleSoft Cloud Manager. The process works exactly the same as the PeopleTools patch process; select the upgrade you would like to apply to your PeopleSoft Environment, and then click the Upgrade button. PeopleSoft Cloud Manager will run the upgrade process in the background. The Upgrade PeopleTools dialogue is shown in Figure 8-22.

Figure 8-22. *Upgrade PeopleTools page*

Provisioning Status

During and after provisioning, a PeopleSoft Cloud Manager environment, the Provisioning Status page, shown in Figure 8-23, is updated with the current status of each phase of the provisioning process. If provisioning is successful, you will see the success messages here. Likewise, if the provisioning process fails, you are also able to see the failure message and other information to help with the start of the troubleshooting process. The error summary will provide high-level information as to the error, along with possible solutions or resolutions to the encountered problem.

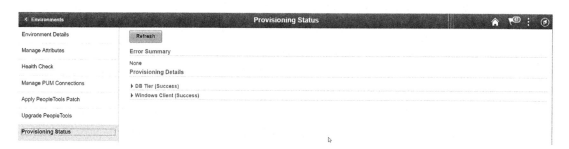

Figure 8-23. *Provisioning Status page*

Logs

This page allows you to search and view the log files created during the provisioning process and also during the normal operation of your PeopleSoft environment. This allows you one simple location to go to track down any log information you may need to for troubleshooting issues, improving performance, or understanding the behavior of your environment. The Logs page and the search logs dialogue are shown in Figure 8-24.

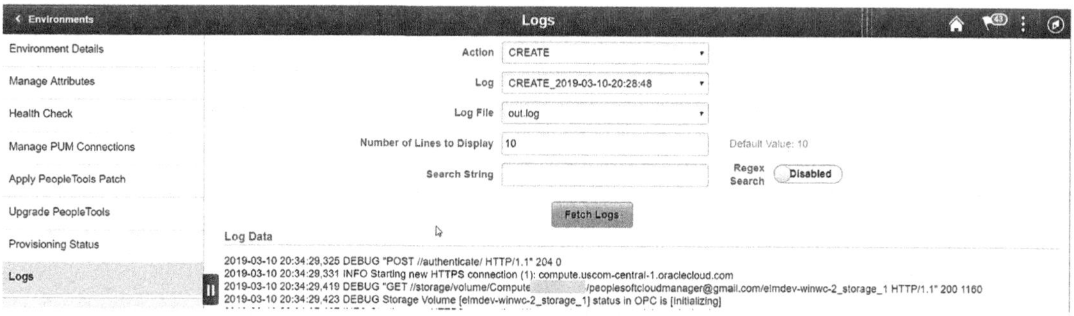

Figure 8-24. *Logs page*

PART II

Advanced PeopleSoft Cloud Manager

CHAPTER 9

Moving to the Cloud: Lift and Shift

One of the most difficult parts of any project to move an on-premise application to the Cloud infrastructure is the actual migration of that environment to the cloud – whether the cloud is AWS, Google Cloud, Oracle Cloud, or other cloud infrastructure. Oracle has streamlined and simplified this process for customers looking to move PeopleSoft applications to the Oracle Cloud and PeopleSoft Cloud Manager by providing the Lift and Shift utility. This utility helps simplify the packaging, migration, and deployment of PeopleSoft applications to the Oracle Cloud.

Moving your PeopleSoft applications from your on-premises data center to the Oracle Cloud Infrastructure and PeopleSoft Cloud Manager will require planning and may possibly require configuration changes that could necessitate the need for application or PeopleTools upgrades to your application stack. The process and cost of moving PeopleSoft applications to the cloud should not be underestimated nor should it be taken lightly; the lift and shift process needs to be properly analyzed in regard to the status and configuration of your current environment, and the required changes to your applications must be thoroughly assessed.

Before diving into the requirements for utilizing the lift and shift functionality within PeopleSoft Cloud Manager, we should first have an understanding of what lift and shift is and how it is designed to work within PeopleSoft Cloud Manager. In the simplest terms, lift and shift allows for an automated process to migrate on-premise PeopleSoft applications to the Oracle Cloud. This automated process is accomplished by first lifting the application. The Lift part of the process consists of packaging the PeopleSoft application and Oracle Database into a DPK format and uploading that DPK to the Oracle Storage Cloud. Next, the Shift part of the process is completed by PeopleSoft Cloud Manager by first downloading the DPK from Cloud Storage and then creating a new cloud environment based on that DPK. This two-step process, lift then shift, allows

© Aaron Engelsrud 2019

A. Engelsrud, *Managing PeopleSoft on the Oracle Cloud*, https://doi.org/10.1007/978-1-4842-4546-0_9

229

the administrator the ability to scale up or scale down the application as needed and also allows for multiple copies of the application to be created in the Oracle Cloud Infrastructure and managed through PeopleSoft Cloud Manager.

Minimum Requirements for the Lift and Shift Process

It is important to note that many PeopleSoft Application configurations will not be able to easily utilize the lift and shift functionality. The next section of this chapter will cover in detail the requirements that PeopleSoft applications must meet in order to lift and shift to the Oracle Cloud.

Database Requirements

There are quite a few database specific requirements that may need to be addressed prior to moving an application and database to the Oracle Cloud. First and foremost, the application must be running on an Oracle Database, further the supported Oracle Database versions are 11g and 12c. Given this, Microsoft SQL Server, DB2, and other non-Oracle database platforms are not supported by the lift and shift process. Short of first migrating your on-premise database from your current non-Oracle database to Oracle, there is no work-around for this requirement.

Many Oracle customers are currently running their Oracle Databases in a RAC configuration, and unfortunately, this configuration is not supported for the lift portion of the process. While PeopleSoft applications can be shifted to a RAC configuration, they cannot be lifted. Additionally, Transparent Data Encryption (TDE) enabled databases are supported for lift and shift to OCI-Classic only, and the source environment must be encrypted using TDE before the lift is completed.

Further, for Oracle customers that have existing non-unicode PeopleSoft databases, there are additional requirements that must be met. A non-unicode database must have NLS_LENGTH_SEMANTICS set to "BYTE". To determine what the setting for your database is currently, you can run the following SQL on the source database: SELECT value from V$NLS_PARAMETERS WHERE PARAMETER = 'NLS_LENGTH_SEMANTICS'. If the value is set to something other than "BYTE" for a non-unicode database, the setting must be updated accordingly.

Application Requirements

Any PeopleSoft applications that are being lifted to the Oracle Cloud must have a minimum application version of 9.2. As such, if your PeopleSoft Campus Solutions or HCM applications are currently running an application version of 9.0 or less, you will need to first set out on an upgrade path. Additionally, the application configuration must have a decoupled home which was introduced in PeopleTools 8.54. Oracle's decoupled PS_HOME setup consists of the following:

- PS_HOME (PeopleTools Software)

- PS_APP_HOME (PeopleSoft Application-Specific Software)

- PS_CUST_HOME (Custom Application-Specific Software)

- PS_CFG_HOME (Domain Configuration and logging filesystem)

The lift process will look for these specific home configurations during the process of creating the DPK that will be moved to Oracle Cloud Storage. Without this decoupled home, the lift process will not be able to properly define the structures within the DPK.

PeopleTools Requirements

Along with the requirement for PeopleSoft applications to be running version 9.2, the application must also be running on a minimum of PeopleTools 8.55.12. Any application running a PeopleTools version less than 8.55.12 will require patching/upgrading prior to a lift and shift process being completed.

Operating System Requirements

While PeopleSoft can be run on a variety of operating systems on-premise, lift and shift is only supported for PeopleSoft applications running on Linux, specifically Oracle Enterprise Linux or Red Hat Enterprise Linux (OEL/RHEL). With this, Python 2.7.9 needs to be set as the default Python version on your Linux system. As such, if your PeopleSoft environment is currently running on a Windows server, you will first need to migrate your application to Linux and configure the application properly for that operating system before lift and shift will be a possibility for your application.

Additional Considerations and Requirements

There are few other considerations and requirements that should be addressed when moving from on-premise to the Oracle Cloud. One consideration and assessment that should be made prior to a move to the cloud is having a solid understanding of any specific bolt-on PeopleSoft applications or third-party software that you may be running alongside PeopleSoft and the impact that a move to the Oracle Cloud may have on these applications. These applications will not be moved with the lift and shift migration, so steps should be taken to address moving these pieces of your application stack in a manual process. Additionally, third-party data integration will need to be individually reviewed, assessed, and eventually set up in your new cloud-based environment. Likewise, if your PeopleSoft application requires COBOL, it must be manually installed and configured after the shift process is completed within PeopleSoft Cloud Manager.

Lift and Shift

Once all the requirements noted in the previous section are met and you are ready to move your on-premise environment to the Oracle Cloud, there are still quite a few technical items that need to be completed to make it happen. While it is outside the scope of this book to provide step-by-step instructions for every possible configuration and Lift and Shift possibility, the following sections will outline the basics of the lift and shift process. The pages within PeopleSoft Cloud Manager that help you manage this process will be reviewed, and a basic understanding of how to get started with moving on-premise environments to the Oracle Cloud will be covered.

To get started, the Lift and Shift process really begins within PeopleSoft Cloud Manager. Similar to all the other functionality with PeopleSoft Cloud Manager, start by clicking the Lift and Shift Tile on the Cloud Manager home page. The Lift and Shift tile on the PeopleSoft Cloud Manager is highlighted in Figure 9-1.

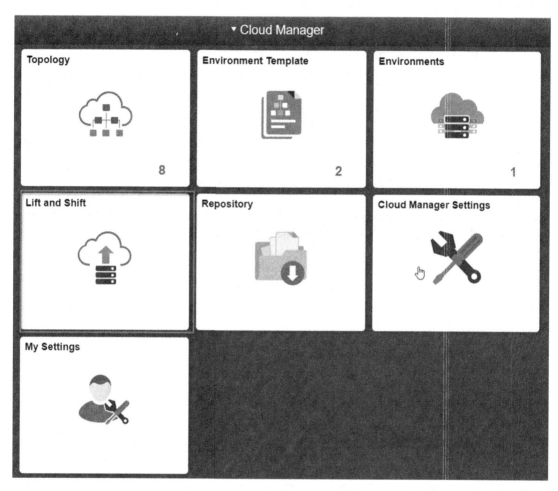

Figure 9-1. *Lift and Shift tile*

Once you click the Lift and Shift tile, you will be directed to the Lift and Shift home page. This page contains everything you need to both get started with lift and shift and manage environments that have already been lifted to Oracle Cloud Storage. The List Object Store Button in the upper left of the page refreshes the list of objects (lifted DPKs) on the page. Additionally, once you have lifted DPKs to Oracle Cloud Storage, you will find detailed information on each DPK stored including

- The name of the object

- Whether the database is TDE enabled or not

- The database character set

- Whether the database is unicode or non-unicode

- The type of PeopleSoft application

- The operating system platform

- The total size of the DPK

- The date the DPK was uploaded

Additionally, from this page you can perform a variety of actions for each DPK using the Action button at the end of each row of data. Figure 9-2 shows you the content on the Lift and Shift home page within PeopleSoft Cloud Manager.

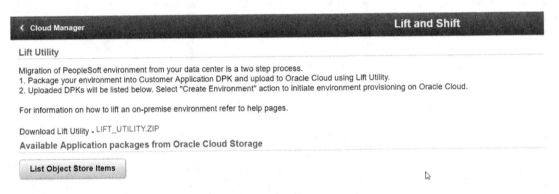

Figure 9-2. *Lift and Shift home page*

To get started, click the blue link to download the lift utility. This is labeled as LIFT_ UTILITY.ZIP. This zip file, highlighted in Figure 9-3, contains everything necessary to lift your on-premise environment DPK including the application and database to Oracle Cloud Storage.

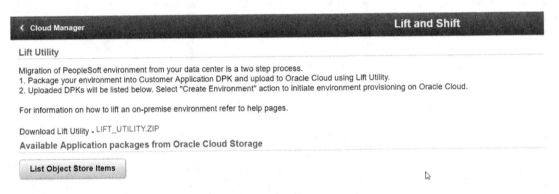

Figure 9-3. *Download the lift utility zip file*

Lift – Moving Applications to the Cloud

Once you have downloaded the lift utility from PeopleSoft Cloud Manager you will need to unzip the zip file to a local directory. This will allow you access to the necessary scripts included in the lift utility to complete the one step lift process.

1. To get started – navigate to the directory where you have the lift utility zip file unzipped. In my case this is the LIFT_UTILITY directory in my home directory. One more directory down you will find the setup directory. Once you are there, run the psft-osl.sh script. Additionally, in the setup directory, there is a PDF document titled psft_onesteplift_setup.pdf that provides detailed instructions as well. Figure 9-4 shows you the unzipped contents of the lift and shift zip utility as well as the location of the psft-osl.sh script.

Figure 9-4. The setup directory and psft-osl.sh script

2. Follow the prompts and answer the questions. First, select either a local or remote lift. A local lift assumes that the application, process scheduler, web server, and database are located on the same node that is running the lift utility. Conversely, a remote lift allows you the option to lift an application that exists on a different node than the one running the lift utility as shown in Figure 9-5.

```
===============================================================================
==============✋==============PeopleSoft One Step Lift========================
===============================================================================
Please Select One of the below options:
===============================================================================
1. Local Lift
2. Remote Lift
===============================================================================

Please enter your selection: (1 or 2): █
```

Figure 9-5. *Local or Remote Lift*

3. If you chose Local Lift (option 1), you will next need to choose
    to either create the DPK and not upload it to the Oracle Cloud
    or create the DPK and upload it to Oracle Cloud Storage as well.
    Figure 9-6 shows the next menu options in the Lift and Shift
    process.

```
===============================================================================
=====================PeopleSoft One Step Lift===============================
===============================================================================
Please Confirm if the Lift Utility should:
===============================================================================
1. Create and Save DPK in APP/DB Environment
2. Create, Save DPK in APP/DB Environment and Upload the DPK to Oracle Public Cloud (Object Store)
===============================================================================

Please enter your selection: (1 or 2): █
```

Figure 9-6. *Create and Upload to the Oracle Cloud or Create only*

4. We will assume that you are looking to upload this to Oracle Cloud
    Storage and select option 2. The utility will then prompt you to
    enter your Oracle Cloud login information to allow access to store
    the DPK in you Oracle Cloud Storage area. This includes your
    cloud username, cloud password, and cloud domain name as
    shown in Figure 9-7.

```
===============================================================================
======================PeopleSoft One Step Lift==============================
===============================================================================
Capturing the OPC Details for Lift:
===============================================================================
Enter Oracle Public Cloud User Name:
Enter Oracle Public Cloud Password:
Enter Oracle Public Cloud Domain Name:
```

Figure 9-7. *Oracle Public Cloud Information*

5. Let the lift utility know if you want to lift the Application Environment by answering Y or N at the prompt as shown in Figure 9-8.

Figure 9-8. *Application Environment*

6. Answer the necessary questions about the application environment.

7. Let the lift utility know if you want to lift the Database Environment as shown in Figure 9-9.

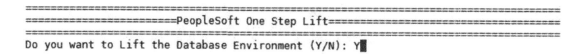

Figure 9-9. *Database Environment*

8. If you choose to lift the database environment, the script will find the database and determine if database version is appropriate for lifting. You will once again need to answer a few questions about the database environment you are lifting.

9. Verify all the information you have provided to this point is correct, and then select Y to proceed with the Lift process.

10. Once the lift process is complete, the DPK zip files created are available locally and, if you selected to upload the DPK to the Oracle Cloud, on your Oracle Cloud Storage and visible through the PeopleSoft Cloud Manager Lift and Shift tile and page.

That's it! Your on-premise PeopleSoft application and database are now packaged as DPKs and ready to be deployed in PeopleSoft Cloud Manager. Obviously, there are other options that could be employed to complete this process including a silent, command line only, lift. This provides additional flexibility and options and would allow for a completely hands-off approach to the lift process. Additionally, the Remote Lift, lifting an application that sits on a different node than the node running the lift utility, requires you to include additional detail around the remote hostname, security and login information, and a few other details. Using the remote lift option could allow you the ability to set up one lift node and lift multiple remote applications without multiple deployments of the lift utility zip.

Shift – Provision Environments in PeopleSoft Cloud Manager

Once you have completed the lift process detailed in the previous section and you have access to your lifted application and database in the Lift and Shift home page, you can utilize the functionality found in the create environment wizard and the included lift and shift topology to properly provision your environment. This is a guided process very similar to creating environments directly from the Environments tab. The Lift and Shift Create Environment Wizard is accessed by finding the lifted environment you want to create in the Lift and Shift home page and selecting the Create Environment option from the Actions drop-down at the end of the associated row.

There are four sections or pages to the guided Lift and Shift Create Environment Wizard:

- General details
- Advanced options
- Custom attributes
- Review and submit

Each of these pages is covered in detail in the following sections. A key aspect to this process and a component that should be validated prior to starting this wizard is the availability of the delivered Lift and Shift topology within PeopleSoft Cloud Manager.

General Details

The general details page is the first page you see in the Lift and Shift Create Environment Wizard. This page allows you to enter three key pieces of information: the environment name, a brief description of the environment, and the zone within which the environment will be deployed. Another piece of information on the general details page is the topology – this will always show Lift and Shift as the only option. Figure 9-10 shows the Lift and Shift General Details page.

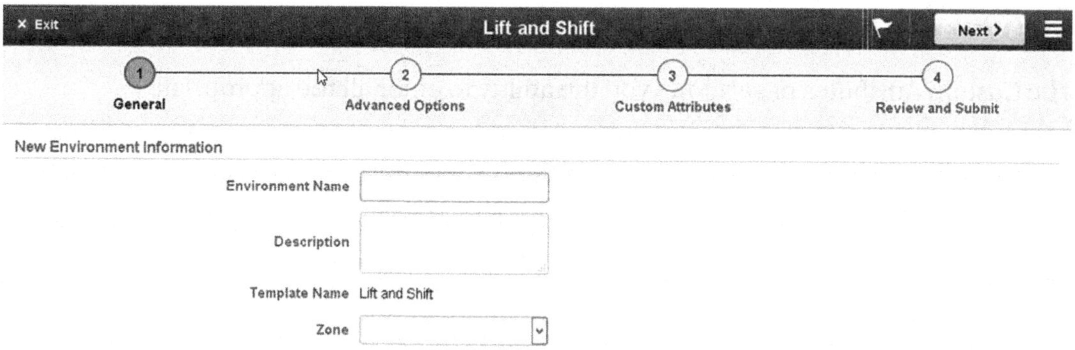

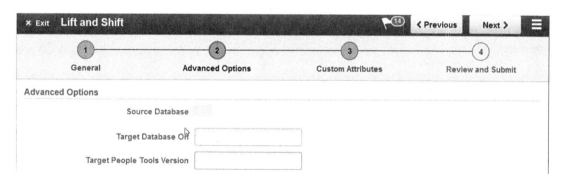

***Figure 9-10.** Lift and Shift General Details page*

Once you have entered the required information on the General Details page, click the next button in the upper right corner of the wizard to move forward to the advanced options page.

Advanced Options

The Advanced Options page in the Lift and Shift Create Environment Wizard allows you to enter specific information about the environment you are going to create including where the database will be created and what tools version will be used to create the DB. Figure 9-11 shows the Lift and Shift Advanced Options dialogue.

***Figure 9-11.** Advanced Options page*

Once you have selected the appropriate information to populate the Advanced Options page, click next in the upper right-hand corner of the page to advance to the Custom Attributes page.

Custom Attributes

The Custom Attributes page allows you the ability to enter all the appropriate passwords and application information required to properly configure your provisioned environment. This includes specific information about the Middle Tier, the Database Tier, and the Windows client as necessary. This allows you to provision an environment to match what you may be using in any of your on-premise environments including password standards, users, and other vital information. Custom Attributes editable in the Lift and Shift process are shown in Figures 9-12, 9-13, and 9-14.

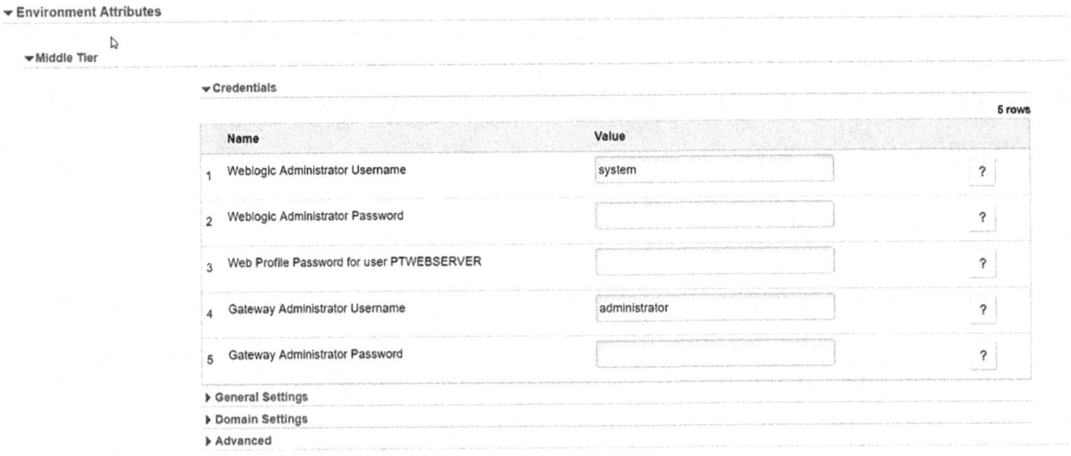

Figure 9-12. *Middle Tier Custom Attributes*

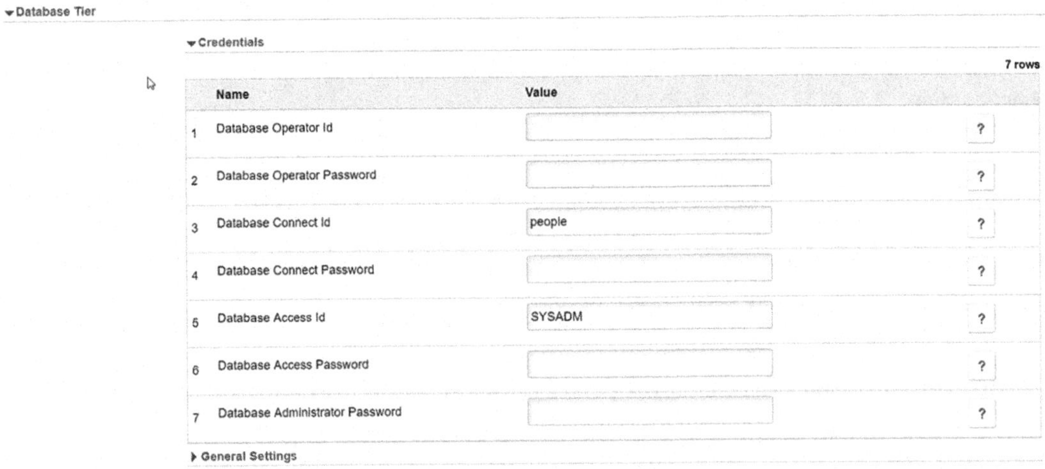

Figure 9-13. *Database Tier Custom Attributes*

Figure 9-14. *PeopleSoft Client Custom Attributes*

Once you have provided all the required information in the Custom Attributes page, click the next button in the upper right-hand corner of the page to move on to the Review and Submit page.

Review and Submit

Review and Submit is the last page in the process before the provisioning of the environment starts. This is your last opportunity to ensure you have everything entered as you would like it and you are ready to start provisioning the environment in PeopleSoft Cloud Manager. Figure 9-15 shows you the detail provided in the Review and Submit page found in Lift and Shift in PeopleSoft Cloud Manager.

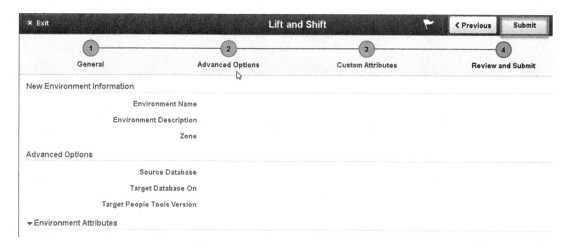

Figure 9-15. *Review and Submit*

Once you have reviewed all the information on this page and you are happy with your configuration, click the Submit button in the upper right-hand corner of the page, highlighted in Figure 9-15, to start the provisioning process.

Like many components of the PeopleSoft application, there are a multitude of variations on this process and many ways to change configurations and settings when leveraging Lift and Shift. This guide is the basic process for moving a PeopleSoft environment from your local datacenter to the Oracle Cloud leveraging the Lift and Shift utility to automate the process. While your source environment will most likely be a variation on this, the requirements to move it and the end result of the process will be consistent with this approach. It is important to keep in mind that every PeopleSoft environment is not ready for Lift and Shift and the Lift and Shift utility and functionality cannot help move every PeopleSoft environment.

CHAPTER 10

PeopleSoft Update Manager in the Cloud

With the advent of PeopleSoft 9.2 and, more specifically, the delivery of new features, bug fixes, and other updates via PeopleSoft Images and PeopleSoft Update Manager, the concept of selective adoption has grown popular in the PeopleSoft community. Selective adoption and the use of PeopleSoft Update Manager allow you to define your own update strategy that works for you and your business. This process allows you to decide what updates you want and when you want to apply them. Given that updates are coming more frequently, it is important to both have a strategy to get the new features you want and allow for the maintenance and support that must happen to keep your PeopleSoft system secure and up to date.

PeopleSoft Cloud Manager can help streamline this process and provides a few key tools that help you deliver on the strategy you defined. First, PeopleSoft Cloud Manager allows for automatic downloads of the newest PeopleSoft Image, getting you the most current functionality with the least amount of effort. Second, using a PUM (PeopleSoft Update Manager) FullTier topology, PeopleSoft Cloud Manager allows you to quickly and easily deploy these new PeopleSoft Images to the Oracle Cloud Infrastructure; test the new functionality and see for yourself how it may benefit your business. Finally, PeopleSoft Cloud Manager also deploys a Windows virtual machine that includes Change Assistant to help you further manage the application of updates, functionality, and fixes to your PeopleSoft Environment.

This chapter will focus on the process of enabling selective adoption in PeopleSoft Cloud Manager. You will learn how to properly provision a PUM image in PeopleSoft Cloud Manager, how to add a target environment to that image, and then how to use that image to apply updates to your target environment. Utilizing this process will help you ensure that you can keep you PeopleSoft environment up to date, functional, and secure with as little downtime as possible.

© Aaron Engelsrud 2019
A. Engelsrud, *Managing PeopleSoft on the Oracle Cloud*, https://doi.org/10.1007/978-1-4842-4546-0_10

Provisioning a PUM Image in the Cloud

There are a few key steps that a PeopleSoft Cloud Manager administrator must complete prior to creating a new PeopleSoft Update Manager image in the Oracle Cloud. First, you need to ensure that the latest required PeopleSoft Image has been downloaded and available in the PeopleSoft Cloud Manager repository. To do this, complete the following steps.

1. If this is a brand-new application that you have not yet downloaded to the repository, start by navigating to the Repository tile on the PeopleSoft Cloud Manager home page and clicking it. The Repository tile is highlighted in Figure 10-1.

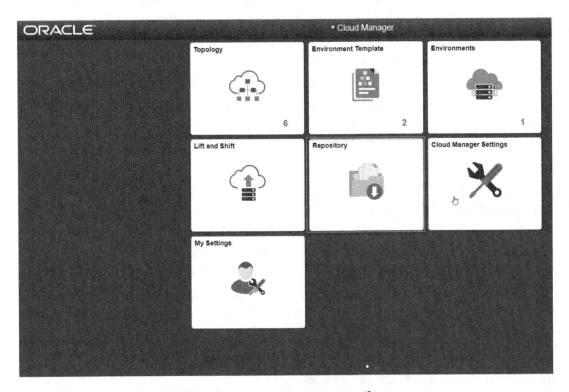

Figure 10-1. *PeopleSoft Cloud Manager Repository tile*

2. Once you are in the repository, click the Download Subscriptions menu option on the left-hand navigation as shown in Figure 10-2.

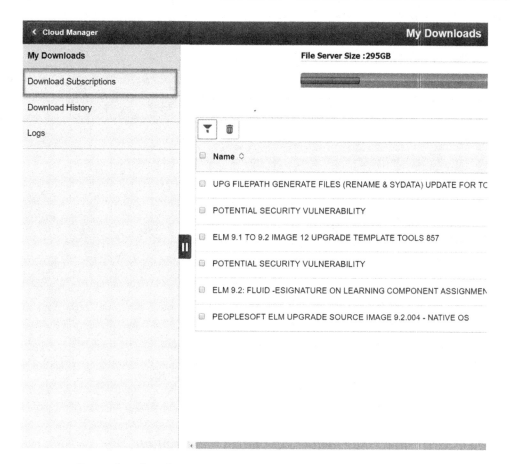

Figure 10-2. *Download Subscription navigation option*

3. From the Download Subscriptions page, click the Unsubscribed button at the top of the page. This will take you to a list of all the images you are not subscribed to. This button is highlighted in Figure 10-3.

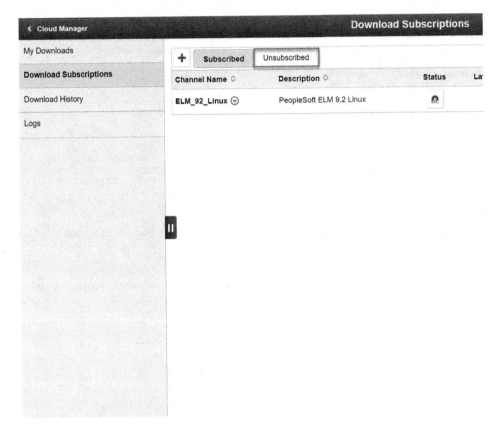

Figure 10-3. *Unsubscribed PeopleSoft Images menu option*

4. Find the PeopleSoft Image (Channel) you want to subscribe to
    from the list of options.

5. Click the small circular arrow to the right of the channel name,
    and select Subscribe from the drop-down list as indicated in
    Figure 10-4.

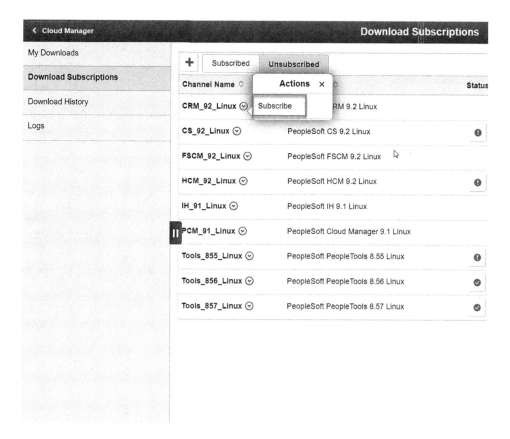

Figure 10-4. *Subscribing to a PeopleSoft Channel on the Download Subscriptions page*

6.   Once this is complete, the image download will begin. This will take some time to complete.

Monitoring the PUM Download

You can monitor your PeopleSoft Image download progress in PeopleSoft Cloud Manager by doing the following:

1.   From the PeopleSoft Cloud Manager Repository page, click the Download History menu option in the left-hand navigation as highlighted in Figure 10-5.

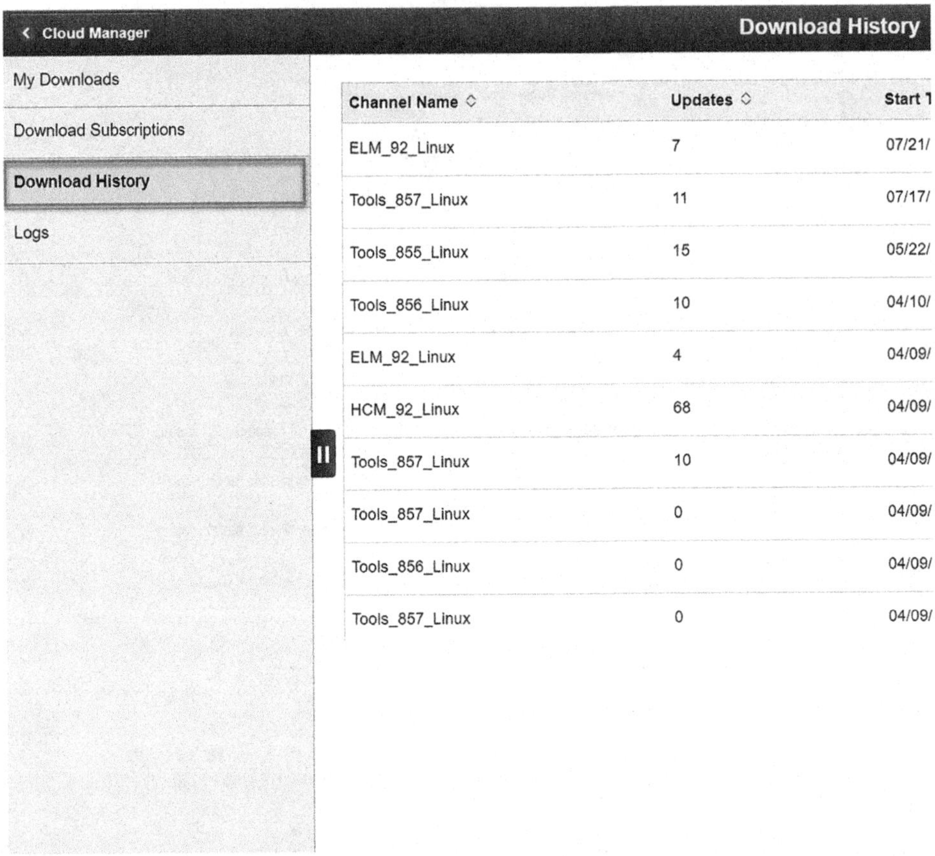
Cloud Manager
Download History
My Downloads
Download Subscriptions
Download History
Logs
Channel Name
Updates
Start T
ELM_92_Linux
7
07/21/
Tools_857_Linux
11
07/17/
Tools_855_Linux
15
05/22/
Tools_856_Linux
10
04/10/
ELM_92_Linux
4
04/09/
HCM_92_Linux
68
04/09/
Tools_857_Linux
10
04/09/
Tools_857_Linux
0
04/09/
Tools_856_Linux
0
04/09/
Tools_857_Linux
0
04/09/

Figure 10-5. *Download History page*

2. From the Download History page, find the channel name you are interested in seeing the progress for, and click the arrow button on the right-hand side of the row. This small arrow is noted in Figure 10-6.

Channel Name ◇	Updates ◇	Start Time ◇	End Time ◇	
ELM_92_Linux	7	07/21/19 12:52PM	07/21/19 1:10PM	>
Tools_857_Linux	11	07/17/19 1:34PM	07/17/19 2:03PM	>
Tools_855_Linux	15	05/22/19 7:53PM	05/22/19 8:59PM	>
Tools_856_Linux	10	04/10/19 2:44PM	04/17/19 12:33AM	>
ELM_92_Linux	4	04/09/19 5:28PM	05/01/19 12:42AM	>
HCM_92_Linux	68	04/09/19 5:26PM	05/22/19 12:30AM	>
Tools_857_Linux	10	04/09/19 4:19PM	05/22/19 12:44AM	>
Tools_857_Linux	0	04/09/19 4:01PM	04/09/19 4:01PM	>
Tools_856_Linux	0	04/09/19 4:00PM	04/09/19 4:00PM	>
Tools_857_Linux	0	04/09/19 4:00PM	04/09/19 4:00PM	>

Figure 10-6. *Download History Detail button*

3. This will provide a list of all the objects that are either downloaded, in progress, or not yet downloaded for the channel selected. The various download status' are highlighted in Figure 10-7.

Tools_857_Linux - Patch List

Download in progress

Patch Download Status

Patch Location ◇	Status ◇	Download Time ◇	Size ◇	Name ◇
/cm_psft_dpks/dpk/linux/tools/857/03/PEOPLETOOLS-LNX-8.57.03_3of4.zip	Download in progress		2.43 GB	PT 8.57.03 PRODUCT PATCH DPK
/cm_psft_dpks/dpk/linux/tools/857/03/PEOPLETOOLS-LNX-8.57.03_4of4.zip	Download in progress		1.3 GB	PT 8.57.03 PRODUCT PATCH DPK
/cm_psft_dpks/dpk/linux/tools/857/custom/ESK-DPK-LNX-6.1.2_05.zip	Download complete	00:00:42	383.57 MB	ELASTICSEARCH AND KIBANA 6.1.2_0
/cm_psft_dpks/dpk/linux/tools/857/custom/ESK-DPK-LNX-6.1.2_04.zip	Download complete	00:02:05	380.93 MB	ELASTICSEARCH AND KIBANA 6.1.2_0
/cm_psft_dpks/dpk/linux/tools/857/custom/p29649415_8570_Linux-x86-64.zip	Download complete	00:00:39	242.24 MB	COBOL DPK FOR LINUX (CLOUD MAN.
/cm_psft_dpks/dpk/linux/tools/857/03/PEOPLETOOLS-LNX-8.57.03_2of4.zip	Download in progress		1.83 GB	PT 8.57.03 PRODUCT PATCH DPK
/cm_psft_dpks/dpk/linux/tools/857/08/PEOPLETOOLS-LNX-8.57.08_2of4.zip	Download in progress		1.79 GB	PT 8.57.08 PRODUCT PATCH DPK
/cm_psft_dpks/dpk/linux/tools/857/03/PEOPLETOOLS-LNX-8.57.03_1of4.zip	Download complete	00:00:26	121.87 MB	PT 8.57.03 PRODUCT PATCH DPK
/cm_psft_dpks/dpk/linux/tools/857/08/PEOPLETOOLS-LNX-8.57.08_3of4.zip	Download in progress		2.46 GB	PT 8.57.08 PRODUCT PATCH DPK

Figure 10-7. *Download History patch download status*

249

4. This view will also show you if downloads have failed and will also
    show the reason for the failure. A failed download can be seen in
    Figure 10-8.

Download History					

Tools_855_Linux - Patch List   ×

Sync finished for the channel. Some of the artifacts could not be downloaded. Review and retry channel subscription

Patch Download Status

Patch Location ◇	Status ◇	Download Time ◇	Size ◇	Name ◇
/cm_psft_dpks/dpk/linux/tools/855/13/PEOPLETOOLS-LNX-8.55.13_1of4.zip	Download not started		190.52 MB	PT 8.55.13 PRODU
/cm_psft_dpks/dpk/linux/tools/855/15/PEOPLETOOLS-LNX-8.55.15_2of4.zip	Download Failed!. Disk Full.		2.58 GB	PT 8.55.15 PRODU
/cm_psft_dpks/dpk/linux/tools/855/16/PEOPLETOOLS-LNX-8.55.16_3of4.zip	Download Failed!. Disk Full.		2.38 GB	PT 8.55.16 PRODU
/cm_psft_dpks/dpk/linux/tools/855/15/PEOPLETOOLS-LNX-8.55.15_4of4.zip	Download not started		1.49 GB	PT 8.55.15 PRODU
/cm_psft_dpks/dpk/linux/tools/855/14/PEOPLETOOLS-LNX-8.55.14_2of4.zip	Download not started		2.58 GB	PT 8.55.14 PRODU
/cm_psft_dpks/dpk/linux/tools/855/14/PEOPLETOOLS-LNX-8.55.14_4of4.zip	Download not started		1.49 GB	PT 8.55.14 PRODU
/cm_psft_dpks/dpk/linux/tools/855/12/PEOPLETOOLS-LNX-8.55.12_1of4.zip	Download not started		174.09 MB	PT 8.55.12 PRODU
/cm_psft_dpks/dpk/linux/tools/855/custom/OPC_EL5U10_X86_64_SES_11.2.2.2_BP4_PVM_3of4.zip	Download not started		3.89 GB	PEOPLETOOLS 8.5
/cm_psft_dpks/dpk/linux/tools/855/12/PEOPLETOOLS-LNX-8.55.12_3of4.zip	Download not started		2.38 GB	PT 8.55.12 PRODU

Figure 10-8. *Download failure*

5. Once your download is complete, the Patch Download Status will
    show sync complete, indicated in Figure 10-9, and all objects that
    have downloaded to your PeopleSoft Cloud Manager.

ELM_92_Linux - Patch List   ×

Sync finished for the channel

Patch Download Status   1 row

Patch Location ◇	Status ◇	Download Time ◇	Size ◇	Name ◇

Figure 10-9. *Download complete in Download History*

You can also verify that the download is complete in the Downloaded Subscriptions page. Downloads in progress will show a status symbol with a small gear, completed downloaded subscriptions will show a small green check, and failed downloads will show a red x. Figure 10-10 shows successfully completed downloads in the repository.

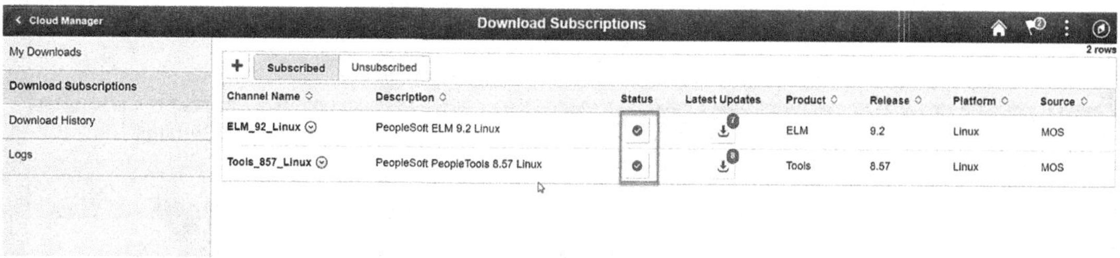

Figure 10-10. *Download status complete in Downloaded Subscription views*

Creating a PUM Environment Template

Once you have verified that your image has successfully downloaded to PeopleSoft Cloud Manager, you are ready to start the process of provisioning the environment in the Oracle Cloud. To do this, start by logging in to PeopleSoft Cloud Manager and clicking the Environment Template tile to go to the Environment Template home page. The Environment Template tile is found in the PeopleSoft Cloud Manager home page and is highlighted in Figure 10-11.

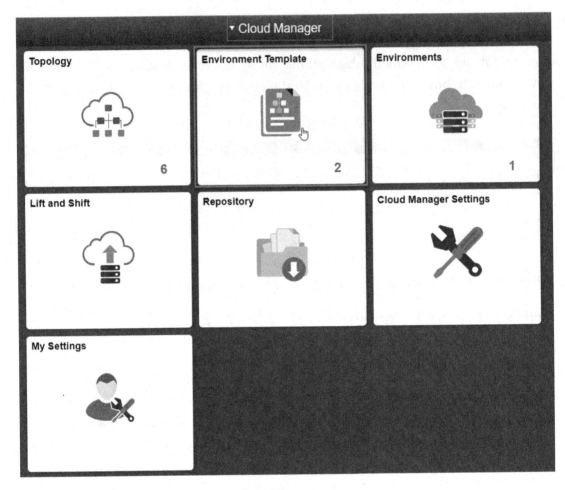

Figure 10-11. Environment Template tile

1. Create a new Environment Template by clicking the Add New
   Template button in the top right-hand corner of the Environment
   Template home page (Figure 10-12).

< Cloud Manager		Environment Template			

Environment Template Definitions   2 rows

Clone	Delete

Template Name	Database	Default Topology	Description		
ELM Non-Prod	PEOPLESOFT ELM UPDATE IMAGE 9.2.018 - NATIVE OS	development (small)	Template to be used to provision non-production ELM instances.		>
Lift and Shift		Lift and Shift	This template is used during the Shift process, in which a customer environment will be moved to Oracle Public Cloud.		>

Figure 10-12. Add New Template button

2. Give the template a name, in this example ELM PUM, and a description, ELM PUM Image.

3. Select the PUM image you want to create from the list of databases in the Select Database dialogue.

4. Click the Next button in the top right-hand corner of the page (Figure 10-13).

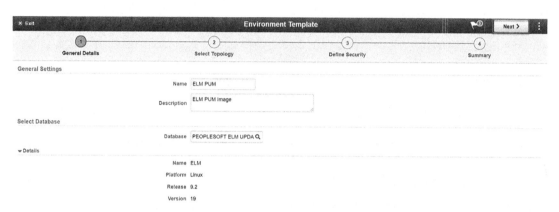

Figure 10-13. *Environment Template General Details*

5. Select the delivered PUM Fulltier topology on the Select Topology page, and click the Next button in the top right-hand corner of the page (Figure 10-14).

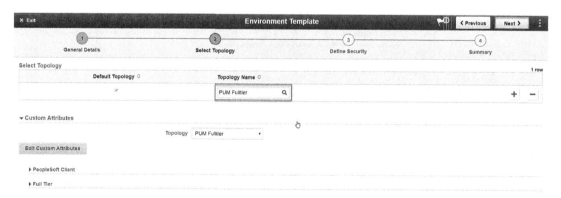

Figure 10-14. *PUM Fulltier Topology*

6. On the Define Security step, select the Development Zone, and
    add any necessary security roles for the PUM Image. In this case
    the Cloud Manager Admin role is enough. Click Next in the upper
    right-hand corner as highlighted in Figure 10-15.

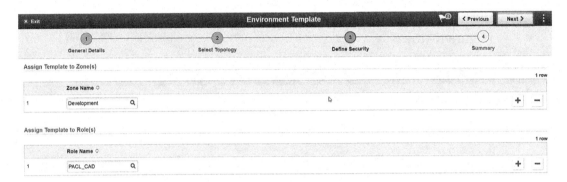

Figure 10-15. *Define Security step in the Environment template*

7. Review the details on the Summary page and, if you are happy
    with the results, click the Submit button in the upper right-hand
    corner of the page. The Summary page and the Submit button are
    shown in Figure 10-16.

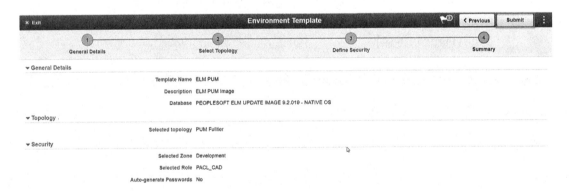

Figure 10-16. *Environment Template Summary page*

8. Your PUM Template is complete.

Creating a PUM Environment

Now that you have created an Environment Template based on the current PUM image and the PUM Fulltier topology, you are ready to create you PUM image in the Oracle Cloud. Start this process by clicking the Environments tile on the PeopleSoft Cloud Manager home page. The Environments tile is highlighted in Figure 10-17.

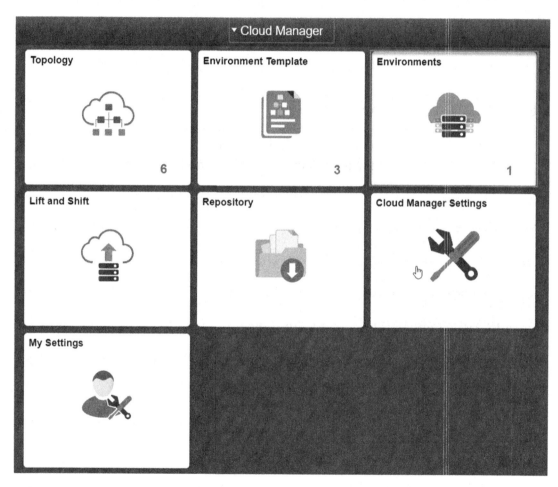

Figure 10-17. Environments tile

1. Click the Create Environment button in the top right-hand corner of the Environments home page (Figure 10-18).

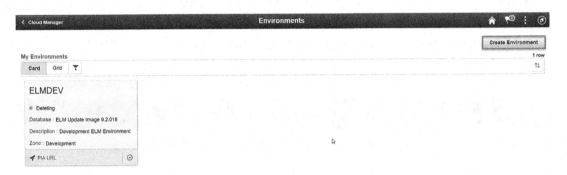

Figure 10-18. *Create Environment button*

2. In the Create Environment window, give the new environment a name, a description, and select the template we created in the previous section (Figure 10-19).

Figure 10-19. *Create PUM Environment dialogue*

3. In the Full Tier Environment Attributes section, fill in the password information in the Credentials section (Figure 10-20).

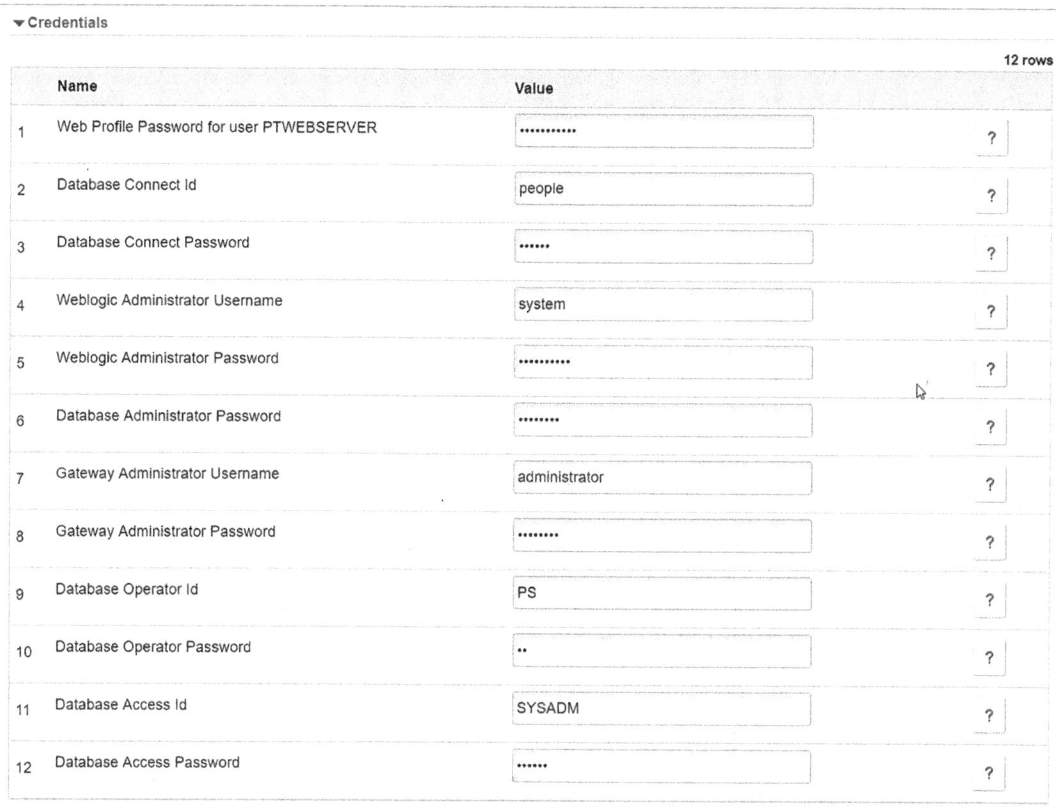

▼ Credentials

12 rows

	Name	Value	
1	Web Profile Password for user PTWEBSERVER	··········	?
2	Database Connect Id	people	?
3	Database Connect Password	······	?
4	Weblogic Administrator Username	system	?
5	Weblogic Administrator Password	··········	?
6	Database Administrator Password	········	?
7	Gateway Administrator Username	administrator	?
8	Gateway Administrator Password	········	?
9	Database Operator Id	PS	?
10	Database Operator Password	··	?
11	Database Access Id	SYSADM	?
12	Database Access Password	······	?

Figure 10-20. *PUM Image Credentials section*

4. Scroll down to the PeopleSoft Client Credentials section and fill
   in the Windows Administrator Password required to start the
   environment as shown in Figure 10-21.

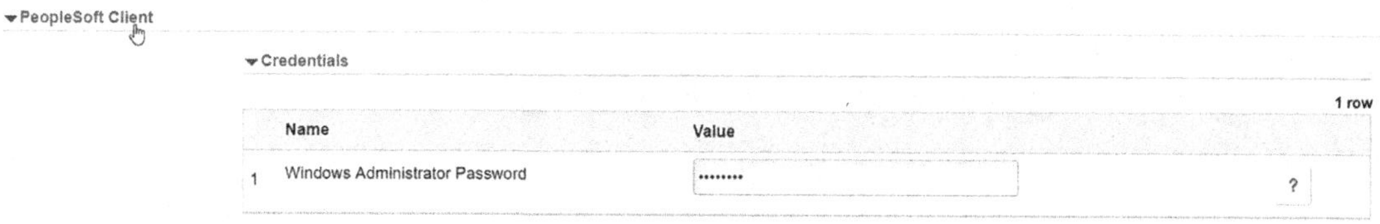

▼ PeopleSoft Client

   ▼ Credentials

   1 row

	Name	Value	
1	Windows Administrator Password	········	?

Figure 10-21. *Windows Administrator Password entry*

5. Click the Done button in the upper right-hand corner of the
    Create Environment page (Figure 10-22).

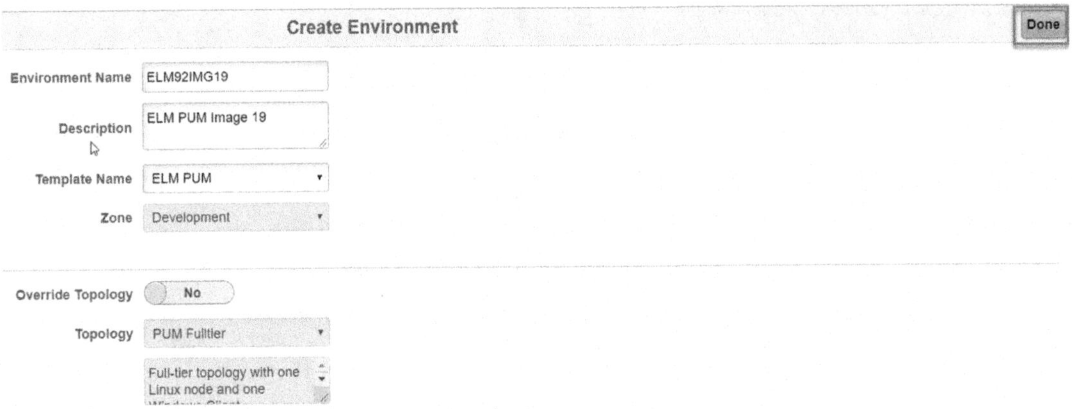

Figure 10-22. *Click Done*

You should now see your PUM image in the list of environments with the status
of Initiating. Allow the environment to full provision before moving on and using this
environment. This is highlighted in Figure 10-23.

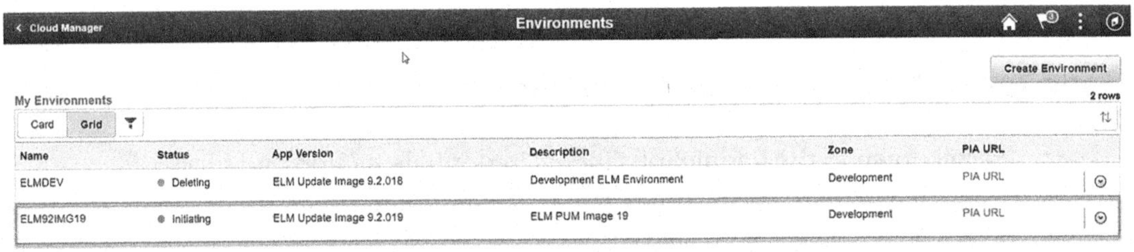

Figure 10-23. *Initiating the PUM environment*

Adding a Target to the PUM Image

Now that you have a fully provisioned PUM image in the Oracle Cloud, you will need to
add your target database (the database you want to update) to the PUM image to allow
for the application of maintenance, new functionality, and bug fixes. To get started
setting this up, navigate to the PeopleSoft Cloud Manager home page and click the
Environments tile.

1. From the Environments home page, click the related actions
   Details button on the far right of the PUM source environment.
   This action item is highlighted in Figure 10-24.

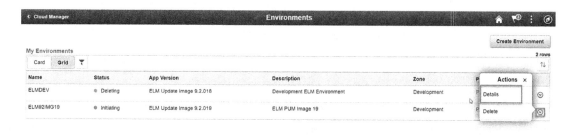

Figure 10-24. *Details of the PUM Image*

2. From the PUM Image Environment Details page, click
   Manage PUM Connections option on the left-hand navigation
   (Figure 10-25).

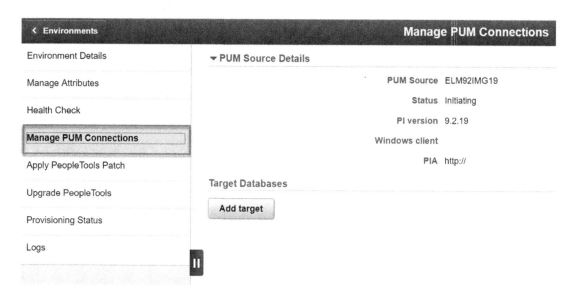

Figure 10-25. *Manage PUM Connections*

3. Click the **Add target** button, highlighted in Figure 10-26, and add
   any environment of the same application type; in this case we can
   select ELM target environments.

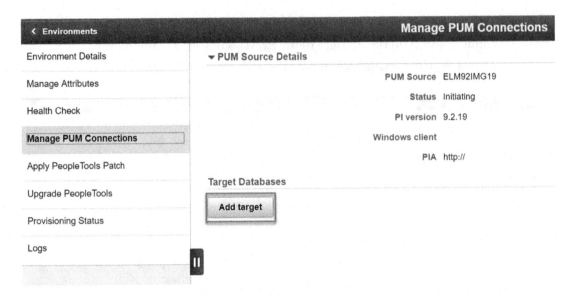

Figure 10-26. *Add target button*

4. Select a target environment from the Target Environment drop-down.

5. Click the Add button in the top right-hand corner of the Select Target window (Figure 10-27).

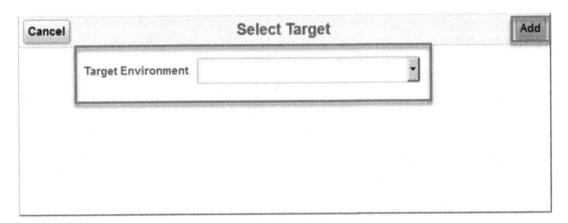

Figure 10-27. *Select Target Environment and Add button*

Completing these steps will start a process to add the target database you selected to the PUM image. This process can take a few minutes for the target database to be configured in the Change Assistant. The Target database is uploaded to the PUM source database for comparison. While the process is running, it will show a status of In Progress. The status of the Target database will change to Complete when this process is done and successful. Conversely, the status will change to Failed if the process did not finish successfully.

Change Assistant in the Oracle Cloud

Just like in your on-premise environment, Change Assistant can be accessed in your Oracle Cloud provisioned environments and utilized to create selective adoption change packages, apply bug fixes, or apply an image true-up to allow you to bring a cloud instance current. To get started connecting to the Windows virtual machine to access Change Assistant, you will need to navigate to the PeopleSoft Cloud Manager home page and click the Environments tab:

1. Go to the details page of the PUM image you are connecting to and find the IP address or the hostname of the PeopleSoft Client (Windows Virtual Machine) that was created as part of the PUM Fulltier topology used to create the environment.

2. Connect to the Windows virtual machine utilizing Remote Desktop Connection.

3. Configure this Windows box to best suit your needs as a Change Assistant box for your update process.

The full Change Assistant life cycle and selective adoption process are outside the scope of this book, but from this point in the process you can accomplish any of the same selective adoption and maintenance tasks you currently complete on-premise with your PUM image in the Oracle Cloud. Please reference the Change Assistant PeopleBooks for any further details on applying or creating change packages in Change Assistant.

CHAPTER 11

Updating PeopleSoft Cloud Manager

Like any other PeopleSoft application, PeopleSoft Cloud Manager requires proper upkeep and maintenance. Also like any other PeopleSoft application, Oracle continues to evolve the functionality of PeopleSoft Cloud Manager, releasing new functionality, break fixes, and updates regularly. Applying these updates to the system is key to ensuring a stable and performant application. Oracle provides two different methodologies to successfully update your existing PeopleSoft Cloud Manager instance in place. First, you can apply updates to PeopleSoft Cloud Manager in a fashion much like updating your other PeopleSoft applications. This process utilizes a PUM image and Change Assistant to create a change package which you can then apply to your Cloud Manager instance. The second option available is to apply updates to your PeopleSoft Cloud Manager instance using a delivered and more automated manage updates functionality within the application.

You will find, when comparing these two update methodologies, that they each offer benefits and drawbacks. Where the more automated and integrated methodology is simpler and less hands on, utilizing PUM and Change Assistant provides the highest level of customization and flexibility possible. While both methods provide benefits, it will be up to you to decide what is the best option for you and your organization based on your requirements.

© Aaron Engelsrud 2019
A. Engelsrud, *Managing PeopleSoft on the Oracle Cloud*, https://doi.org/10.1007/978-1-4842-4546-0_11

Applying Updates to PeopleSoft Cloud Manager Using Change Assistant

The process to apply updates and changes to PeopleSoft Cloud Manager utilizing PUM and Change Assistant involves multiple steps and configurations to complete. First, you will need to provision and configure an Interaction Hub (IH) PUM instance in your cloud infrastructure. Second, you will need to properly configure the Windows virtual machine that was provisioned as part of the PUM Full Tier cloud instantiation. This will include properly configuring the Windows firewall, setting the relevant TNS entry for database access, and updating all the Change Assistant configurations to ensure it works correctly. Third, you will need to upload the target database, in this case the PeopleSoft Cloud Manager database, to the IH PUM source. Fourth, once the target database is uploaded, you will need to create a change package based on that target image. Fifth, you will need to download and run that new change package against the PeopleSoft Cloud Manager database. Finally, you will need to run some final scripts to finish up the update process

Provision an IH PUM Instance

The process to provision an IH PUM (Integration Hub) instance in the Oracle Cloud Infrastructure for use in this upgrade process is no different than the process we have covered in previous chapters to create and instantiate a new image. Let's take a second to review these steps to get this image up and running:

1. Log in to PeopleSoft Cloud Manager as a PeopleSoft Cloud Manager administrator.

2. Click Repository tile on the Cloud Manager home page as highlighted in Figure 11-1.

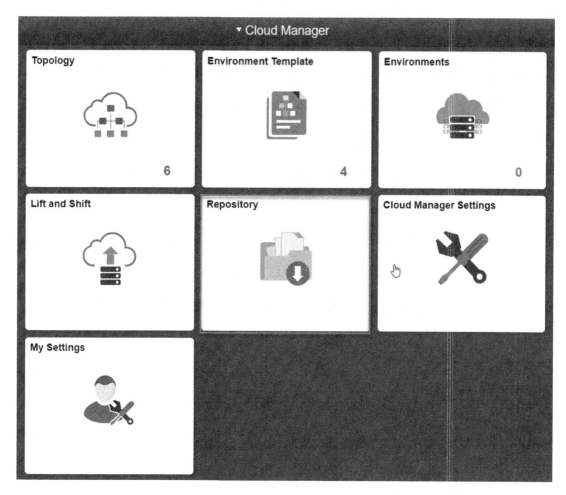

Figure 11-1. *Repository tile*

3. If you have not subscribed to the IH 91 Linux channel, do so now.
    This image is highlighted in Figure 11-2.

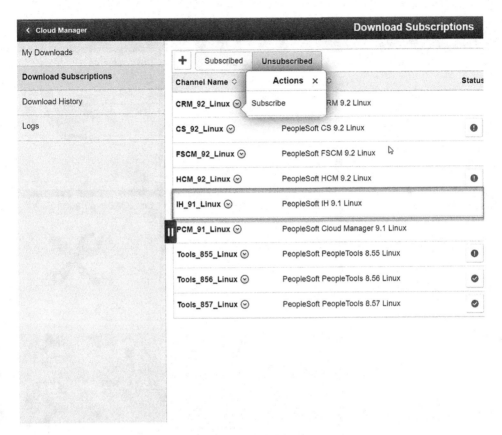

Figure 11-2. *IH_91_Linux Channel subscription*

4. Once the IH image has finished downloading to your cloud repository, you will need to create a new Environment Template specific to the IH image. To do this, click the Environment Template tile from the PeopleSoft Cloud Manager home page as shown in Figure 11-3.

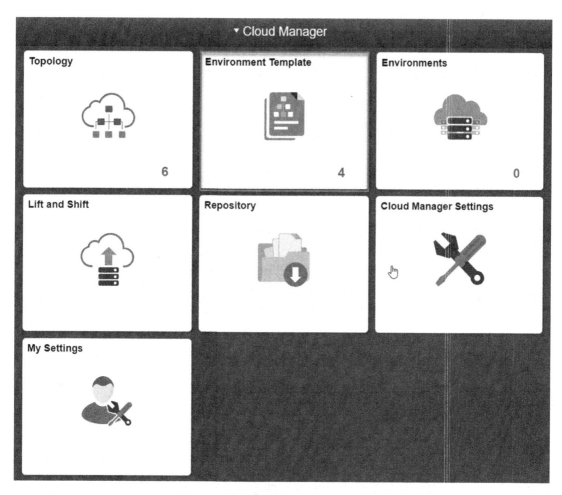

Figure 11-3. *Environment Template Tile*

5. Follow the steps to create a new Environment Template utilizing
    the PUM Fulltier delivered topology. This topology delivers all
    the key architectural components necessary to complete the
    PeopleSoft Cloud Manager update process. This is shown in
    Figure 11-4.

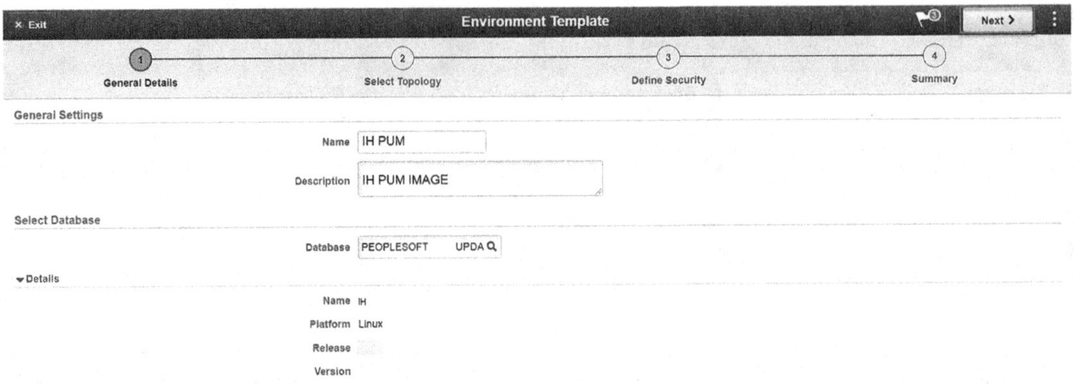

Figure 11-4. *IH Environment Template*

6. Now that you have a new environment template for the IH 91 Linux image, you can create the IH environment. Click the Environments tile from the PeopleSoft Cloud Manager home page.

7. Choose the IH PUM environment template.

8. Enter your environment specific password in the Create Environment dialogue and create the environment.

9. Now wait for your new IH environment to be provisioned.

Configure Change Assistant on Windows Virtual Machine

Now that you have a working IH PUM image, you will need to prepare the environment and the associated Windows virtual machine for use in the upgrade process. There are a few steps that need to happen for this to be completed, but it all starts with connecting to the Windows virtual machine:

1. You can find the Windows virtual machine IP address by navigating to the environment details page and looking at the PeopleSoft Client section. You will need this IP address to provide to the Remote Desktop client.

2. You will also need the Windows password you set at the time you set up the PUM image, shown in Figure 11-5.

Figure 11-5. *Windows Administrator Password dialogue*

3. Plug the IP address, administrator user, and administrator user
    password in to the RDP client and log in to the Window virtual
    machine.

Firewall Configuration

Now that you have successfully logged in to the Windows VM, you need to configure the
machine and allow it to talk to other parts of your cloud architecture. This is necessary
to properly use Change Assistant and work with the PeopleSoft Cloud Manager instance.
Primarily, you will need to add a new firewall rule to open ports 137, 138, 139, and 455.
To accomplish this, you will need to start by navigating to the Windows Firewall with
Advanced Security:

1. Click Inbound Rule (top left-hand side of the window) and then
    New Rule (top right-hand side of the window). Note the two
    highlighted boxes in Figure 11-6.

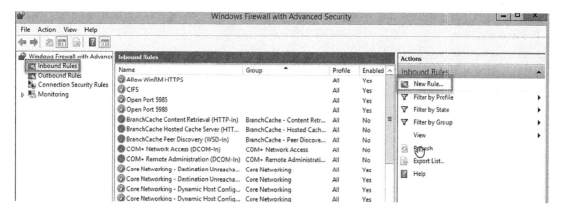

Figure 11-6. *Windows Firewall with Advanced Security*

2. Complete the steps in the New Inbound Rule Wizard.

    a. On the Rule Type step, select the Port option (Figure 11-7).

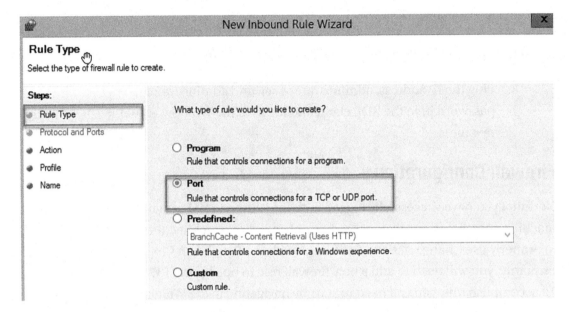

Figure 11-7. *New Inbound Rule Wizard, Rule Type*

    b. On the Protocol and Ports step, select TCP and enter
137,138,139,445 in the Specific local ports text box (Figure 11-8).

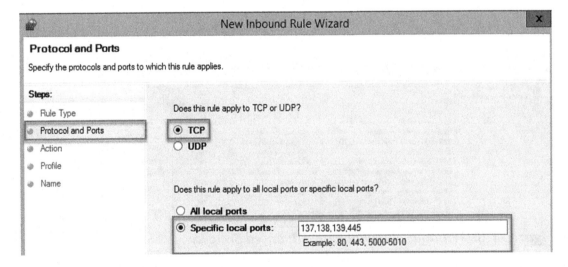

Figure 11-8. *New Inbound Rule Wizard, Protocol, and Ports*

c. On the Action step, select the **Allow the connection** option
(Figure 11-9).

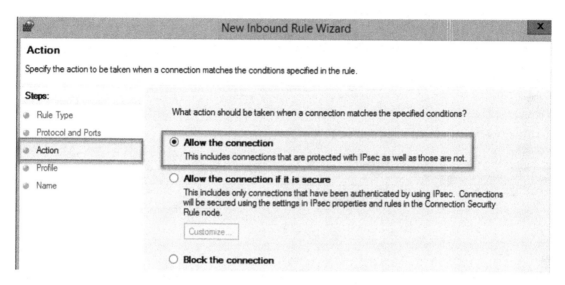

Figure 11-9. *New Inbound Rule Wizard, Action*

d. On the Profile step, select all the options for applying when the
rule applies (Figure 11-10).

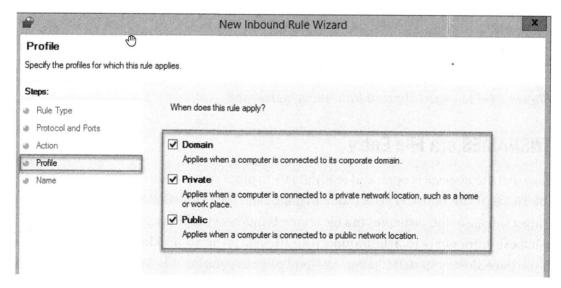

Figure 11-10. *New Inbound Rule Wizard, Profile*

e. On the Name Step, enter the name **CIFS** and click Finish
   (Figure 11-11).

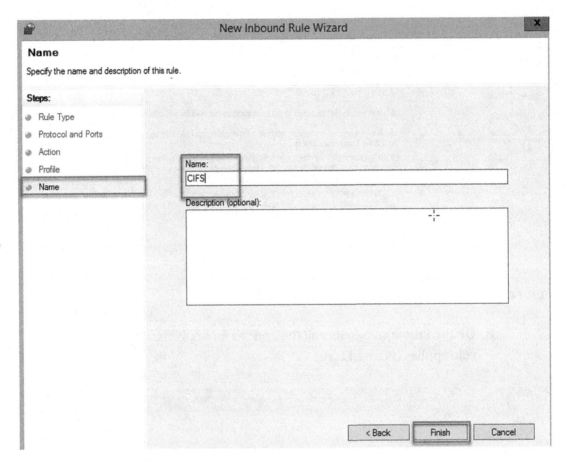

Figure 11-11. *New Inbound Rule Wizard, Name*

TNSNAMES.ora File Entry

Now that the Firewall is open and ready to talk to other components, you need to add
the TNS entry for both the PUM (Source) image and the PeopleSoft Cloud Manager
(target) image to the tnsnames.ora file on the Windows virtual machine. You will need to
put these entries in D:\oracle\product\12.1.0\client_1\network\admin\tnsnames.ora.
If you have already started Change Assistant prior to entering this database connection
information, you will need to close Change Assistant and restart the application. Change
Assistant picks up details including new entries and changes, from the tnsnames.ora file
at application start-up.

Change Assistant Configurations

With both the source and target databases defined in the tnsnames.ora, you can now start the process of completing three different configuration tasks within Change Assistant. First, you need to define your source database, in this case your IH image. Second, you will need to configure Change Assistant and set the proper settings on the Update Manager options page including the General page, the PUM Source (remember, that is your IH image), EM Hub page, and any additional configuration as needed. Finally, you need to define your target database, your PeopleSoft Cloud Manager database.

Define Database Options

To define first your source database and later your target database in Change Assistant, you will need to define a new database. You can open the New Database option in Change Assistant by navigating to File ➤ New Database. Once this dialogue is open, you will need to provide the information required for the source (PUM image) database and also the target (PeopleSoft Cloud Manager) database as shown in Figures 11-12 and 11-13, respectively.

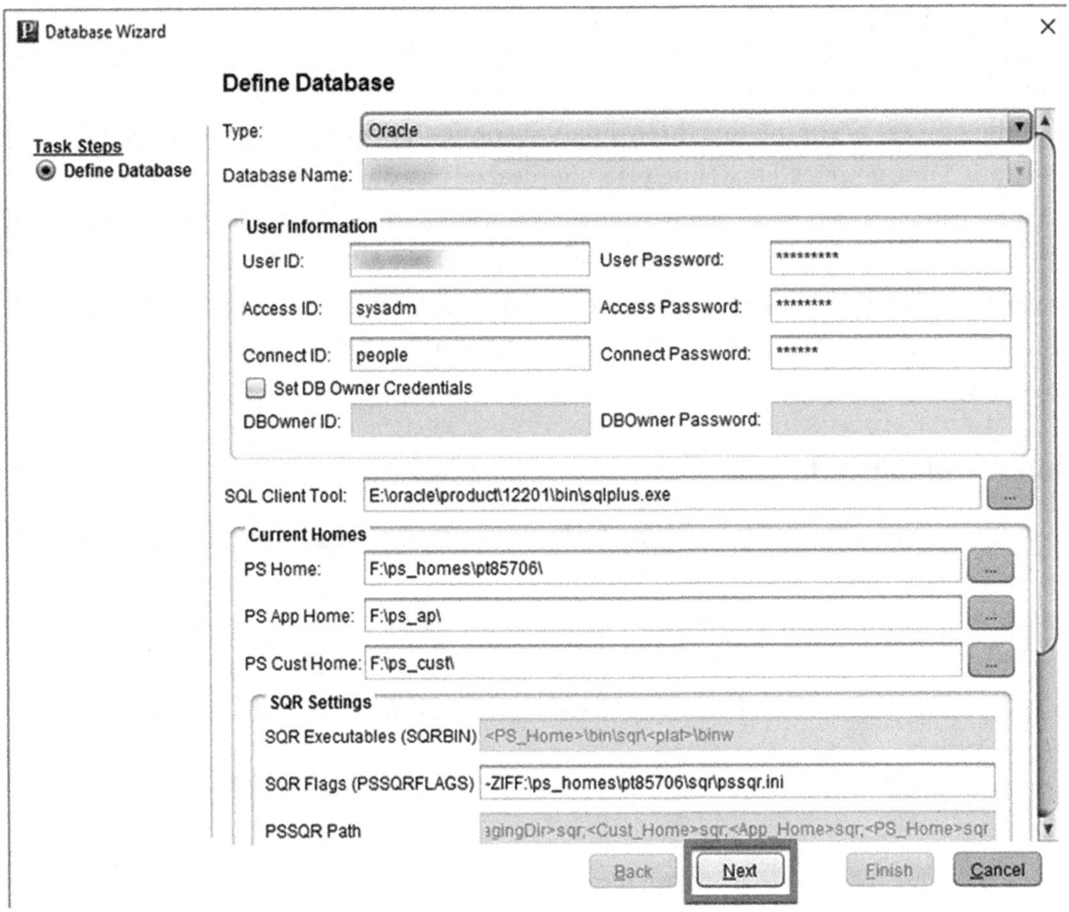

Figure 11-12. *Define Database*

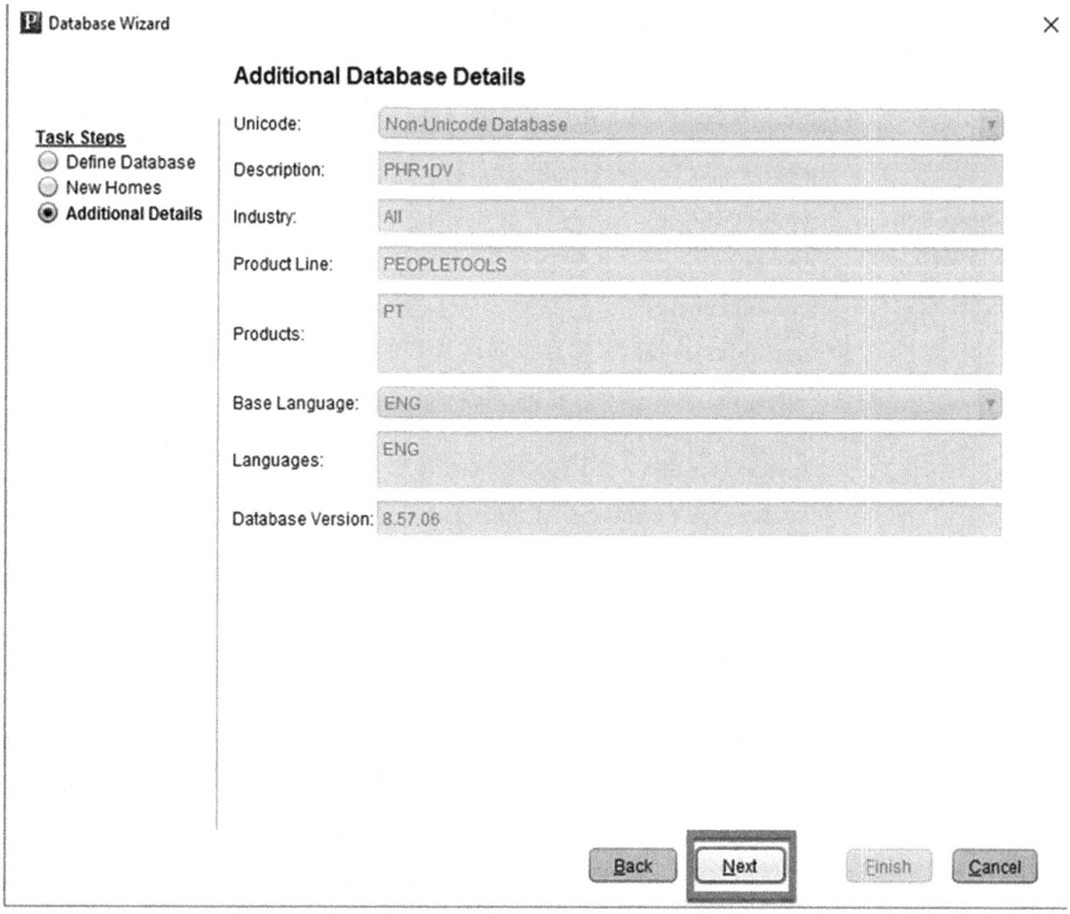

Figure 11-13. *Additional Database details*

Figure 11-14 shows the settings you have defined while creating a new database in Change Assistant.

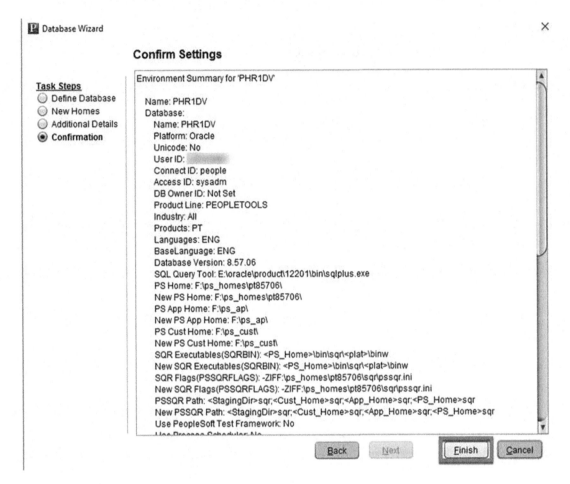

Figure 11-14. Confirm Settings

Update Manager Options

The Update Manager options can be found by opening Change Assistant and navigating
to the Tools ➤ Options. You will need to complete the first three tabs of the Update
Manager options dialogue. Provide the basic Change Assistant setting in the first tab. Set
the newly created target database as the PUM image on the second tab. Finally, define
your EM Hub in the third tab. The details required for these pages are shown in the
following images.

Figure 11-15 shows the General information tab and allows you to enter your
PS_HOME location, the Change Assistant download, output, and setup directories, and
where the SQL Query tool is located.

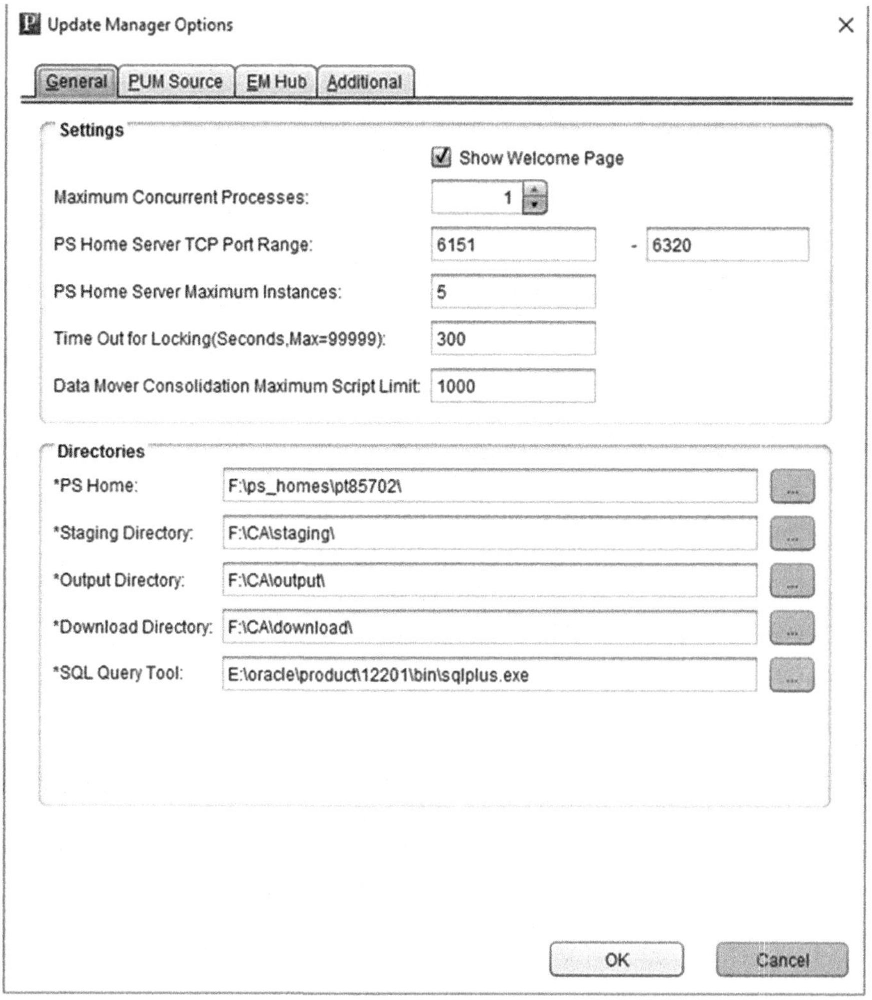

Figure 11-15. *Update Manager Options, General tab*

Figure 11-16 is PUM Options tab and allows you to select PUM home for Change Assistant to use.

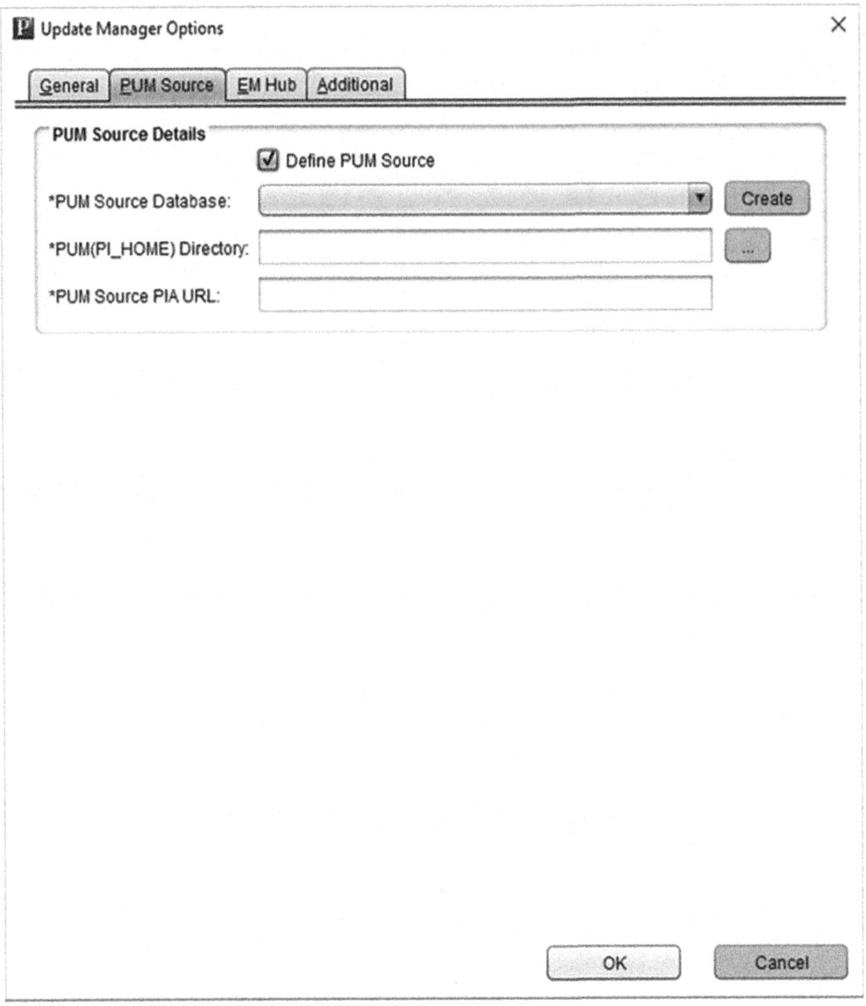

Figure 11-16. *Update Manager Options, PUM Source*

Figure 11-17 is Environment Management (EM) Hub tab. The EM Hub is used to help Change Assistant understand where file objects can be migrated to.

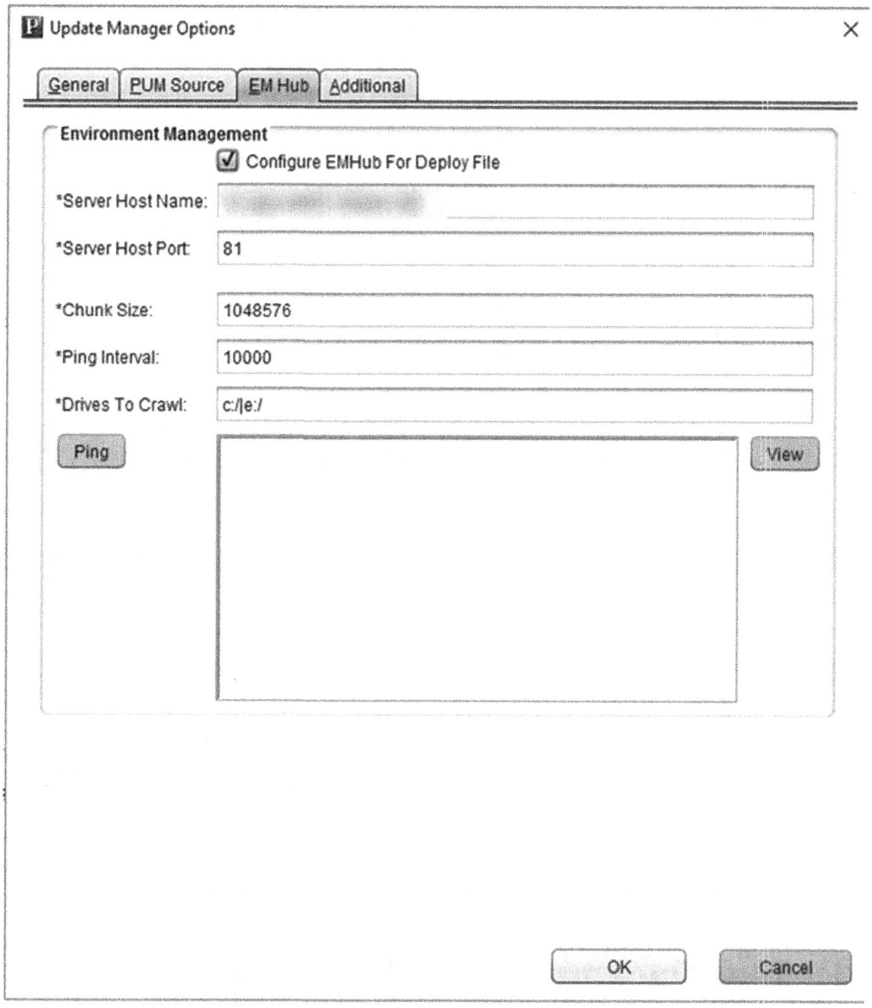

Figure 11-17. *Update Manager Options, EM Hub*

Upload Target Database to IH Instance

Now that you have successfully defined both your source and target databases in Change Assistant, you next need to upload your target database to your PUM source. This is a fairly simple process once you have your PUM Home defined and your source and target databases created in Change Assistant. To upload your source database to your PUM home, select Tools ➤ Upload Target Database Information to Image from the Change Assistant application. Once the upload dialogue opens, select the database you want to upload and click Finish at the bottom of the window. The Upload Target Database Information to Image dialogue window is shown in Figure 11-18.

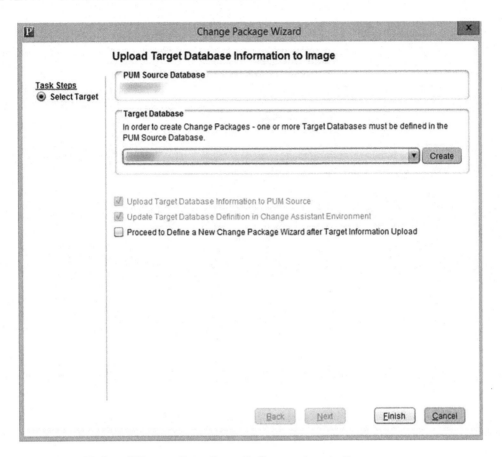

Figure 11-18. *Upload Target Database Information to Image*

Define Change Package in the IH Instance

Once the target database, PeopleSoft Cloud Manager, has completed the upload process to the PUM image, you will next need to log in to the PIA (PeopleSoft Internet Architecture) for the source PUM image, in this case the IH instance we created at the beginning of this process. In the PUM, you will navigate to the Update Manager Dashboard, select the source database in the left-hand navigation, and define a new change package. You will need to give the change package a name and select the correct Product/Severity/Image criteria for PeopleSoft Cloud Manager. Your selection should look like Figure 11-19 to avoid including unnecessary content in your change package. Click Search for Bugs, select all the bugs, and click OK to finish creating your change package.

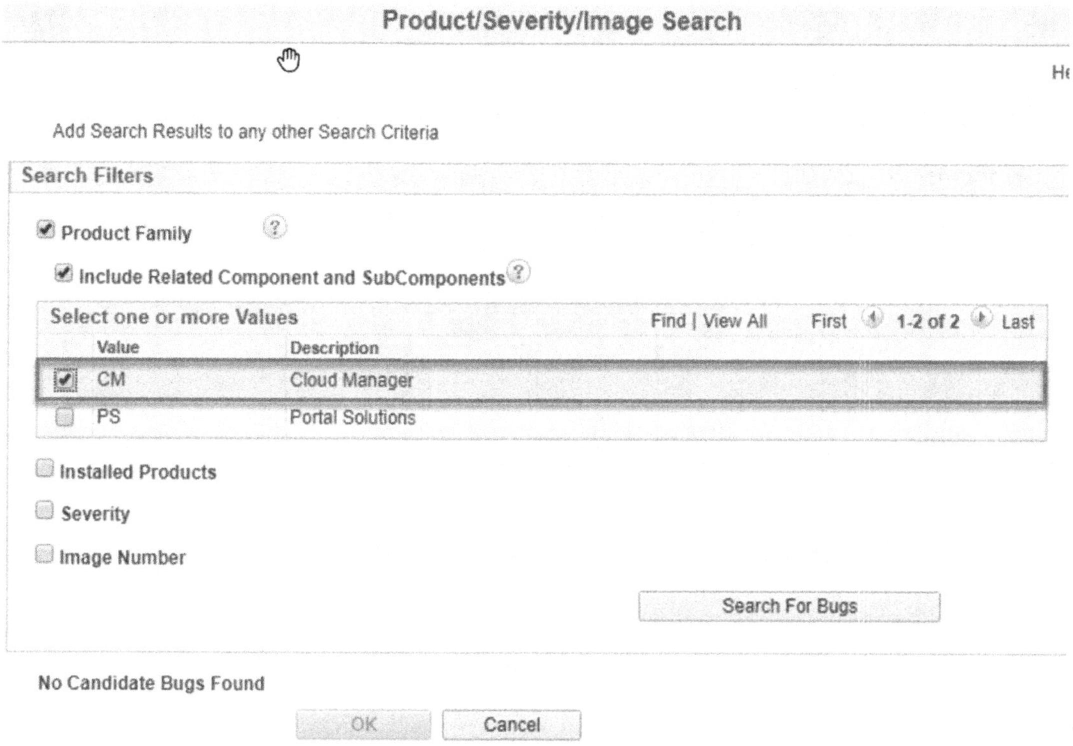

Product/Severity/Image Search

He

Add Search Results to any other Search Criteria

Search Filters

☑ Product Family   ⑦

☑ Include Related Component and SubComponents ⑦

Select one or more Values   Find | View All   First ◉ 1-2 of 2 ◉ Last

	Value	Description
☑	CM	Cloud Manager
☐	PS	Portal Solutions

☐ Installed Products

☐ Severity

☐ Image Number

                                                        [Search For Bugs]

No Candidate Bugs Found

                        [OK]   [Cancel]

Figure 11-19. *Cloud Manager Search criteria for defining the change package*

Once the change package is defined, you will need to go back to Change Assistant and download the change package by navigating to Tools ➤ Define or Create New Change Package. You can select the change package you created from the drop-down menu, click finish, and wait for the download to complete. Finally, once the change package is downloaded, you are able to navigate to Tools ➤ Apply Change Package, select your target database, and apply the change package to your PeopleSoft Cloud Manager database. You will select your change package from the drop-down menu highlighted in Figure 11-20.

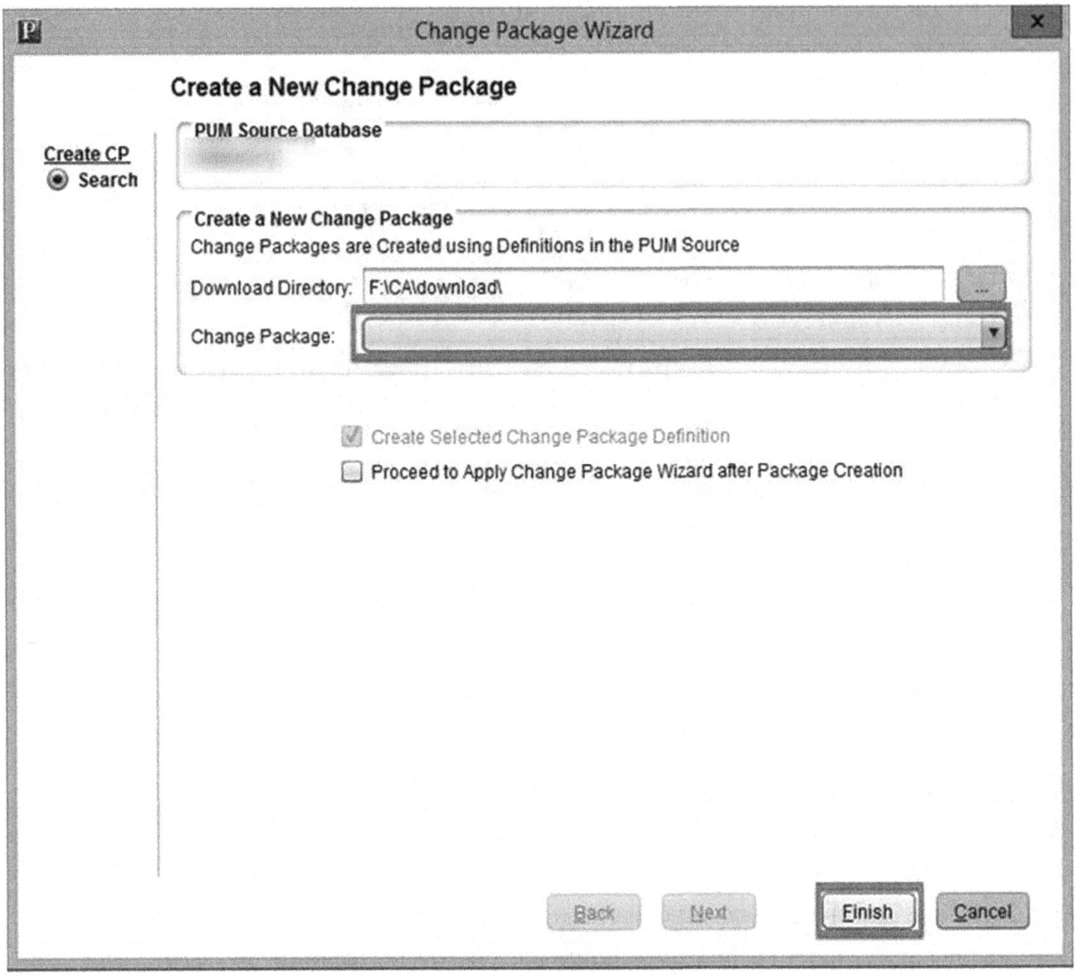

Figure 11-20. *Create a New Change Package in Change Assistant*

Copy and Run the Customization Script

To complete the PeopleSoft Cloud Manager update process, you will need to run a shell script against your PeopleSoft Cloud Manager environment. This script can be found on the PUM Source host in the following location:

- <ps_app_home>/cloud/cm_update_customizations.sh

This delivered script will update files form PUM source, synchronize code to the file server, clean up old files, and restart the host domains when copied and run against the PeopleSoft Cloud Manager Linux instance. To accomplish this task and successfully run this script, you will need root access on the target image. Once this script is complete, you can verify you updated PeopleSoft Cloud Manager environment, and the update process is complete.

Applying Updates to PeopleSoft Cloud Manager Using the Manage Updates Functionality

Since the delivery of PeopleSoft Cloud Manager Image 5, functionality has been included in the application which allows an administrator the ability to update PeopleSoft Cloud Manager in place without using Change Assistant. This simplifies the change process but also removes some of your ability to selectively adopt incoming changes from the PUM image. Your organization will need to address these differences and determine which upgrade procedure is best based on your business requirements.

Pre-update Tasks

There are a few steps that need to occur prior to starting the Manage Updates process in PeopleSoft Cloud Manager. First, like the more manual described previously, you must manually subscribe to the IH and PCM download channels. Second, you must have a Windows image available in your cloud infrastructure. Next, you need to make sure that your PeopleSoft Cloud Manager instance has the Windows image path properly configured in the Cloud Manager Settings page. Finally, you need to make sure that you have the downtime required to apply the updates, that no users are in PeopleSoft Cloud Manager, and that you have the proper backups of your PeopleSoft Cloud Manager application and database.

Manage Updates Steps

To successfully start the automated manage updates process in PeopleSoft Cloud Manager, you need to log in to the application as a Cloud Manager administrator and click the Cloud Manager Settings tile on the PeopleSoft Cloud Manager home page. The Cloud Manager Setting tile on the PeopleSoft Cloud Manager home page is highlighted in Figure 11-21.

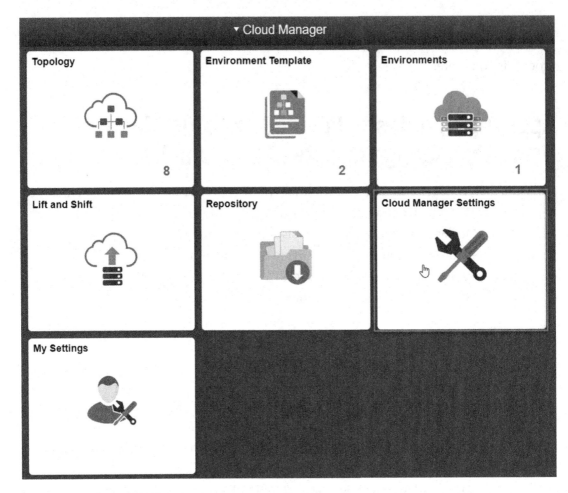

Figure 11-21. *Cloud Manager Settings tile*

1. On the left-hand navigation of the Cloud Manager Settings
    page, click the Manage Updates option, and then click the Edit
    Attributes button (Figure 11-22).

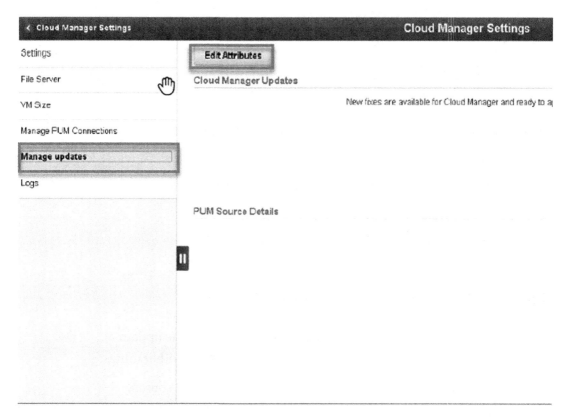

Figure 11-22. *Manage Updates, Edit Attributes*

2. Input the credentials needed to deploy a PUM source environment, and click Save.

3. Click Apply in the upper right-hand corner of the Manage Updates page (Figure 11-23).

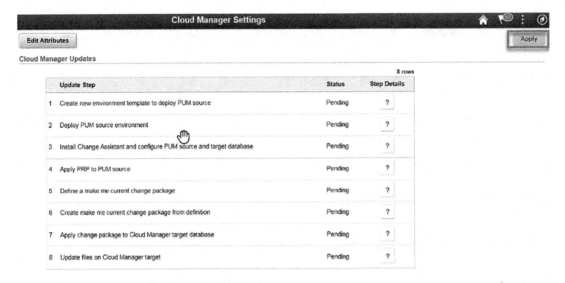

Figure 11-23. *Manage Updates, Apply button*

4. This will start the following eight steps to complete the update process, shown in Figure 11-24, while you go and do other things:

   a. Create new environment template to deploy PUM source.

   b. Deploy PUM source environment.

   c. Install Change Assistant and configure PUM source and target database.

   d. Apply PRP to PUM source.

   e. Define a make me current change package.

   f. Create make me current change package from definition.

   g. Apply change package to Cloud Manager target database.

   h. Update file on Cloud Manager target.

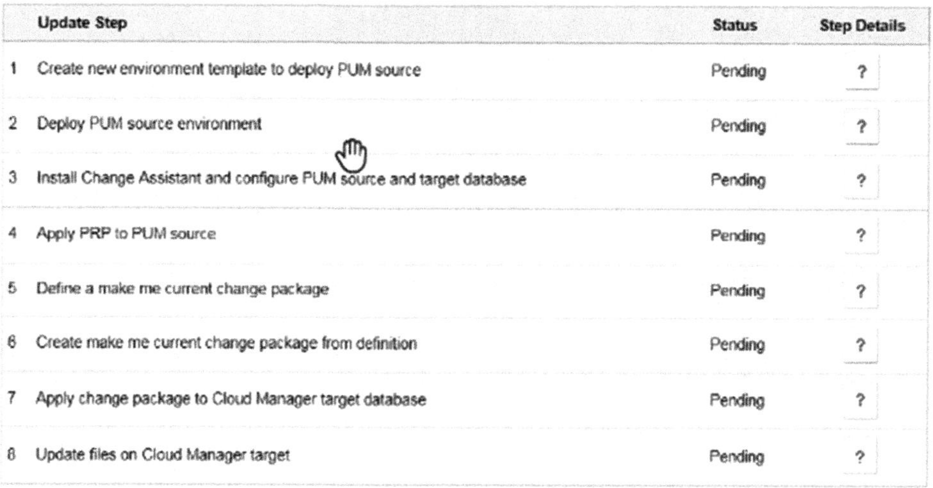

Update Step	Status	Step Details
1 Create new environment template to deploy PUM source	Pending	?
2 Deploy PUM source environment	Pending	?
3 Install Change Assistant and configure PUM source and target database	Pending	?
4 Apply PRP to PUM source	Pending	?
5 Define a make me current change package	Pending	?
6 Create make me current change package from definition	Pending	?
7 Apply change package to Cloud Manager target database	Pending	?
8 Update files on Cloud Manager target	Pending	?

Figure 11-24. Manage Update steps

Index

© Aaron Engelsrud 2019
A. Engelsrud, *Managing PeopleSoft on the Oracle Cloud*, https://doi.org/10.1007/978-1-4842-4546-0

T

U, V

Printed in the United States
By Bookmasters